Consultation at Work

Consultation at Work

Regulation and Practice

Mark Hall and John Purcell

OXFORD
UNIVERSITY PRESS

OXFORD
UNIVERSITY PRESS

Great Clarendon Street, Oxford, OX2 6DP,
United Kingdom

Oxford University Press is a department of the University of Oxford.
It furthers the University's objective of excellence in research, scholarship,
and education by publishing worldwide. Oxford is a registered trade mark of
Oxford University Press in the UK and in certain other countries

Impression: 1

British Library Cataloguing in Publication Data
Data available

ISBN 978–0–19–960546–0

Printed in Great Britain by
MPG Books Group, Bodmin and King's Lynn

To my parents, Joe and Molly Hall, with love and thanks (MH)

In memory of my uncle, Hugh Clegg, who strove to advance industrial democracy (JP)

Contents

List of Tables

List of Boxes

Preface and Acknowledgements

We have, in our separate ways, been interested and involved in consultation and its regulation for much of our careers. Having worked at the Trades Union Congress (TUC) during the 1980s, Mark came to Warwick to research the impact of EU employment law on the United Kingdom. He was soon seconded to the European Commission in Brussels where he worked on drafting the European Works Councils (EWCs) directive and revising the collective redundancies directive. Back at Warwick his research focussed on the operation of EWCs and the emerging EU legislative proposals on employee information and consultation. He wrote papers for the TUC on adapting the works council model of employee representation to British conditions. He also acted as a consultant to the then Department of Trade and Industry (DTI) during the 1997 Labour government's first term of office, advising on UK implementation of the EWCs and information and consultation directives. John's interest came initially from his first job as secretary to the Joint Consultation and Negotiating Committee at Perkins Engines, then the world's biggest diesel engine factory. The focus of his work at the Commission of Industrial Relations was on the reform of collective bargaining systems in companies with terrible strike records. Consultation was squeezed out by extreme adversarialism that marked relations in these workplaces. This experience was the start of a long interest in 'good industrial relations' which has to include consultation. Later, as an academic specializing in the management of employment relations, and latterly human resource management, his passion was finding ways for employment relations to make a positive contribution to company performance and worker well-being. The search for effective worker participation, what later became 'employee voice', was a central concern. And, as a deputy chairman of the Central Arbitration Committee, he has been much involved in the application of the Information and Consultation of Employees (ICE) Regulations.

Our paths converged a decade ago when we worked on a plan to study the impact of the information and consultation directive which had just been adopted by the EU and was about to be transposed in the United Kingdom in the shape of the ICE regulations. In due course, our research proposal was funded by the DTI (now the Department for Business, Innovation and Skills

(BIS)), the Advisory, Conciliation and Arbitration Service (Acas), and the Chartered Institute of Personnel and Development (CIPD). Between 2006 and 2010 we, with our colleagues on the research team, studied twenty-five organizations, usually over a period of twenty-four months, seeking to assess how consultation occurred, and with what outcomes, asking how far the ICE regulations had influenced practice. The final report from the project was published by BIS at the end of 2010 (Hall et al., 2010).

We were very conscious in writing this book that yet another research report would not be appropriate. The broader story of consultation in Britain is much more interesting and compelling. There has been a long, and largely unhappy, history of attempts to gain acceptance for the simple idea of management and employee representatives jointly reviewing and discussing company plans and performance and raising matters of mutual concern. Meanwhile, over three or more decades, the EU was trying, and eventually succeeding, albeit in a watered down form, to put legislation in place to promote consultation in the face of opposition from employers and some governments, notably the British government, whether Conservative or Labour. The British approach was one of employer opposition, union indifference, and government obfuscation. Yet despite this lack of enthusiasm, the ICE regulations eventually came into force in the United Kingdom and apply to all enterprises with fifty or more employees. We felt it important to trace the impact of the regulations and provide a picture of what consultation entails in practice. It is here that we draw on our research findings. One final influence has been an acute awareness that virtually all previous research and writing on consultation was at a time when the paradigm of high levels of union membership and extensive collective bargaining was widely accepted. Consultation was always seen, in these circumstances, as the poor cousin but this view is no longer sustainable, at least in the private sector. The radically changed context means that the case for the regulation and practice of consultation has to be made afresh. It is now the last chance for collectivism in employment relations.

There are many people who have helped us during the past decade as we sought to study and write about consultation. We are very grateful to our colleagues on the research team—Michael Terry, Sue Hutchinson, and Jane Parker—who shared, over five years, the task of gathering data and working through, in many team meetings, what it all meant. Thanks are also due to freelance researcher Jill Smith who undertook three of the case studies. We could not have carried out the study without the active participation of managers, employee representatives, and trade union officers in the twenty-five organizations which allowed us repeated access. We thank them, and those people in other organizations who we interviewed. Bernard Carter (BIS), Gill Dix (Acas), and Ben Willmott (CIPD) were members of the funders' advisory group who oversaw the research project. We are grateful for their support. Colleagues in the Industrial Relations Research Unit at Warwick Business School, notably Linda Dickens, Paul Edwards, and Paul Marginson, have always been willing to share their experience and offer corrective advice when asked. Val Jephcott has provided invaluable administrative assistance. Lastly, we thank our families and especially our wives, Ruth and Kate, for their love, support, and patience during the long gestation of this project.

We are grateful to Penguin Books and Random House for permission to reproduce an extract from Jonathan Coe's novel, *The Rotters' Club*.

MH
JP

January 2012

List of Abbreviations and Acronyms

Acas	Advisory, Conciliation and Arbitration Service
BIS	Department of Business, Innovation and Skills
CAC	Central Arbitration Committee
CBI	Confederation of British Industry
CEEP	European Centre of Employers and Enterprises providing Public Services
CEO	Chief Executive Officer
CIPD	Chartered Institute of Personnel and Development
CST	Catholic Social Theory
DGB	Confederation of German Trade Unions
DTI	Department of Trade and Industry (now BIS)
EAT	Employment Appeals Tribunal
ECJ	European Court of Justice
ECS	European Company Statute
EEA	European Economic Area
EEF	Engineering Employers' Federation
EI	Employee involvement
ETUC	European Trade Union Confederation
EU	European Union
EWC	European Works Council
GPMU	Graphical, Paper and Media Union
HR	Human Resources
HRM	Human Resource Management
ICI	Imperial Chemical Industries
I&C	Information and Consultation
ICE	Information and Consultation of Employees
IPM	Institute of Personnel Management (now CIPD)

IRRU	Industrial Relations Research Unit, Warwick Business School
JCC	Joint Consultative Committee
JCNC	Joint Consultation and Negotiating Committee
JPC	Joint Production Committee
LRD	Labour Research Department
MNC	Multi-national Company
PEA	Pre-existing agreement
SNB	Special Negotiating Body
TICE	Transnational Information and Consultation of Employees
TQM	Total Quality Management
TUC	Trades Union Congress
TUPE	Transfer of Undertakings (Protection of Employees)
UNICE	Union of Industrial and Employers' Confederations (now Business Europe—the Confederation of European Business)
Unite	Unite the Union
WERS	Workplace Employment Relations Survey
WIRS	Workplace Industrial Relations Survey

'This is the beginning. In a couple of years' time, employee participation is going to be codified. It's going to be government policy.'

'Which government?'

'It doesn't matter. Doesn't make a blind bit of difference. I'm telling you, we're going to be entering a whole new phase. Management and workers—elected representatives, that is—are going to sit around the table and take decisions *together*. Looking at the forward plans of the company *together*. Mutual interests. Common ground. That's what we are looking for. And it's got to happen . . . '

The Rotters' Club, Jonathan Coe 2001 (pages 17–18, Viking 2001)

1

Consultation at Work: Competing Agendas, Differing Expectations

What is consultation?

Consultation between managers and employees, both individually and collectively, has been part of the world of work, or at least paid employment, for well over 150 years, yet it is quite hard to define. This ambiguity can be advantageous since it becomes easier to assert that 'joint consultation', as it was often called, is mutually beneficial if important differences in meaning and intention are conveniently overlooked. But this can also mean that consultation, seen in first flush as a way of getting 'all sides' in industry to work together, is found to be riddled with competing agendas and differing expectations such that enthusiasm can quickly turn to cynicism and participation to withdrawal. Yet, where it seems to work, participants can be passionate enthusiasts. Governments have a habit of promoting joint consultation not just as a 'good thing', especially when times are hard and conflict seems to be escalating, but also much more fundamentally by asserting that consultation is an employment right alongside the right to fair treatment and a safe working environment. This has long been the position of the European Union (EU) resulting in a series of EU directives promoting consultation. The most recent, dating from 2002, covers all enterprises with fifty or more employees. Employees have rights to be provided with information and to be consulted on big issues that affect them, and they can demand these rights be provided by their employer.

The aim of this book is to unpack the different meanings and approaches to consultation and explore how they have evolved. It will provide explanations on how and why this area has been subject to regulation, especially when, in the United Kingdom at least, very few people—employers, trade unions, or government ministers—were pushing for statutory rights to consultation while in parts of continental Europe it is an accepted practice. Despite what may, at times, seem a lack of enthusiasm for consultation, in practice, it, or some form of it, is quite widespread in the United Kingdom and we review the evidence not just on coverage and content but also on why management set up consultative bodies in the first place. We need, too, to look at the practice of consultation in some detail to see what is involved and what effect, or outcome, consultation has, if any. Our research project (see Appendix) over four years in twenty-five organizations was able to trace how consultation operated. In some cases it appeared to be effective to the satisfaction of all involved; in other cases less so and in two cases the consultation scheme was abandoned after only a few years. This then leads us to consider the future of consultation in the United Kingdom in the light of experience elsewhere.

So what is consultation? The Oxford English Dictionary (OED) defines 'consult' as to 'seek information and advice from someone, especially an expert or professional' while 'consultation' is the 'action of formally consulting or discussing; a meeting with an expert or professional in order to seek advice'. Chambers's Twentieth Century dictionary adds an extra twist that 'consultative bodies [are] without vote on decision'. In short, to consult is to seek advice but such advice is non-binding. But who is consulting whom and over what sort of issues in the world of work? It is virtually impossible to engage in consultation without providing relevant information to enable considered opinions, the basis of advice, to be reached. One person or party can provide the information to enable others to offer an opinion, provide advice or proffer support. In most cases the assumption is that consultation means management providing information about plans, prospects, and performance since it is management who are appointed by owners to take decisions and formulate strategies.

Who then is seeking advice? Employees may want information and explanation and ask managers, as the experts and professionals, for advice on how a decision is to be implemented, why something was decided or the implications of a course of action. This is largely unexceptional although some managers may complain of the time needed to do this and others suggest it is nothing to do with the employees whose job is just to obey instructions. But what some executives fear is the 'upside-down' world where managers are expected to take advice from their subordinates, the employees. And this, indeed, is the normal expectation of consultation at work: managers consult employees about the decisions that are about to be taken. As Acas put it 'managers must be committed to consulting early in the decision making process, listening to contributions and explaining final decisions' (Dix and Oxenbridge, 2003: 4). The Chartered Institute of Personnel and Development (CIPD), the professional body for human resource managers, says that 'consultation involves managers taking account of employees' views before making a decision' (CIPD, 2004: 9). Earlier, in 1981, the CIPD (then the IPM) was even more explicit in saying that consultation 'allows employees to influence the proposals before the final management decision' (quoted in Bratton and Gold, 1999: 317). Employees, through their representatives in consultative committees, 'advise' managers on decisions and their implications. This can be controversial if it is taken to mean that managers must take account of employee opinions and change aspects of the decision. What, then, is the difference between consultation and negotiation? And if, alternatively, consultation in practice means that employee views are disregarded, or there is scant opportunity for them to be formulated, then it can easily become a sham or worthless exercise.

This may be inconsequential if the decision being consulted about is relatively low level and unimportant such as the price of tea in the canteen. But strategic level decisions on capital investments, the location of production and staff, responses to the recession and such like, impact on employees' lives and futures and can be fundamental to the success of the enterprise, matters over which employees can be expected to have a strong interest. It is here that 'an exchange of views and the establishment of dialogue' can be expected to take place in consultative meetings. This is the definition of consultation to be found in the EU directive on information and consultation. Consultation over such matters would have to take place between senior managers or executives and would require there to be elected or appointed employee representatives acting on behalf of employees. Such representatives could be appointed by a trade union where it is recognized by the employer and, in some circumstances, sit alongside non-union representatives. In non-union organizations, increasingly found in the private sector, employee representatives will be drawn from among the staff, either elected or appointed.

Consultation on strategic issues and policy decisions would be very difficult to undertake with the whole workforce in all but the smallest enterprises even with all of the advantages of social media (Smith and Harwood, 2011). How would such a dialogue take place? It is common for meetings of all employees to be held once a year, what the Americans call 'town hall meetings', but these revolve around senior managers giving out information with some time, but not much, devoted to Q&A (questions and answers). More commonly consultation, or the establishment of dialogue, will involve senior managers meeting employee representatives and it is highly likely that this will happen on a regular basis. Consultation needs an institutional structure, a consultative body, and some rules of conduct or a constitution. The consultative body can have various names. Traditionally, in the United Kingdom they were called 'joint consultative committees' (JCCs) while in Germany the term is 'works council' and some organizations in the United Kingdom use that. We have come across a wide variety of titles such as 'Voice' or in one case the

Love Where You Work Forum (the LWYWF), a title chosen to reflect the marketing slogan for the service provided to clients. It is quite common to find reference to the 'employee forum'. We use the term 'staff council' here, reserving 'works council' for when we refer to the much more extensive German experience of consultation (Frege, 2002). The term 'council' more accurately reflects the type of constitutional bodies set up as the focal point for consultation and dialogue.

The creation of a consultative committee, the staff council, will nearly always be initiated by management, sometimes following a request from employees or a trade union. A whole set of decisions needs to be taken to get consultation to take place, from the election or appointment of employee representatives, arrangements for meetings, choices on which senior managers are to attend, and how much time representatives have to communicate with each other and with their constituents, and so on. More significant, perhaps, are decisions concerning the topics of consultation to be raised at meetings. Unlike collective bargaining, where the subjects discussed can be expected to cover terms and conditions of employment, in consultation there is no obvious core agenda. It can be very broad ranging concerning the success of the company, future prospects, and planned decisions. Or it can have a much narrower remit dealing with information about past performance and an opportunity for employees to raise matters that concern them. Most critical is how far management wish to go in discussing policy options or potential decisions before plans have been decided and how prepared they are to change plans in the light of employee opinions and advice. Labour law can establish 'a right for employees to be informed of planned measures in advance and to have an opportunity to express an opinion prior to implementation' (Budd and Zagelmeyer, 2010: 492), but it cannot specify exactly which planned measures are to be discussed, nor can it specify how management should respond to employee opinions.

Indeed, the whole point of consultation is 'the establishment of dialogue', with no requirement to search for an agreement, unlike negotiation where an agreement is a necessary outcome. In consultation the 'right of last say' always rest with management unless, as in Germany and the Netherlands, the law specifies certain HR policies, such as payment systems, to require agreement, or codetermination. Not surprisingly, working through the ambiguities of decision-making in consultation can be a source of frustration for both managers and representatives if one believes the other has gone too far or not gone far enough in providing information, expressing opinions, and responding to them. The premise of consultation is working together in cooperation. Senior managers used to unilateral decision-making can find it a shock to have to consult. Trade union representatives experienced in collective bargaining and adversarial posturing can also find consultative behaviours difficult to adjust to. Non-union employee representatives when they first experience meetings of a staff council can be at a loss, not knowing quite what is expected of them. It takes time to learn how to consult effectively (Heller et al., 1998: 187).

The consultation explored in this book, and the subject of contentious regulation in the EU and the United Kingdom, is what Boxall and Purcell (2011: 168) call 'power centred', involving senior managers and 'indirect' forms of employee participation via employee representatives in a staff council, or some such body. They point out that there are other forms of 'power centred' employee voice mechanisms and it is often the relationship between these which can be a source of tension. In Germany, for example, provision is made for worker directors while trade unions will undertake collective bargaining often at the sectoral level. A crucial issue there is the relationship between trade unions and the works council, the location of collective bargaining, and the relationship between the works council and worker directors. Within the United Kingdom the critical interaction is between collective bargaining, where unions are recognized by employers, and staff councils. Where a union and an employer have created a 'partnership committee' (Samuel and Bacon, 2010), it may be that there is no role for a separate employee forum. But in other cases the relationship between collective bargaining and consultation has been fraught especially from the unions' perspective. Will a focus on consultation be at the expense of a union's traditional adversarial role in collective bargaining? We will return to the union dilemma in a number of places in the book, initially in the next section where we consider lessons from history.

'Power centred' forms of employee voice are not the only avenues open to managers to communicate with and seek the opinions of employees. In the last twenty years there has been a marked growth in the use of employee attitude surveys, team briefings by line managers, 'town hall' meetings of staff, problem solving groups, and high involvement work practices (Kersley et al., 2006: 135; Boxall and Purcell, 2011: 166–7). These are all examples of direct forms of employee voice involving each employee without a representative intermediary. The growth of these direct forms of voice can often change the role of indirect employee forums and, at times, makes them appear irrelevant. The contemporary search for 'employee engagement' (MacLeod and Clarke, 2009) places emphasis on participatory leadership, inclusive organizational cultures and the role of the line manager, with only limited room for formal mechanisms of consultation. In its broadest meaning, consultation must include the wide range of initiatives taken within companies to communicate with employees and give them opportunities to express their views whether in weekly team briefing sessions, in employee attitude surveys or via staff councils. The most sophisticated employers will tend to use multiple channels of consultation to create an 'embedded' culture of involvement or participation (Cox et al., 2006). These days, assessing the role of collective consultation through staff councils must take account of the broader context of employee voice systems. This is a very different context from the experience of consultation in much of the last century, yet the historical experience can point to wider principles of relevance today.

Lessons from history

Early examples of management style and union substitution

Clegg and Chester (1954), in one of the earliest analyses of joint consultation, record some examples of consultation in the late nineteenth century. Consultative arrangements were established by some firms, either those 'with an unusual interest in the welfare of their workers or... firms with an interest in using a system of direct workers' representation as an alternative to trade unionism' (Clegg and Chester, 1954: 329). Both types of employer are still clearly evident in the twenty-first century and have been features of employers' approaches throughout the history of consultation. Firms vary according to the style of management they adopt in dealing with employees and creating systems of employment relations—showing a concern for the welfare of employees in Clegg and Chester's terms, but it is much more than that. Management style fundamentally affects strategic choice in this area of activity with some adopting a 'sophisticated modern' approach which places emphasis on consultation or what would be called today 'partnership' in some unionized firms (Purcell and Sisson, 1983: 115; Boxall and Purcell, 2011: 182–5). It is often noted in research on participation that 'managerial attitudes are key.... Underpinning highly developed participation practices is a relationship based on a high level of trust between management and employees' (Wilkinson et al., 2010: 12). Managements' approach to consultation is of fundamental importance and we look at this in detail in Chapter 2 and in Chapters 6 and 7.

A managerial style supportive of consultation is likely to be very different from that where a staff council is created to thwart trade unions by providing an in-house system of employee representation. This 'union substitution' activity is especially evident where there is 'a viable union threat' (Gollan, 2010: 215) or as a deliberate pre-emptive response to the possibility of unionization. It has always taken place among a minority of firms. Trade union ambivalence towards consultation, and at times hostility, is clearly understandable in cases where the prime purpose of the staff council is the avoidance of unionization and collective bargaining. And if the EU directives, as applied through regulations in the United Kingdom, on consultation are seen to provide opportunities for employers' to create non-union bodies, then unions may show a marked lack of enthusiasm towards the regulations. The lesson from history is that unions have long memories and will inevitably be suspicious of some management's proposal for staff forums. Of course, few employers are explicit in their union substitution aims, preferring instead to emphasize the need for better communications and cooperation. We need to be careful in working through management action and intent.

Consultation in times of war: expansion and controversy

The biggest boost to consultation came in periods of major wars, both the First and the Second World Wars. There were three elements to this. First, with large numbers of workers away in the armed forces there was a shortage of labour even despite the enlistment of women to the factories—'Rosie the riveter' in the famous American recruitment poster. Second, pressure on production was huge especially in engineering and manufacturing and production blockages and material shortages affected the war effort, and not just employers' profits. The assumption was that there would be a common interest in trying to tackle production problems and that consultation over such matters would be workable and certainly preferable to the rash of strikes which broke out during the First World War. Third, these factors combined to change the nature of management authority, as Clegg and Chester (1954: 328) make clear. 'The customary sanction of industrial authority (command and control) having lost most of its force, they (employers) have had to make use of persuasion and have found it necessary to construct means of communication in order to reach their workers to persuade them'. This latter is a familiar refrain today where the growth of customer service work and the rapid expansion in knowledge working in conditions, until recently, of full employment, has meant that communication and persuasion were at a premium in trying to gain employee commitment and engagement. Managers in these circumstances become reliant to a much greater extent on employees using their discretion in the way jobs are done, and employees are more able to move to another company if they find communication and 'persuasion' lacking.

It is unclear how far modern managers have to go to gain workers' consent. Clegg and Chester record, in what to us now seem like extreme circumstances in the 1914–18 war, that 'in the factories themselves, especially in those producing munitions, managers found themselves having to cherish their labour force, and often unable to carry out their plans unless these met with the consent of their employees' (ibid.: 330). This vividly raises the question of power: consultation may be felt more necessary where employees exert actual or potential power over the production process or where consent is needed for the achievement of organizational change. In these circumstances the purpose of consultation, at least from the workers' point of view, may be much less about solving production problems and the pursuit of efficiency than the redistribution of power from 'capital' to 'labour'.

The vexed question of who would represent the workers in consultative discussions with management had to be dealt with. This remains controversial today and helps explain union ambivalence towards consultative committees. The First World War saw the emergence of shop stewards, lay union officials in the place of work, who dominated the consultative committees yet were 'a part, even if a rebellious part, of the trade unions' (ibid.: 331). The 'rebellious part' was the tendency for shop stewards to act independently of the trade union leaders or full-time officers. At the time, collective bargaining was predominantly multi-employer, conducted at an industry level like the whole of the engineering industry (as still applies to a great extent in Germany). The union bargainers were therefore in large part full-time officers. What, in these circumstances, was the role of the shop steward at the workplace beyond collecting subscriptions? Shop floor power over production in the context of the war effort and the consequential need for regular meetings between management and shop stewards in joint committees came to be the emerging pattern (Gospel, 1992: 82).

Something of a battle for control took place within the trade union movement. In the Second World War, joint production committees (JPCs) become commonplace but many feared that the shop stewards were often communist party members or sympathizers (Dukes, 2008: 106; see also Kelly, 2010: 50). It was feared that they had a more radical agenda than held by union leaders: 'the development of cohesive and self confident workplace organisation, able to apply pressure directly at the point of production' (Hyman in Goodrich, 1975: xxvi). In contrast, 'for official trade unionism, order and stability depend on maintaining the established relationship and the established balance of power and the negotiation . . . of order and consent are central to the trade union function' (ibid.). 'It is no accident' writes Hyman (1975: xxvii) 'that British labour organisations insist that industrial democracy be exercised through a "single channel of representation" subordinating workplace institutions to the official union hierarchy'.

Official union support for consultation during and after the Second World War was luke warm since there was always a fear of losing control over militant shop stewards in consultative committees. 'The growth of JPCs . . . was feared by many trade union leaders to mean the growth of influence of the grass roots and the CP' (communist party) (Dukes, 2008: 106). Better, in the circumstances, to favour collective bargaining. When, after the Second World War, the Labour government nationalized a number of industries like coal and electricity, members of consultative committees established by statute were almost always full-time union officers.

The term 'single channel of representation' had two meanings at this time. Not only should members on the workers' side in consultative committees be controlled by the union but also there was absolutely no room for non-union representatives. The historic claim of trade unions is to be the only legitimate body able to represent workers' interests. If 'many union leaders were fearful of shop stewards as a potential challenge to their own control... the whole movement was intensely suspicious of "house unions" which were set up in fair numbers after the General Strike (1926), often in the form of non-union works committees or councils' (Clegg and Chester, 1954: 336).

One such non-union consultative committee was established in Imperial Chemical Industries (ICI) in 1927 with a national central committee, divisional committees, and works committees at plant level. In this famous company, although unions were recognized for collective bargaining, the consultative councils remained non-union, elected by all the employees, until the 1970s when the shop stewards were allocated all the worker seats (Roeber, 1975: 221–3). The unions thought that these non-union councils were 'sinister from the start as they were not based on union channels' (Marchington, 1989: 379). Another example comes from the successful and largely strike-free Vauxhall Motors. In this American owned motor manufacturer, the 'highly intelligent managing director', Sir Charles Bartlett (who liked to be called 'the Skipper'), promoted 'the Management Advisory Committee (to which each area of the factory sent a representative elected by secret ballot) as a forum for meaningful rather than fig leaf consultation' while 'the union was kept relatively marginalised' (Kynaston, 2007: 489–90). The committee was established in 1941 not long before the union was recognized. It, too, later became a union-only committee.

This employer tactic of creating an innocent enough sounding staff council elected by all employees is sometimes called the Trojan Horse effect by trade unions. They see employers using the excuse of creating a staff council as means of overwhelming union organization in a company before it has been recognized. Not to be outdone, employers complain also of a Trojan Horse problem where unions use the creation of a consultative body inside a company as a device for organizing and recruiting members. Consultation becomes a precursor to full recognition for collective bargaining purposes. This is what happened in the Second World War (Dukes, 2008: 109). What such repeated references to the Greek trick to enter Troy illustrates is the low level of trust between unions and employers at the national level in creating a joint agenda for the adoption of consultative arrangements. This low trust makes it difficult for consultation to thrive.

If members of consultative committees are to be union members, how then are they to be elected? The solution in JPCs in the Second World War, and set out in joint national agreements covering much of manufacturing, was for all employees to have a vote but candidates standing for election had to be 'card carrying' union members (Dukes, 2008: 106). And where there were no union members then direct workers' representatives could be elected. What this meant was that the workers' side of JPCs represented all employees, as all had a vote, and not just the segmented interests of the manual or clerical workers' unions. This arrangement came close to the system in Germany, then and now, where a union nominates candidates for works council elections, and non-union staff can be put forward. It is clear on the ballot paper who is a union nominee. The unions win around three-quarters of the elections (Gumbrell-McCormick and Hyman, 2006: 476). In the United Kingdom, this war time solution no longer applies. Recognized unions now usually nominate representatives to be members of the staff council. These are usually shop stewards who have often already been elected or selected by the union members to the wider representative role. They may well sit alongside elected or appointed non-union representatives in the staff council in what are called 'hybrid bodies' but they do not themselves generally stand for election to the council. This strict interpretation of the meaning of 'single channel of representation' has been controversial and was debated within the union movement in the 1990s when there were moves afoot to adopt a 'continental' works council model, as we explore in Chapter 4.

The rapid growth in joint consultation in the two periods of war, and in the immediate aftermath, was not just something employers and unions agreed to off their own bat. The government strongly endorsed the adoption of consultation and, especially in the Second World War, put strong pressure on both trade unions and employers to adopt JPCs. It took two sorts of pressure from the robust Minister of Labour, Ernest Bevin, to persuade the unions and employers to create JPCs in 1941 and 1942. He found the unions 'apathetic, disorganised and unwilling to take on new responsibilities', as he told the Prime Minister, Winston Churchill (cited in Dukes, 2008: 106). He threatened that the Minister for Aircraft Production would deal directly with the communist shop stewards in that vital sector. Once the system for the election of union representatives, discussed in the previous paragraph, had been put forward by Bevin, the unions came into line since elected representatives would, in most firms, be union members. His solution to employer 'hostility to the idea of JPCs... (was to) threaten them with using statutory powers to render the committees compulsory. Recognising that the only way to avoid this was to negotiate their voluntary establishment with the unions, the employers capitulated' (ibid.: 107).

There are three lessons of relevance today that can be taken from this unusual war time experience. First, trade unions rarely want consultation but will go along with it if they have to, provided it does not damage the prime role of collective bargaining (Tomlinson, 1996: 35). Second, employers are generally hostile to the idea of consultation especially if it means, or they fear it means, sharing power. Third, what employers hate even more, in the United Kingdom at least, is legislation, and, as we will see, would be prepared to adopt voluntary measures if it staved off regulation, or failing that will fight to modify or weaken proposals especially those put forward by the EU.

In the immediate post-war periods, governments had an interest in boosting productivity and securing industrial peace. Towards the end of the First World War, the Whitley Committee recommendations in 1917 on how to bring about a permanent improvement in relationships suggested three tiers of joint committees at works, district and national levels. The 'works committee', Whitley suggested, 'should always keep in the forefront the idea of constructive co-operation in the improvement of the industry to which they belong' (cited in Clegg and Chester, 1954: 332). The national level committees, the joint industrial councils, would also ensure 'the better utilization of the practical knowledge and experience of the workpeople' (ibid.). The government called a National Industrial Conference in 1919 to get unions and employers to set up the three-tier committees but the conference 'disappeared unnoticed in 1921' (ibid.: 333). All that was left were some Whitley Committees in the Civil Service (which still exist under this name) and around a thousand works committees in 1922 (Brannen, 1983: 41–2, cited in Marchington, 1989) but most of these disappeared by the end of the 1920s in the depression after the General Strike (Gospel, 1992: 91). It is hard to avoid the conclusion that all the parties—employers, trade unions, and the government—lost interest and without their support the fledgling consultative movement could not survive. Legislation was ruled out by the Whitley Committee which feared that 'works committees might be used in opposition to unions'; the union substitution problem (Dukes, 2008: 98).

Much the same happened after the Second World War. Clegg and Chester (1954: 342) note that 'the general enthusiasm for JPCs evaporated rapidly' and many JPCs 'fell back into the ambiguity surrounding consultation', as Phelps Brown (1983, cited in Gospel, 1992: 144) wonderfully put it. However, by 1947 the Labour government, faced with an economic crisis of low productivity, sought to resurrect joint consultative machinery for 'the regular exchange of views between management and workers on production matters' (Clegg and Chester, 1954: 343). In a debate in the House of Commons in 1950, 'speakers from both parties vied with each other in bestowing praises on consultation and in stressing its good effects on production' (ibid.). The key question, of much relevance in more recent periods, is why did the Labour government not legislate to establish consultative machinery throughout the economy? Just like his successor, Tony Blair, Clement Atlee, the Labour Prime Minister, had a massive majority and consultation did not appear to be a particularly contentious issue.

The answer to this conundrum, why the legislative dog did not bark, is normally given by reference to the British tradition of voluntarism and collective laissez-faire: the belief that the system of industrial relations can and should operate without a legal framework of regulation provided by the State. In other words, it is up to employers and trade unions to agree on forms of social regulation. Dukes (2008: 116–20) argues that other, specific factors were important. Attempts to create JPCs were increasingly resisted by employers and certainly they had no interest in legislation. The trade union position appeared to be confused. While they favoured consultation, and at times suggested that compulsion should be used against recalcitrant employers, their prime aim was the avoidance of independent shop steward power and working at industry and national level to preserve their role and influence (Kynaston, 2007: 457). In fact the only group pressing the Labour government to legislate in this area were the communist shop stewards themselves (Dukes, 2008: 91). This was guaranteed to raise the suspicions of employers and unions both of whom feared consultation being used as a basis for worker control under communist stewards: 'joint consultation represented the thin end of the wedge of pressure for workers control' (Tomlinson, 1996: 36). And it is suggested by Hinton (1994: 5–6) that 'reluctance to embrace an alliance with communist shop stewards was itself a major cause of government indifference to industrial democracy' (cited in Dukes, 2008: 120).

Nevertheless, a Labour government with a big majority could have legislated in the period up to 1951. After all, governments in continental Europe were doing so in France in 1945 and in Germany in 1952 (following establishment by the Allied Control Council in 1946). This legislation has been of continuing influence in these and other countries. Dukes (2008: 120) adds another reason for government reluctance to legislate. This hinged on what consultation was for and how it was meant to improve productivity. If consultation was about power-sharing or was seen as an inviolable worker's right, then legislation would be both necessary and appropriate. If, however, the purpose of consultation was more psychological, seen in the generation of trust, then compulsion would be unlikely, it was argued, to produce this desired end. You cannot force people to cooperate. Tomlinson (1996: 35) records that certain members of the government became influenced by the human relations school of thought, then becoming fashionable, which implied that the effect of cooperation between management and labour was to be found in building mutual trust. 'Management, by paying attention to their non-economic, social and cultural needs increase worker satisfaction and productivity' (Marsh and Evans, 1973: 142). We have now discovered yet another purpose of consultation: building relationships of trust and confidence.

Ultimately, Dukes (2008: 121) concludes that the 'failure' to legislate was due to trade union preference for union-only representation and an insistence that JCCs remained firmly under union control. The dogged defence of the single union channel of representation in consultation may have scuppered the chance of statutory regulation of consultation then, and it did do again later in the 1990s. Towers (1997: 217) is blunter: 'the biggest obstacle to introducing works councils into Britain . . . lies in the need for an historic shift in trade unions' perspectives'. When Michael Young, one of the leading centre-left thinkers of his generation, wrote a Labour party pamphlet on 'industrial democracy' in 1948, 'privileging the rank and file worker above the union leadership and even flirting with the idea of workers' control', he was forced to withdraw it by two Labour ministers close to the trade unions, Ernest Bevin and Herbert Morrison (Kynaston, 2007: 225).

The post-war retreat and possible resurgence of consultation

In the early 1950s, Clegg and Chester (1954: 344) were able to ask rhetorically 'why should a device which is given almost universal public approval meet with such limited success?' Their answer was to list many of the issues raised here summed up as 'the suspicions and ignorance which determine the attitude of many managers, trade union officers and workers, despite public approbation and government propaganda . . . the consequence of these sort of attitudes is apathy' (ibid.: 346). What they did not list, as advocates of 'voluntarism', was the failure of the government to legislate in this area. This was almost certainly even more important, given the experience in the Continent.

It is widely assumed that consultation declined further in the 1950s and 1960s (Marchington, 1989: 380). Marsh and Coker's 1963 study of the engineering industry found by the early 1960s that only one in five firms employing over 150 retained a consultative committee, the number dropping sharply every year after 1955 (cited in Ramsay, 1977: 493).

No new major national initiatives were to be taken until the establishment of the Bullock committee on industrial democracy, concerned with the appointment of worker directors, in 1975. This was when the EU began to put forward legislative proposals for employee rights to information and consultation. This is discussed in Chapter 3 while the Bullock report and its aftermath are considered in Chapter 4.

What did change was the context which shaped the demand for consultation and arguments about its relevance. There were two distinct phases. First, in the period up to 1979, especially the 1960s and 1970s, the power and position of shop stewards was consolidated. Collective bargaining began to be decentralized to the single employer level and spread to new sectors of the economy; the subject matter broadened beyond pay and conditions to wider areas of joint regulation and the style of negotiation changed in some areas to integrative bargaining or joint problem solving in productivity bargaining (Walton and McKersie, 1965; McKersie and Hunter, 1973). The most famous of the productivity bargains at the Esso Refinery at Fawley (Flanders, 1964) led Allan Flanders, one of the leading industrial relations academics and theorists, who charted the deal, to reappraise the value of joint consultation. According to Kelly (2010: 120), his biographer, having been disillusioned with consultation in the early 1950s (ibid.: 105), Flanders 'radically revised his assessment and now believed there was an important role for joint consultation as an adjunct to collective bargaining... what impressed him was that joint consultation could serve as a vehicle for "reasoned discourse" and "rational persuasion" based on an examination of the facts'. Esso management was open and prepared to discuss a wide range of items and plans and the local union shop steward body was well organized to respond.

By the end of the 1970s, both collective bargaining and union membership reached their peak. Some two-thirds of workplaces with twenty-five or more employees recognized unions for collective bargaining purposes, covering 70 per cent of employees (the equivalent figures in the private sector were 50 and 54 per cent) (Brown and Forth, 2009: tables 2.1 and 2.2). Trade unions' membership density, the proportion of the workforce in union membership, peaked in 1979 at 55.4 per cent, some 13.5 million workers (Bain and Price, 1983: table 1.1). Consultation was almost completely overshadowed by collective bargaining in practice and in fashionable academic discourse about industrial relations. The irrelevance of consultation had been made abundantly clear by the Director of Research to the Donovan Commission, Bill McCarthy, in the mid-1960s when he asserted that consultative committees 'either must change their character and become essentially negotiating committees carrying out functions which are indistinguishable from the formal processes of shop floor bargaining or they are boycotted by shop stewards and... fall into disuse' (McCarthy, 1966). The assumption then was that consultation would inevitably be with union representatives, the shop stewards. McCarthy (1988) did subsequently modify his views in the light of declining union membership in the 1980s and proposed 'joint councils' in enterprises with 500 or more employees.

McCarthy's conclusion in 1966 was probably more an extrapolation of trends than an accurate measure. Consultation is not so easily dismissed. A survey of manufacturing industries in 1977–8 with fifty or more employees revealed that consultative committees were present in 42 per cent of establishments. Just under 20 per cent of JCCs for manual workers and just over 20 per cent of staff JCCs included non-union representatives. Overall, non-union representatives were found in over a quarter of establishments (Brown, 1981: 74–7). This is evidence of the long existence of 'hybrid' union and non-union staff councils.

The survey gave an indication for the first time of the views of managers who were involved in consultation. As Brown reported, 'managers showed a cheerful view of their committees' success. Over two thirds considered them to be usually successful' (ibid.: 77). This, and the prevalence of consultative committees, led Brown to modify the McCarthy thesis on the grounds that shop stewards were now so well established that they were 'unlikely to be threatened by the introduction of consultation' (ibid.: 80). Again the assumption was made that shop stewards would be the employee representatives even although around one in five of JCCs included non-union representatives and 'over half of representatives on the JCCs were not automatically part of the collective bargaining process' (ibid.: 77). Consultation and collective bargaining were often separate activities.

Brown's survey picked up something else of interest, indicative of another phase in consultation. The majority of the consultative committees (61 per cent) had been set up within five years of the survey, post-1972. Was this an indication of a resurgence of interest and if so why? The survey report noted that managerial enthusiasm for the consultative committees was 'markedly less where the committees had been (recently) established' (ibid.: 77) and speculated that 'perhaps recent moves on consultation had included hasty and cosmetic attempts to adjust to the spirit of the Bullock Committee' (ibid.). The implication, which became clearer later when there was a real prospect of EU initiatives (MacInnes, 1985: 93), was that managements were rushing into consultation in order to show that 'voluntary' action could be relied upon and there was no need for legislation. Sometimes consultation is embarked on by employers without any desire by managers to consult!

Further evidence of a possible resurgence in consultation came from the first Workplace Industrial Relations Survey (WIRS) in 1980. This showed that some 16 per cent of the consultative committees had been established in the five years before the survey (Daniel and Millward, 1983: 132) and establishments with newly introduced committees outnumbered those that had abandoned them by about nine to one. 'We can be sure that some growth has taken place' (Marchington: 1989: 381). However, by 1984 it seems this growth had petered out (Millward and Stevens, 1986: 140). In both surveys the overall incidence of consultative committees was one-third (34 per cent) in establishments with twenty-five or more employees. The surveys noted that the adoption of consultative committees was more likely the larger the workplace. Looking at all of the evidence of consultative committees since the war, MacInnes (1985: 98) found that the incidence of committees was remarkably even with between 'at least half and two thirds of establishments with 200 or more employees having some form of joint consultation at any time'. This did not imply stability, however. MacInnes noted that 'the high birth rate and apparent "renaissance" of consultation is paralleled by an equally high but less visible death rate' (ibid.: 106). Some consultative committees have a short life, a curious feature of consultation which we will return to later.

One dominant explanation for this strange phenomenon of birth and death in consultative committees came from Ramsay (1977) who placed emphasis on the 'politics of participation' (Martinez Lucio, 2010: 118). His argument was that in moments of conflict and labour mobilization, employers had little choice but to develop strategies of worker and union incorporation as seen in cooperation (in consultative committees, for example) and other means of defusing power. When these moments passed, employer interest in consultation waned. This line of reasoning is very similar to earlier work by Fox (1974: 307) on management style. 'A common phenomenon in industrial history has been the employer who, at times of high labour bargaining strength or a fashionable mood of sympathy toward the less favoured manifests signs of a shift to a pluralistic strategy, but reverts to unitary attitudes and behaviour when a slack market returns or when the fashionable mood passes'. He describes this as the 'standard modern style', implying it is the modal characteristic of employers in the second half of the twentieth century. This oscillation in styles was often the result of different coalitions of managers coming to power inside the organization.

How far does Ramsay's 'cycles of control' theory fit the period? We have already noted how collective bargaining spread and union membership grew to its peak. The early 1970s was also marked by very high levels of strike action peaking in 1972 with virtually 24 million working days lost in disputes and the number of strikes never fell below 2,000 a year in the decade with 2,703 strikes taking place in 1977 (Edwards, 1983: table 9.1). By way of comparison, in 2009 there were ninety-eight stoppages leading to just under half a million working days lost (Hale, 2010: 47). At the same time in the second half of the 1970s, the Labour government was attempting to forge a 'social contract' with unions and had set up the Bullock Committee which was expected to recommend the appointment of worker directors. Purcell (1981) noted that 'the change in managerial attitudes between 1977, when industrial democracy and consensus politics were popular, to 1980, when a new abrasive Conservative government was in power in a period of a major recession', provided a good illustration of such a shift in style.

Consultation in a period of union decline

The recession in the early 1980s was especially severe in manufacturing leading to major job losses and a scaling back in shop steward workplace organization and collective bargaining over job controls (Terry, 1983). But the period was also marked by a renaissance in joint consultation in some firms with discussions now much more likely to be focussed on key strategic decisions: 'investment plans, the development of new products, problems of productivity and competitiveness, national and international amalgamation, takeovers, rationalisation' (ibid.: 56). Marchington (1987: 344) noted the same trend in his research among manufacturing companies a few years later. 'The context within which revitalised consultation is more likely to take place . . . is one which management see the best response to external competitive pressure as increased employee involvement—both direct and indirect—and do so in a climate of relatively high trust between the parties'. The 'market conditions caused the parties to see more value working with each other to overcome their jointly perceived difficulties' (ibid.: 342). At this time of recession there were real issues to consult over. Sometimes consultation can struggle to be meaningful when not much of any importance is happening, and sometimes the news is so catastrophic that consultation is useless: 'where relations are unfrozen by adversity, but not paralyzed by calamity' (Cutcher-Gershenfeld and Verma, 1994: 560).

The early 1980s was the start of a prolonged and profound period of change. The decline in trade union membership and the proportion of companies, especially in the private sector, recognizing a union has been marked since the 1980s. One effect of this has been the decline in the single union channel as a form of employee voice. This fell from 24 per cent in 1984 to 6 per cent in 2004 in workplaces with twenty-five or more employees (Gomez et al., 2010: 388) with a fall noted in each of the survey years in between. There are two explanations for this marked change. First, there are now many more non-union companies in the private sector. Trade union recognition fell from 50 per cent in private sector establishments with twenty-five or more employees in 1980 to 38 per cent in 1990 (Millward et al., 2000: table 4.6) and 23 per cent in 2004 (Kersley et al., 2006: 121). Consultative committees have always been more prevalent in unionized companies so that declines in recognition also lead to a drop in the use of consultation, although the relationship between the two is not linear.

Second, a new development in the 1980s was the growth in direct forms of employee 'voice' often at the level of the team or work group within the workplace. This typically can involve team briefing sessions led by the line manager or team leader, problem solving and direct forms of communication. If some time is given in team briefing sessions for employees to ask questions and express their views, then it can become a form of consultation. In addition, there can be meetings of all employees addressed by senior managers.

The combination of these direct forms of 'voice' with indirect staff councils is called 'dual channel' by Gomez and his colleagues. They note that the growth of dual channels was especially prevalent in 'older' workplaces, meaning established companies (Gomez et al., 2010: 393).

This double change in the context of consultation in the last three decades—union decline and new forms of employee voice—was observed by Marchington et al. (1992) in one of the first studies to combine direct and indirect forms of employee involvement. They noted that 'these new employee involvement initiatives have been much more management sponsored than in the past, and as a result have been more concerned with employee motivation and commitment to organisational objectives and performance than with issues of joint regulation and power-sharing' (Marchington et al., 1992: 1). They showed in their case studies how initiatives came in waves. For example, in manufacturing 'the JCC wave was central to participation in the 1970s and it has been sustained, albeit at a lower level . . . However, the 1980s saw the spawning of a series of initiatives' (ibid.: 27). Examples given were team briefing in Southern Shoes where joint consultation 'remains a key feature of employee relations but team briefing was introduced in the early 1980s and now operates in conjunction with the JCC' (ibid.). Another company was Midbank where initiatives included team briefing, profit sharing, and total quality management (TQM).

The importance of the wave analysis is that it requires 'account to be taken of the fact that initiatives come from different sources, are of different levels of intensity and can sometimes directly contradict each other' (ibid.: 30). The HR manager may push for consultation, a production manager want team briefing, and the finance director think in terms of profit sharing. In the new coalitions of the 1990s, where 'the emphasis on customers and competitors is much more explicit than it was in the 1970s' (ibid.: 1), those managers favouring 'collectivist' forms of employee voice tended to lose out. This broadening of the scope and location of employee voice means that collective consultation through staff councils can no longer be treated in isolation.

The periodic national surveys of employee relations from 1980, the WIRS, now WERS (Workplace Employment Relations Surveys) series allows us to plot developments in this crucial period between 1980 and 1998. Table 1.1 shows the incidence of JCCs while Table 1.2 gives the use of various forms of direct employee voice methods. Millward and his colleagues (2000: 108) use a definition of a 'functioning consultative committee' where the JCC meets at least every three months. This sensibly avoids sham committees which rarely, if ever, meet. The decline in JCCs is very clear, and this was true in each size range. By 1998, only one in five workplaces with twenty-five or more employees had a JCC. Meanwhile the use of briefing groups, or team briefing, rocketed from one-third to two-thirds in workplaces between 1984 and 1998. We look at data from the 2004 WERS in Chapter 5 when we chart contemporary practice.

Table 1.1. Incidence of joint consultative committees, 1980–98 (% of workplaces)

	1980	1984	1990	1998
All establishments	30	31	26	23
25–49	21	21	18	14
50–99	29	32	31	25
100–199	39	47	37	32
200–499	60	54	43	49
500 or more	66	70	61	58
Private sector	26	24	18	20
Public sector	39	42	45	32

Establishments with twenty-five or more employees.
Source: Millward et al. (2000: table 4.10).

Table 1.2. The take up of direct communication methods, 1984–97 (% of workplaces)

	1984	1990	1997
Regular meetings with senior management	34	41	48
Problem solving groups	–	35	49
Briefing groups	36	48	65

Establishments with twenty-five or more employees.
Source: Millward et al. (2000: table 4.12).

Further analysis shows that establishments which only had representative voice arrangements, whether union or non-union, fell from 29 per cent in 1984 to 14 per cent in 1998; those with a mixture of indirect and direct fell from 45 to 39 per cent. The proportion of establishments which used only direct forms of employee voice, without staff councils, grew from 11 to 30 per cent (ibid.: table 4.15). The decline in the use of consultative bodies was evident across the board in all size ranges and sectors. Overall the use of direct methods, whether in combination with JCCs or on their own, rose from 56 per cent in 1984 to 69 per cent in 1998.

The evidence that collectivism, which includes consultative committees, was losing out to more individualistic forms of communication and involvement was vividly revealed by the surveys when they looked at how old the establishments were. The authors refer to 'stark differences between workplaces entering the population and those leaving it' (ibid.: 124). Among new establishments, which had been at their current address for five years or less, only 2 per cent had union-only voice, a quarter had dual union and direct systems while two-thirds had solely non-union arrangements. In older workplaces only a quarter had non-union-only direct forms of involvement. In short, 'dual channel replaced union solutions for older workplaces and stand alone non-union voice became the norm in newer workplaces' (Gomez et al., 2010: 393).

The big change was just as predicted by Marchington and his colleagues in their wave theory: the introduction of direct forms of employee involvement. The majority of continuing workplaces with union-only voice arrangements in 1990 had switched to dual-channel arrangements in 1998 (Millward et al., 2000: 124). In this period, union density in establishments with recognized unions fell from 66 to 53 per cent (ibid.: 90). It became harder to claim single-channel representation rights when only a half, or less, of the workforce are union members. The big growth was in direct voice mechanisms. This was especially noticeable in smaller manufacturing sites. And among those with consultative committees and direct methods 'there was a large shift to non-union employee representatives on the (consultative) committee' (ibid.: 125). This was not simply a move away from union-based arrangements. All forms of indirect, representative-based systems declined in the period 1984–98 (ibid.: 126). These were seismic shifts or 'the end of institutional industrial relations' (Purcell, 1995: 101–19) calling into question, by the time of the election of the Labour government in May 1997, the continuing relevance of collective consultation and starkly showing the weakness of trade unions especially in the private sector. By then the first moves to put consultation onto a statutory basis had already begun in the EU. This is the topic of Chapter 3.

Conclusion

There is a form of institutional memory in Britain, as most probably elsewhere, which means that history, or our selective experience and memory of it, shapes interpretations of current events and the choice of futures, what is termed in organizational studies as 'path dependency'. Consultation is so difficult to define with precision and has been embarked on at different times over the last 100 or more years for very different reasons that there is little shared agenda. The views of employers and trade unions differ widely even although they were party to the same events.

Employers and employers' organizations have often viewed consultation with suspicion not for the act of consulting itself but because other outcomes or effects came as the price. There was, certainly from the 1920s, a fear that trade unions would use consultative bodies as a means of organizing: the union Trojan Horse. This fear remains today but how realistic it is we will explore later. Employers also became concerned when governments began to flirt with consultation as a 'good thing' whether to raise productivity, reduce employers' arbitrary power or as a fundamental employee right. If this government interest, in times of social and economic difficulty, should lead to the threat of legislation, it was especially disliked, as in the Second World War and again in the 1970s.

These fears were symptomatic of the long-running low level of trust between employers and trade unions at the national level. The fact that consultation, unlike collective bargaining, was premised on cooperation, not conflict, cut little ice since it was the side effects which were feared more. On the ground inside workplaces, away from the corridors of power, employers, or at least a significant minority of them, have always engaged in consultation, most often with trade union representatives but sometimes with non-union bodies. For some this came out of a choice of management style while for others it was more pragmatic.

Unions have always been ambivalent about consultation. It is seen as a much less attractive option than collective bargaining since no agreements are made and few obvious benefits can be delivered to the members. Where consultation is an adjunct to collective bargaining, as it was in the Esso Fawley productivity deal, then it can be helpful. These days it would be seen as a part of partnership activity where it is hard to say quite where bargaining ends and consultation begins since the premise is a search for mutually acceptable understandings. Consultation in the shadow of collective bargaining can be a sham or of marginal importance as the experience in the 1960s and 1970s showed. But the real union fear of consultation is that employers will introduce it as a substitute for unionization: the employers' Trojan Horse. Employees will see no need to belong to a union if there is an effective consultative body in place, and it will be in the employer's interest to ensure that consultation is effective. Unions experienced this in the late nineteenth century, in the inter-war years and again in the post-war era up to the present day. And it was fear that employers would adopt this tactic that led the Whitley Committee of 1917 to eschew recommending statutory enforcement.

Unions were always anxious to ensure that the 'single channel of representation' meant that only their nominees would attend consultative committees, or at least be able to stand for election. This was introduced in part to limit the communist threat in the Second World War but also to reduce the likelihood that non-union representatives would be chosen. Unions have, until recently, been no more interested in legislation to enforce the adoption of consultation than employers. This was due to the general preference for voluntarism in the whole area of industrial relations but also to specific fears about the impact of consultation on the primacy of collective bargaining. Governments have shown interest in consultation in periods of national emergency and industrial unrest but only once considered legislation, and this was a device to coerce employers into setting up 'voluntary' consultative committees in the Second World War.

The last two decades of the twentieth century radically changed industrial relations and, within it, the context in which consultation was practised. The decline of trade unions in the private sector seen in membership levels, and especially in collective bargaining, has meant the disappearance of a collective voice, except where there is a consultative committee, in much of the sector. At the same time the introduction of direct forms of employee involvement, seen most obviously in team briefings on a weekly basis, has provided an extra dimension to consultation in the same way as employees increasingly gain information from their employer via social media.

Consultation in staff councils with employee representatives can seem old fashioned if it is only about communication. But if it is about sharing information on business plans and decisions before they are taken and holding high-level discussions where implications and alternatives are explored in mutual dialogue, then it remains a radical agenda. If this agenda is backed by law, as it is now via EU legislation, then there remains the potential for a new era of consultation. For trade unions this may be 'the least worst option' (Hyman, 1996: 65). For companies it may provide better opportunities to gain employee engagement and improve performance when linked with direct involvement methods, since it is backed by statute and in many places does not involve contamination by the collective bargaining agenda.

In Chapter 2, we look at the competing logics for introducing consultation: is it to improve efficiency, to change the balance of power and reduce arbitrary employer decision taking, or is consultation a basic human right, a form of democracy? Regulation can say something on each of these justifications for consultation but where does regulation come from? In Chapter 3, we look at the unfolding and changing approach of the EU to regulating in this area, something that has been planned since the early 1970s. Chapter 4 explores the response to the EU directives in the United Kingdom. How have they been turned into statute law to create the system of consultation that applies in Britain? Chapter 5 asks what impact these various forms of information and consultation regulations and statutes in the United Kingdom, and their enforcement, have had on the practice of consultation. Chapter 6 uses evidence to look in detail at how consultation is practised and identifies the necessary prerequisites for staff councils to operate effectively. Chapter 7 uses case histories drawn, in the main, from our research project to show the dynamics of consultation. As staff councils are formed, participants learn and adapt their behaviour sometimes to strengthen and in other circumstances to weaken consultative practice. In the final chapter, we ask what future there is for consultation in the United Kingdom, especially in the private sector where most firms now are non-union. We do this in the light of comparative experience from continental Europe.

2

Justifications for Consultation

Ambiguities over the meaning of consultation reflect the differing intentions of employers, trade unions, and governments in promoting, or at least concurring with, consultative schemes. These intentions are themselves never fixed as the review of the history of consultation in Chapter 1 showed. The purpose of this chapter is to explore the different functions that consultation can serve. There are many variations, as we will show, but three dominant reasons for embarking on consultation can be identified.

Employers tend to emphasize the effect on organizational and employee *efficiency* but quite how this comes about is far from straight forward. The effect of consultation on efficiency can be positive but it can also have negative connotations in the sense of avoiding something worse. Using consultation for union avoidance purposes fits this negative view.

Where trade unions and labour relations analysts on the political left have promoted consultation, they have done so often for reasons of *power-sharing*—a means of reducing or curbing the arbitrary power of employers to take decisions unilaterally without accounting for the interests of employees. Of course, a justification for this can be that it will result in better decisions and it may be more acceptable to promote power-sharing under the guise of efficiency.

The third justification, more often, but not exclusively, used by governments, is that consultation is a *right* that employees should have in the modern world of employment; a right to be told and a right to express a view and for that opinion to be treated seriously. It is often portrayed, especially at the EU (European Union) level, as a 'fundamental' right implying it is indivisible and not something that can be qualified by circumstances. It is one thing to proclaim consultation as a fundamental right but quite another to give effect to that right through enforceable legislation. Yet again the justification for this right to information and consultation is often dressed up, or indeed camouflaged, by reference to the effect on efficiency especially in circumstances of major organizational change where to consult is to manage consent.

The language of consultation, participation, and involvement

These three justifications for consultation tend to be associated with different descriptive terms. The language used to describe the consultative process has changed over the years, reflecting the ebbs and flows of the different justifications. *Industrial democracy* is rarely used now but was in quite common parlance especially at the time of the Bullock Committee of Inquiry on Industrial Democracy in 1975–7 (see Chapter 4). The remit of the committee was to determine how the representation of trade unions on company boards of directors could best be achieved. This clearly would have been a form of power-sharing in management decision taking had anything come of the recommendations: 'the right to share in the control of industrial decisions' (Clegg, 1960: 3). The origins of industrial democracy go back to the Guild Socialism and syndicalism of the early part of the twentieth century as modified forms of worker control: the replacement of the capitalist industrial system. With these antecedents it is not surprising that most managers, and quite a number of trade union full time officers, were never in favour of anything that smacked of industrial democracy in the board room. However, another interpretation is to see industrial democracy as a form of industrial citizenship; 'a belief that citizens of liberal democracies should have the right to participate in the governance of industry in the way that they participate in the governance of the wider society' (Heery and Noon, 2001: 173). This is consultation as a right and, to emphasize this, power-sharing is replaced by 'participation in governance', a much vaguer and less threatening term.

Workers' participation or just *participation* (to avoid the dated feel of the word 'worker', now replaced in some organizations as 'colleague' or 'staff member') is much more acceptable since it avoids connotations of power-sharing: 'the inclusion of employees or their representatives in the process of management decision making' (ibid.: 253). This allows for participation at the level of the work group or team by individual employees in association with their line manager on the sort of decisions made at that level. These can be on the job, for example through semi-autonomous work groups allocating tasks and being concerned with the achievement of quality, or off the job (Adler et al., 1999) participating in problem-solving activities like quality circles and Keizen teams. At this level, participation can have a beneficial effect and be valued by most employees since they have a direct say in the process.

What direct participation at this level cannot do is to provide an input into organization-wide decisions taken by senior management or the board of directors. This is the role of employee representatives in consultation. The dual approach implied by the term participation has become more important as organizations have increasingly implemented both forms, at the work group and in higher level decision forums. A further advantage of participation is the emphasis placed on decision-making: the process of making a decision before the final act of taking a decision. The board of directors may well take a decision on restructuring, for example, but the process of making the decision will have involved a lot of considerations and reviewing of options as well as determining how the decision can best be implemented. Participation in this process is likely to be more meaningful and influential than the final stage of taking or agreeing the decision. The down side of participation as a descriptive term, especially the full term 'worker participation', is that it came to be associated with trade union-based consultative activities often aligned to collective bargaining, the 'adjunct model' (Marchington, 1989: 392), with a fear that it would thus be conducted in a spirit of adversarialism rather than cooperation (Kaufman and Tarras, 2010: 273).

The alternative term much favoured since the 1980s is *employee involvement* (EI). This 'describes those practices which are initiated principally by management, and are designed to increase employee information about, and commitment to, the organisation. EI does not therefore involve any *de jure* sharing of authority or power with employees, though some forms of EI may give employees new channels through which their influence is advanced' (Marchington et al., 1992: 7). What EI means in practice is the use of a range of techniques to increase information flows to employees such as team briefing, 'town hall' meetings and company social media, and ways to give employees some form of 'voice' whether through the use of employee attitude or engagement surveys or opportunities to ask questions and contribute in team briefing sessions. EI places emphasis on direct forms of involvement. This can include consultation through staff councils but usually does not. It is a very vague term: 'management clearly intends that these forms of voice will either lift productivity *without* challenging managerial power or provide consensus around the implementation of major workforce decisions' (Boxall and Purcell, 2010: 43). EI places emphasis on the role of the line manager or team leader as the prime conduit for communication with employees. As we will see later, the relationship between EI and consultation through staff councils, especially where these are non-union, can be complementary but at times becomes competitive to the detriment of consultation systems. We give case histories illustrating this problem in Chapter 7.

At the time when EI first came into vogue, worker or employee participation was still the widely used term. What was the relationship between them? The sometime director of the Industrial Society (now the Work Foundation), John Garnett, used to explain the difference through a fable. The pig and the hen decided to give the farmer a special breakfast for his birthday. 'I know', said the hen, 'let's give him bacon and egg!' 'Perhaps', said the pig, 'but the trouble is you are only involved but I am participating'. Participation, if it means inclusion in the process of management decision-making, is much more demanding for both employee representatives and managers. Almost nothing is expected or required of an employee being 'involved' except perhaps giving passive consent, although some hope it will lead to employees working 'beyond contract'. To participate is to debate and exchange, involving the examination of proposals. At its heart it is a political process. Perhaps because of this, the term 'participation' fell out of common use among managers and now the emphasis is on EI. The contribution of collective consultation through staff councils has been over-shadowed by EI precisely because the former is focussed on 'power-centred' decision-making which can sometimes challenge the management prerogative.

The pursuit of efficiency through consultation

Management nearly always dominate the consultative process in determining what is to be discussed, what form the discussion takes, and what notice is to be taken of points raised by representatives. Management beliefs and values on the purpose of consultation and why it is necessary will carry considerable weight in these circumstances. Studies in the early 2000s (Wilkinson et al., 2004) concluded that 'for the majority of firms in the UK, managers tend to view consultative structures as means of building mutual cooperation with the workforce and promoting an understanding of company policy' (cited in Wales and Landsbury, 2010). It was commonly noted in the 1970s (e.g. Ramsay, 1977) and 1980s (e.g. MacInnes, 1985) that such beliefs were typical of unitarist views of the firm where there were, or should be, shared goals emanating from top management with all members of the organization working together to the common end. In this unitary frame of reference conflict was an aberration either imported into the organization by militant trade unionists or more commonly was attributed to failures of communication. The essential function of consultation was to improve communication flows to allow cooperation to flourish. The alternative, pluralist frame of reference placed emphasis on the inevitability of conflicts of objectives between management and labour and the need for collective bargaining to allow for differing goals to be accommodated in the short term.

What is interesting now in the long-running debate between pluralism and the unitary perspective is that there is evidence from large-scale surveys in Anglo-American countries (including the United Kingdom) that private sector workers 'want forms of voice that will help them deal with problems cooperatively and improve their firm's performance' (Boxall et al., 2007: 219). 'All the studies [in five countries] underline the message that workers want more cooperative styles of engagement with management' (ibid.: 216). The growth in professional and administrative occupations, which require high-level qualifications, often now called 'knowledge workers', may help explain this desire for cooperative engagement with management. 'Employees who enjoy more autonomy in their job tend to have a greater preference for participation' (Green, 2006: 98) and 'a qualified workforce is important for cooperative relationships between works councils and management' (Jirjahn and Smith, 2006: 12). This evidence may provide support to management views on the cooperative purpose of consultation but the consultation process would have to be genuine and effective to meet the representational gap that many workers in the survey identified (Purcell and Geogiadis, 2007: 191).

How does management-inspired consultation contribute to organizational efficiency? 'Efficiency' needs to be defined quite broadly and not just in terms of income and profit. It needs to 'include the continuing survival of the firm... thus economic outcomes include efficiency, productivity and adaptability to changing economic circumstances' (Frege, 2002: 243). There are a number of streams of data suggesting causal relationships although the evidence is generally thin (Bryson et al., 2007: 442). The problem of measurement is that the efficiency effects can come through at least six different processes: gaining access to top management, improving the quality of decisions, easing the management of change, inculcating a participative management style, adopting progressive HR policies, providing effective grievance handling and building employee commitment. These justifications are considered in turn in the following sections. In exploring each of these attributes, the assumption is made that management is actively wishing to engage in consultation rather than trivialize it. There is plenty of evidence that this trivialization does occur; for example, Gollan (2006b) notes the lack of financial, investment, and strategic data provided to non-union consultative committees (cited in Wales and Landsbury, 2010: 580). There is no point searching for efficiency outcomes if management is not committed to making consultation work.

Access to top management

One of the most distinctive characteristics of staff councils is the attendance of top management not just from HR but often including operations and facilities management as well as the CEO or the most senior site manager. The active involvement of senior managers meeting employee representatives in the staff council can influence efficiency in a number of ways.

- Top executives can sometimes value access to junior staff since they can hear about issues and attitudes without these being channelled through middle managers 'who can filter and distort information' (Dundon and Gollan, 2007: 1186, citing Kaufman, 2000). This leads to more accurate information, aiding decision-making.
- The provision of company information and discussion of trends and challenges faced in the business environment can lead to a reinforcement of management authority. Top managers show that they are competent and on top of events while educating representatives on the complexity of organizational decision taking. 'Managers tried to show that their prerogatives and the right to manage were not authoritarian but a function of their expertise and the requirements of business efficiency. Consultation was therefore a forum for management to show common interest [with] the workforce' (MacInnes, 1985: 102). MacInnes calls this the 'negotiation of legitimacy' (ibid.: 105). Marchington (1987: 350) noted from his research that 'some organisations prided themselves on their consultative arrangements and see these as synonymous with the earning of managerial legitimacy'. This often meant top management 'using their information about the environment in order to justify to employees any decision they wish to make, or have taken' (Marchington et al., 1992: 44).
- This legitimating process does not imply or require that management alter any decision but merely be present and open in discussion. The outcome can mean that decisions are less likely to be challenged and proposed business changes more likely to be accepted.
- Representatives are drawn into the complexities of organizational decision-making and are less able to maintain independence of thought or action. This is the sin of incorporation, much feared in union circles. 'Unions fear that participation would subject them to the charge of having "sold out" to management' (Heller et al., 1998: 114). It may even be a deliberate ploy 'to weaken unionism by the back door' (Marchington, 1989: 391).

Improving the quality of decisions

From the earliest efforts to establish consultation, it was assumed that tapping the practical knowledge of workpeople would improve decision-making since employees often have unique perspectives on work processes. The act of representatives scrutinizing management-proposed decisions may lead to more careful deliberation and 'improve the quality of the decisions as well as giving them greater legitimacy' (Heller et al., 1998: 26). This can happen in three ways.

- The most obvious is that it results from the debate in the staff council. We give an illustration of this in the case histories in Chapter 7.
- 'Management changes the way in which decisions are framed from the outset, in the light of the requirement to (consult)' (Marginson and Sisson, 2004: 212). They anticipate employee concerns and adapt proposals in advance of a council meeting.
- The third way in which this participation in decision-making can take place is through sub-committees or joint working parties exploring a particular management proposal in detail before further discussion in the staff council. In one of our cases, call out payments had to be scaled back. The complexity of the rules covering call outs, and the loss of income anticipated, made a working party an ideal forum for this topic.

High-level consultation on business decisions can be demanding. To be credible it needs management to bring proposed decisions or areas of concern to the discussion. To be able to do this there has to be a high degree of trust in the capacity of the representatives to handle material on a confidential basis as well as having the capability to review and respond. Many commentators have observed that it is managements' overall orientation to consultation and participation which is more important than the mechanics of consultation, and, of these orientations, trust and responsiveness are the most important (Bryson et al., 2006; Wood and De Menezes, 2008).

Contribution to the management of change

Consultation has always been seen to be most necessary at times of organizational change. A two-way process is common. Management use discussion of proposed changes as a means of seeking employee cooperation and consent. Consultation can also improve the ways changes are designed and implemented by allowing employee ideas to be considered. Senior management often do not have the intimate level of knowledge of operations necessary to ensure that changes can be introduced in a cost-effective manner or to ensure successful implementation. Consultation can 'enable management and employees to highlight issues of concern at an early stage thus reducing potential conflict at the implementation stage' (Gollan, 2010: 225).

Change management has a number of phases from first initiation of an idea or policy decision through development to finalization and implementation (Heller et al., 1998: 21). At what stage should and does consultation take place? A study of employee participation in technological change in five countries (Fröhlich and Krieger, 1990) concluded that consultation and participation was much more likely in the latter stages and that full participation remained relatively low in all countries for all stages (cited in Beardwell and Holden, 1994). Research in the Netherlands confirmed that 'works council involvement in decision-making tends to be strongest towards the end of the decision-making process' (Marginson and Sisson, 2004, citing Looise and de Lange, 1987). This led Cressey and Williams (1990) to conclude on the basis of their study of twelve EU countries that there was a 'paradox of participation', a point echoed later by Visser (1995): 'although the probability of participation is higher, the magnitude of impact at the implementation stage is smaller' (Marginson and Sisson, 2004). The focus on the implementation stage is understandable. Employee representatives may feel they have less to contribute to a business decision per se, a merger or takeover for example, but have a great deal of interest in the consequences of the decision for the organization and employees' jobs and employment prospects. It is these that will dominate discussion and it is these matters which link to cooperation and consent. It is debatable whether this means, as Visser asserts, that the impact is smaller.

Failures in the implementation stage of change can be damaging. In redundancy it is commonly noted that there can be a 'survivor syndrome' where remaining employees feel a sense of guilt and loss leading to a collapse of employee commitment (Baruch and Hind, 2000). One of the justifications for consultation is that it allows for proper and wider consideration to be given to how a change is to be implemented and its aftermath since this will be of particular interest to employees but can overlooked by senior managers. The outcome most required is a perception of fairness (Dietz and Fortin, 2007: 1168), closely allied to feelings of justice about the fairness of the decision-making process (Folger and Cropanzano, 1998).

Inculcation of participative management style

This requirement for fairness—'worker representatives' views on consultation could be summarised as the demand for management to manage "fairly"' (MacInnes, 1985: 102)—underlines the connection between consultation and management style especially by reinforcing a participative style. This is where the interconnection between indirect participation through the staff council and direct participation or employee involvement via line managers is most obvious. The act of senior managers meeting employee representatives and being prepared to share information and establish dialogue on proposed changes provides visible proof of a participative style which can influence line managers in their leadership roles. And should a particular manager adopt a less than helpful style the way is open for complaints to be made to senior management since staff council members have regular formal and often informal contact with senior managers (Kersley et al., 2006: 163). In a medium-sized snacks company we studied, there were allegations of sexual harassment. The chairman of the non-union staff council, a worker representative, was able to raise this informally with the plant manager who dealt with the matter. It reflected a high level of trust between the two forged in the staff council.

The effect of being consulted can influence perceptions of fairness even if the management decision under discussion is not changed (Dietz and Fortin, 2007: 1162). Process can be more important than outcome. 'In the end, the extent to which the... system delivers either distributive fairness (in outcomes) or procedural fairness (in processes) depends on managerial fairness' (Kaufman and Tarras, 2010: 269). Management style in participation is often associated with other initiatives in human resource management (HRM) typically found in high-involvement work systems. 'There is considerable evidence that participation is generally more effective when associated with complementary human resource practices' (Heller et al., 1998: 122), what Wilkinson et al. (2010: 9) call an 'integrated approach to employee participation'.

There is a symbiotic relationship between consultation in staff councils and the wider management style adopted; a process of mutual reinforcement provided consultation is seen to be meaningful. Where there is an avoidance of collectives such as trade unions or staff councils, or where the relationship is adversarial, consultation is unlikely to be successful whatever the way employees are managed. Where, however, cooperative relationships flourish in the staff council, and between senior managers and employee representatives, the full beneficial effect cannot be reached unless there is also a style of management based on high-commitment, or high-involvement management (Boxall and Purcell, 2011: 182–5). Walton et al. (1994) make a similar distinction in the management of major change seeing relationships with employees as a 'social contract' which needs to be 'fostered' unless there are specific circumstances when the only option is 'forcing': 'when management want a social contract based on high individual commitment with behavioural compliance and strong labour-management cooperation, they will be likely to emphasise fostering' (Boxall and Purcell, 2011: 177). Comparative research in the United States and Germany on work reorganization in call centres suggests that in Germany, where consultation is strongly embedded, 'collective voice can be a critical factor encouraging management to adopt high-involvement employment systems where pressures to rationalize work are strong' (Doellgast, 2010: 378).

Providing an effective means for handling grievances and complaints

Both management and representatives can put items on the agenda of meetings of the staff council. In many cases, issues and complaints raised by employees will be housekeeping matters. These can be trivialized as 'tea and toilets' and in the least successful consultative committees, as we explore in Chapter 7, come to dominate with items sometimes discussed at successive meetings: 'the hole in the smoking shed roof' as it was known in one company. This is often a process failure as no effective means has been adopted to filter out trivial matters which are better dealt with through other channels. When a consultative committee is first established, especially in non-union companies where there is no prior experience of representation, early meetings often deal with a backlog of problems concerned with perceptions of unfairness in management action or inaction. Once these have been resolved, the council can have less relevance if management use it only for communication purposes and do not, themselves, put items on the agenda. 'The pay off from further participation is then perceived to decline; frustration and resignation result' (Heller et al., 1998: 60). But the ability to raise items and get a resolution helps establish the credibility of consultation, what Marchington and Wilkinson (2002: 439) call 'the safety valve effect'.

In non-union companies it is sometimes the case, although it is not common, for representatives to play a role in discipline and grievance matters by accompanying an employee at hearings and providing advice. This role is normally played by union representatives even where a union shares the staff council with non-union delegates in a 'hybrid' committee.

Improving employee engagement and commitment

The efficiency outcome of consultation comes from improvements made to management decisions and implementation and in the way change is managed. This is where consultation leads to changes in management behaviour. A quite different outcome derives from the way consultation impacts on employees' attitudes and beliefs about their organization and their assessment of managers becomes more positive. These positive feelings and attitudes must then translate into improved performance valued by the company. The common shorthand is 'employee engagement': a combination of worker attitudes, like commitment, plus action or behaviour (MacLeod and Clarke, 2009). The sort of behavioural outcomes normally associated with increasing levels of organizational commitment are reduced absence, lower quit rates, willingness to learn and adapt, and the exercise of discretionary behaviour, sometimes misleadingly called 'going the extra mile'. The causal chain from HRM to organizational performance is hard enough to prove (Purcell and Kinnie, 2007) but the link with consultation is even more difficult. For one thing, employees' knowledge of what happens in consultation is understandably often sketchy. Gollan (2006a: 630), in his study of consultation in Eurotunnel, showed that half of all respondents (in his survey) were never in contact with, or did not know, their consultative committee representative. Roughly the same proportion is reported by Hall et al. (2010: 37). Direct attitudinal outcomes are not likely in these circumstances but when mediated through management style and perceptions of managerial fairness, both influenced by consultation, there may well be an effect.

Searching for the effect of consultation by itself reveals very little evidence either of a positive or negative impact. The very few instances where there is a staff council but no evidence of direct participation meant in Purcell and Geogiadis's analysis (2007: 185) of the 1998 WERS data that these had to be excluded from the analysis. However, once consultation is combined with direct employee involvement systems, the outcome effect on organizational commitment, intrinsic job satisfaction, and job discretion is almost 10 per cent greater than direct-only systems, where there is no collective consultation. 'In line with previous research, the existence of dual systems was found to have the strongest link with employee attitudes' (ibid.). Cox et al. (2006) found much the same outcome effect where employee voice was embedded in terms of scope and depth. Bryson (2004: 228) differentiated between union and non-union consultative bodies and came to the stark conclusion, based on careful analysis of large-scale data, that 'it is the combination of direct voice with non-union representative voice that is particularly beneficial and it is the only voice regime which performs better than "no voice"'. The explanation for this is that 'it seems that on-site union representation engenders greater critical awareness on the part of workers and perhaps increases voice-induced complaining' (ibid.: 235) and that 'unionism raises the number of reported problems while firm-based non-union channels reduce reported problems' (Bryson and Freeman, 2007: 90). We will look at the operation of union, non-union and hybrid (union and non-union) staff councils in detail in Chapter 6.

An overall assessment of the link between participation and employee attitudes and behaviour is provided by Gallie and White (1993: 44) from their large-scale survey of employees. 'Participation is of fundamental importance for employees' attitude to the organisation for which they work. It is strongly related to the way they respond in changes in work organisation and with their perception of the quality of the overall relationship between management and employees'. One reason suggested for this is that employees feel they have more control over their organization and as a result 'they will develop property sentiments. This, in turn, may express itself in various forms: commitment, involvement, participation or responsibility' (Heller et al., 1998: 45). When the authors suggest that employees feel they have 'more control', this does not mean that management necessarily have less control. It is the total amount of control in the organization which increases as suggested in German research (Frege, 2002: 239). One benefit of this increase in control, or what could be termed 'self-control', is that it can 'reduce costly monitoring of employee behaviour' (Spreitzer and Mishra, 1999: 162, cited in Dietz et al., 2008: 248).

Summarizing their findings in 2001, ten years after their initial case studies in a large number of organizations, Marchington et al. (2001) concluded that there are three positive impacts of employee voice:

- valuing employee contributions leading to improved employee attitudes and behaviours, loyalty, and cooperative relations;
- improved performance, productivity, and individual performance, lower absenteeism and, in a few cases, new ideas arising from employee voice;
- improved managerial systems—tapping into managerial ideas, informative and educational role of voice, improved relations with trade unions.

There are many routes through which consultation can improve organizational efficiency but there are many pitfalls, too. If management commitment to consultation is shallow, for example in order to head off a trade union recognition campaign or as a device to show legislators that there is no need for statutory intervention, the outcome is hardly likely to be beneficial in terms of productivity. As Hendry notes (1995: 49), 'the history of joint consultation is littered with schemes adopted as a last resort to ward off perceived greater evils'. It is possible, though, that the parties may find consultation more helpful than they expected. We give an example of this in Chapter 7.

Even when a staff council has been established for positive reasons there can be complaints. Some managers may resent the slowing down of decision taking while consultation takes place (Heller et al., 1998: 14). Others may complain that the representatives are not qualified to debate strategic management decisions: the 'competence deficit' (ibid.: 151). There can be a fear that confidential information will leak out. Middle managers and supervisors can complain of being 'the last to know' and feel their authority is undermined (Marchington et al., 1992: 35) when an employee representative reports back about latest information gleaned from the CEO. They can disrupt future meetings by making it difficult for a representative to get the necessary time off.

Managers can be surprised that a process designed to emphasize cooperation can be a forum for disagreement. There are often fears that adversarial behaviour will dominate consultative committees, especially where unions nominate representatives more used to collective bargaining. This negativity and low trust is not the same as expressing a difference of opinion in a cooperative endeavour: 'the research evidence suggests that participation allows disagreements to increase, but there is also evidence that when participation works well, disagreements are resolved smoothly' (Heller et al., 1998: 147). Although 'higher levels of participation were positively related to the frequencies of disagreement the counter evidence is that (the conflict) facilitates innovation and consensus' (ibid.: 46). An effective consultative committee is not a focus group (Koukiadaki, 2010: 380). It can involve differences of opinion and a search for shared outcomes in a process sometimes akin to negotiation. Nightingale (1982) showed that participative organizations use 'problem solving' as a conflict resolution technique rather than 'forcing' or 'ignoring' (cited in Heller et al., 1998: 46–7). It is not surprising that sometimes 'representative participation threatens top management . . . top management support is often symbolic and uncertain' (ibid.: 200). Nor is it surprising that there can be greater enthusiasm for consultation when times are bad. 'Management hope it will cut costs and improve the competitive position. Unions and employees see it as possibly saving jobs, what Cressey et al. (1985) call "life boat democracy"' (ibid.: 210). A counter view, where managers are secretive and dislike sharing information, is that 'consultation is for good times' only (Terry, 1999: 27). They revert to unilateral decisions and announcements in challenging times, but such Janus-faced treatment of consultation is hardly likely to imbue confidence and commitment in employees.

Most damaging of all, perhaps, is that there can be a lack of employee enthusiasm (Marchington and Wilkinson, 2002: 440) which can make it difficult to get employees to stand in elections for membership of the staff council. There is 'considerable research evidence [which] suggests that, even when given the opportunity to participate, relatively few employees take advantage of this opportunity' (Heller et al., 1998: 200). Bull (2010: 289–90) in her case study research observed that 'employee apathy was a notable constraint to the sustainability of information and consultation arrangements . . . The extent to which employees felt involved was contingent on . . . the visibility and effectiveness of representatives, line management style, leadership and the presence of other employee involvement mechanisms. Employees were largely disinterested in the operation of the forum'. Twenty years earlier, Marchington et al. (1992: 59) noted from their case study research that 'it could be argued that most employees do not want more influence over activities . . . and a number of attitude surveys . . . would appear to support this proposition'. One explanation for this provided by Heller and his colleagues is that the subordinate position of employees leads to the creation of 'dependency thought habits and compliant behaviour' (Heller et al., 1998: 148). That is, the challenge implied in high-level consultation may be too daunting for many. The alternative perspective is that the growth of independence and individuality, which is a more developmental orientation to work based on self-help and personal growth (Boxall, 2008: 221), leads to a belief that the individual has no need or desire for a 'protective agency' like a trade union (or a staff council) (Dundon and Gollan, 2007: 1190). The purpose of the staff council in conditions of high individuality, 'to encourage and promote an alignment of interests' (ibid.), may well be worthy but can still be of little interest.

It can, of course, be argued that if industrial citizenship is akin to political citizenship, then low participation rates are to be expected. Low participation rates do have a number of largely negative consequences. The causal model linking consultation to performance through employee engagement must be damaged, although the positive effects on management decisions logically remain. Second, given differences of opinion among managers on the value of consultation, low levels of participation gives succour to those who think it is at best a waste of time and at worst a damaging diversion. Third, if legislation is designed to be 'triggered' by a proportion of employees indicating that they want information and consultation arrangements, as it is in the United Kingdom, this becomes harder if there is a lack of enthusiasm. We discuss this in subsequent chapters.

Consultation as power-sharing

Power-sharing to some extent is an inevitable feature of effective consultation and Heery (2010: 547) is correct to assert that 'representative institutions must be *redistributive*' (emphasis in original). The same could be said even for some forms of direct participation. It is commonly noted, for example, that high involvement work practices, at the heart of most EI arrangements, require a decentralization of authority seen most obviously in autonomous and semi-autonomous workgroups and in problem-solving groups. Power is shared with the line manager. This, however, is not what is generally meant by power-sharing forms of consultative systems. Power-sharing arrangements are generally a built-in feature of the system as agreed with a firm's management or, more likely, built-in to the statutory system underpinning consultation. The most obvious example here is provision for worker directors in some industries nationalized in the late 1960s such as British Steel or long-running public enterprises 'reformed' in the same period such as the Post Office (Brannen et al., 1976; Batstone et al., 1983). Serious proposals were made for worker directors by the industrial democracy committee chaired by Lord Bullock in 1975–6. The terms of reference made it plain that the purpose of industrial democracy was 'the control of companies': 'accepting the need for a radical expression of industrial democracy in the control of companies by means of representation on boards of directors' (Bullock Report, 1977). We discuss this report and its aftermath in Chapter 4. Worker directors are commonly found in continental European countries such as the Netherlands and Germany as well as in worker cooperatives. The term 'codetermination' neatly captures the power-sharing agenda. Worker directors, as a form of power-sharing, are beyond the scope of the book.

A second form of institutionalized power-sharing is linked to trade unions through modifications or additions to collective bargaining. Here, as noted earlier, consultation becomes an adjunct to collective bargaining. It is more common to refer to this as union partnership agreements. We noted in Chapter 1 how consultation was seen to play a major role in the Esso Fawley productivity deals. As Samuel and Bacon (2010: 433) note, 'it is claimed that partnership agreements extend joint regulation to address issues previously decided only by managers'. They suggest, on the basis of their research, that these agreements 'have delivered little' (ibid.: 444) but they do often mean that the topics for discussion go well beyond traditional collective bargaining into management decisions. Power-sharing, if it happens through partnership agreements, comes about because the discussion of strategic management decisions then informs the topics and outcomes of collective bargaining where an agreement is required. This does not mean that the strategic decision itself is necessarily subject to negotiation but its application and implementation may well be, for example, the introduction of technical change in terms of jobs and work organization. The style of bargaining is likely to change with more emphasis on 'integrative bargaining' and less on 'distributive bargaining' (Walton and McKersie, 1965).

It is widely noted that the 'adjunct model' of consultation is the most effective since it combines union bargaining power with discussion of a wider agenda. Heller et al. (1998: 121–3) summarize the evidence:

- unions increase job security; consequently employees are less likely to fear that increased productivity caused by participation will cost them their jobs;
- union approval increases the chance that changes will be viewed as fair and legitimate;
- experience in union activities may increase consultative committee members' competence and effectiveness;
- a union can negotiate how to share the benefits of increased cooperation;
- unions provide expertise which is not available locally.

These benefits do not flow just from union recognition. Overall union–management relations must be good and the union must feel strong and secure (ibid.: 114). As we have noted, where unions feel insecure and have a low membership, they can be suspicious that in consultation management may establish a rival power centre and worry that reaching an accommodation with management will subject them to charges of 'selling out'. Power-sharing as an adjunct to collective bargaining requires strong, self-confident unions and leadership. This is hard to achieve in the twenty-first century.

The *raison d'être* for power-sharing forms of consultation is the view that 'traditional autocratic relationships are inherently unjust and inconsistent with the values of a democratic society' (Heller et al., 1998: 9). Employers are judged not simply by their economic achievements but by their 'social legitimacy' (Boxall and Purcell, 2011: 19–22). Institutional pressures towards social legitimacy can lead to institutional and social change. There are three sorts of pressure (Scott, 2008: 50–9). 'Regulative' pressure is when the state steps in to right an injustice or curb 'bad' behaviour: 'the unacceptable face of capitalism' as the Prime Minister, Edward Heath, put it in 1973 (Sandbrook, 2010: 526). 'Normative' pressure is where firms need to conform to prevailing social values and norms about how to treat people at work. 'Cultural-cognitive pressure' includes the way people customarily think and behave in society. Outrage at employers who breech these norms can lead politicians to enact regulations to curb such excesses. Public opinion can be mobilized to 'name and shame' employers who breach these norms and values. It is, of course, highly unlikely that consultation, or a lack of it, would feature in such feelings of outrage, but it would have to for power-sharing to return to the political agenda.

A lesser form of power-sharing can be seen in certain periods when a 'stakeholder perspective' (Donaldson and Preston, 1995) is favoured with labour as one of the dominant interest groups to be accommodated. This is seen most clearly in EU regulations on collective, or large scale, redundancies and on company mergers, acquisitions, and takeovers referred to as 'transfers of undertakings'. We explore these regulations later in the book but for now the importance is to note that as well as requiring an employer to provide information in advance of a decision and to explore ways of ameliorating the consequences on employment and work organization, the need is to do so with representatives of the workforce 'with a view to reaching an agreement'. This requirement to seek an accommodation of interests with employees via their trade unions or representatives comes close to a statutory definition of power-sharing in consultation. But it is only a requirement to make the effort, not to actually share decision-making. It implies a process 'close to negotiation' but 'ultimately leaves (management prerogative) intact' (Deakin and Morris, 2009: 791, 816).

The ambiguity in power-sharing is not just in the meaning of 'share'—what sort of share: big, small, trivial?—but also the process of sharing in a temporal sense (how far in advance of a decision should sharing start) and in a behavioural sense, how is the sharing conducted? Early on, Clegg and Chester (1954: 326) noted the distinction between bargaining 'as a process of haggling between opponents, and consultation as a process of co-operation between partners'. Bargaining implies the ability or power of one party to veto the other's proposals, and, sometimes, recourse to arbitration if no agreement can be reached. In consultation, no such outcome is possible since 'the employer has the last say'; the right to decide. Employers must be willing to share power but in consultation they cannot be coerced to do so. Boards of Directors with worker directors may vote on a decision but voting has no place in consultation. Power-sharing in a meaningful way is not possible in consultation unless the employer wishes to cede power. Some may do so to aid the management of change, and we provide an example in Chapter 7, but it is not a requirement of consultation to go beyond 'the establishment of dialogue'. Consultation does not require an outcome.

It is ironic that the power-sharing justification for consultation has waned at a time of significant changes in company ownership, scale of operations, and the primacy of shareholders especially in liberal market economies. The dominance of 'shareholder value' and the consequent weakening of efforts to promote a stakeholder perspective are well documented by Jacoby (2005) in his comparisons between the United States and Japan. This is associated with more pronounced short-termism linked to viewing the firm as little more than a nexus of contracts where restructuring is a permanent condition (Sisson and Purcell, 2010: 91–9). Within Europe the 'varieties of capitalism' debate points to differences in corporate governance and the management of labour (Gospel and Pendleton, 2003). The problem, in part, is globalization and the growing dominance of multinational companies (Marginson and Meardi, 2010) where, despite the creation of European Works Councils (EWCs), executives at the centre are beyond the reach of national consultative arrangements. No national government, nor trade unions, could adopt a power-sharing consultative agenda, however radical, which would dent such corporate power, even if they wanted to.

Consultation as an employee right

Justifications for the adoption of consultative systems for reasons of efficiency maximization and power-sharing place most of the responsibility for action in the hands of management, and to a lesser extent, trade unions and employees themselves. Once consultation is seen as a fundamental human right in employment, the justification changes to moral and ethical reasoning and the call to action turns to the state. The moral case has often been made on grounds of the de-humanizing nature of the workplace, as in the view of the Catholic Church, for example: 'Catholic Social Theory (CST) sees the economistic mindset (the view that labour is an immaterial commodity) as the ultimate source of practices which degrade the worker' (Lower, 2010: 96). This is made clear in Pope John Paul II's encyclical *Laborem exercens* 1985 which sets out the basis for the church's views on worker participation. It follows that 'it is impossible to understand the central purpose of the firm, and to think how it adds value, without bringing employment into the picture' (ibid.: 98–9). Through this analysis 'CST has stressed and explained the ethical importance of employee participation in corporate governance' (ibid.: 127).

An 'ethical socialist' perspective, put forward, for example, by Allan Flanders, referred to the 'worker's resentment against arbitrary or contemptuous treatment by the "boss" and the desire for self respect. Such demands could even be said to embody a "conception of human dignity . . . the claim to be treated as an equal"' (Kelly, 2010: 77). The implication is obvious: 'the worker's claim to be consulted by management before decisions are taken . . . is fundamentally a moral one . . . As human beings they have dignity and are entitled to respect' (Flanders: 1951: 150, cited in Kelly, 2010: 94).

It is a short step now, given union weakness, from espousing the moral case for participation to calls for legislation. While the Catholic Church hesitates to suggest how this might be done, there is an understanding that it will not come about by market forces. 'It may . . . be that serious market failures play a part in obstructing the spread of co-determination. In any event, there are moral and political issues at stake that markets are not capable of addressing' (Lower, 2010: 128). The need, in whatever form, is to 'recast corporate governance and labour law to promote workplace democracy' (ibid.: 107, citing Klare, 1988). 'The state may sometimes legitimately feel that it has to intervene; indeed, Bellace (1994: 460) suggests that it is crucially important for the state to devise mechanisms that will "serve as bulwarks for independent employee voice"' (ibid.: 125).

It is commonly noted by those who research in employee participation that 'regulatory rules and laws encourage or force certain behaviours that otherwise would not have taken place' (Gollan, 2010: 221). The clearest example of this is found in continental Europe in countries like Germany and the Netherlands. Freeman and Lazear (1995, cited by Bryson et al., 2006: 441–2) 'argue that the legally mandated nature of continental works councils may embed labour management cooperation more deeply than voluntary arrangements. This is because management have a stronger incentive to maintain cooperation with the works council and so have less incentive to defect by abolishing it or ignoring it'. Looking across a wide range of countries in their comprehensive study of participation, Heller et al. (1998: 14) conclude that 'indeed laws and other legally binding rules provide a major explanation for differences in the extent of actual participation across countries'. This is because 'the law legitimises participation . . . and gives employees clout to insist that participation takes place' (ibid.: 214).

The prevailing view is that consultation is unlikely to become widely adopted and practiced unless it is supported by laws and regulations which can be enforced. This sits uneasily in Britain with its traditions of voluntarism and has meant that continental practice of legally supported works councils tended to be resisted if there was a chance, or a danger, of them being adopted by the EU as a template to be imposed on the United Kingdom as a member state. This is explored in Chapters 3 and 4.

Conclusion

Consultation needs to be justified in every period of industrialization since the case for it has never been widely accepted. Heller et al. (1998: 212) observe that 'most organisations are non-participative, so participation exists in a hostile environment'. It is not surprising that there are periods of high birth rates for consultation in certain conditions of economic uncertainty, growing challenges from trade unions, and threats of state intervention. But, as MacInnes (1985) showed, there are equally high rates of collapse of consultative bodies. The economic justification for consultation has never been strong enough, in itself, to ensure the widespread diffusion of consultative practices, and even if there was sufficient evidence, it would not be enough to overcome managerial resistance and the deep-seated belief in the managerial prerogative. Boxall and Purcell (2011: 22–4) note that one of the objectives of HRM at the level of the firm has always been the preservation of managerial power: 'a goal to maximise control over an uncertain environment including threats to its power base from work groups and trade unions'. It is seen, too, 'at industry and societal levels in the tendency of employer federations to lobby, over time, for greater freedom to manage and to resist new employment regulations seen to be diminishing managerial prerogative' (ibid.). At first sight it can seem surprising that something benign, premised on cooperation and mutual trust, can be so contentious. Marchington, who has studied consultation and employee involvement for as long as anyone, suggests that 'voice' (the contemporary term covering all forms of participation) 'is probably the area of HRM where tensions between organisational and worker goals, and between shareholder and stakeholder views, are most apparent because it connects with the question of managerial prerogatives and social legitimacy' (Marchington, 2007: 233).

Calls for consultation to be adopted in order to share power between management and labour are never convincing since consultation does not provide for joint decision taking. This requires negotiation and agreement, or the radical transformation of capital in new forms of ownership and control. In any case, power-sharing had greatest resonance in the age when the majority of workers had blue collar jobs, and many worked in very large factories where antagonistic relationships were the norm. It sits oddly now in a period of individualism and emphasis on knowledge and discretionary behaviour.

Now the justification for employee voice systems is EI seen in direct methods of two-way communications and the tapping of attitudes and ideas in surveys, focus groups, and team briefing sessions. Managers are now responsible for ensuring that their team members are 'engaged'. Power-centred consultation, it is argued, is an old-fashioned irrelevance. Modern, participative managers can be relied upon to have the interests of their staff at heart and communicate directly with them.

There remain three objections to this assertion. Even if were true that modern managers are much more participative than their forebears, something challenged by the growth in work intensification (Green, 2001), job insecurity (Standing, 2011), and financial engineering (Sisson and Purcell, 2010), it does nothing to influence strategic business decisions taken by executives. Indeed, these participative middle and junior managers are as powerless as their subordinates to influence big decisions. Their job is to enact a strategy, not to make it. Second, there is little opportunity for employees to seek redress if things do not go well and EI processes are ignored. Of course, grievance procedures can be used but without representation this can be difficult and recourse to an Employment Tribunal is nearly always only embarked upon once the person has left the organization. The most obvious objection to reliance on EI is that 'good management' can never replace the right for employees to be told and have a say in decisions which affect them. Consultation is not just a means to an end to achieve a 'better' workplace, but an end in itself. As a fundamental right it is indivisible. This 'right' has never been universally recognized and it remains a contentious assertion. The struggle to recognize it and turn it into effective legislation in Europe and in Britain is the subject of Chapters 3 and 4.

3

Legislating for Employee Consultation: The Significance of EU-Level Regulation

European Union (EU) requirements have played a central role in shaping the United Kingdom's contemporary legislative framework regulating employee consultation. The growth since the mid-1970s in British statutory provisions requiring employers to inform and consult employee representatives has been driven primarily by EU legislation—often adopted in the face of strong opposition from UK governments of both main parties. Successive legislative initiatives by the European Commission, not all of which were adopted, reflected the long-established systems of board-level employee representation and works councils existing in most of the original EU member states, thus presenting major challenges for the United Kingdom's 'voluntarist' industrial relations traditions. This chapter analyses the basis and reasoning for EU intervention in this area, charting the changing approaches to EU-level regulation and the emergence of employee consultation as a 'fundamental right' and key element of the 'European social model'. Over a thirty-year period there has been a shift from the Commission's initial focus on 'industrial democracy' towards a greater emphasis on employee consultation and 'social dialogue', and from seeking to generalize best national practice ('upward harmonization') to establishing minimum standards. These more flexible legislative strategies were prompted by the failure of key employee participation initiatives and the wider industrial relations diversity among member states as a result of EU enlargement. This changing approach to EU regulation has meant that, while in the 1970s and 1980s only narrowly-framed, issue-specific employee consultation directives, such as that relating to collective redundancy, won the approval of member states, by the 1990s and 2000s EU measures entailing more general and systematic information and consultation provisions, including the 2002 information and consultation directive, successfully reached the EU statute book.

The evolution of EU intervention

There has been a long and controversial history of EU employee participation initiatives. Formal legislative proposals from the European Commission date from 1970, but the earliest initiatives in this area had been under discussion since the 1950s (EIRR, 1991). Debates surrounding successive proposals in this area have been protracted and highly contentious, reflecting the political and technical challenges of attempting to harmonize (i.e. align more closely) diverse national provision as well as polarized trade union and employer attitudes towards EU intervention. Not all the measures put forward by the Commission have become law, while others have taken many years (in the case of the European Company Statute (ECS), decades) to complete the legislative process.

The first Commission proposals to be adopted successfully—the 1975 collective redundancies directive and the 1977 transfers of undertakings directive—were confined to requiring information and consultation in respect of specific issues. The earlier draft ECS (issued in 1970) and draft fifth company law directive (1972) had focussed much more ambitiously on promoting institutionalized employee participation in corporate decision-making procedures but had failed to make progress within the Council of Ministers. A further issue-specific consultation measure followed in 1989 with the adoption of the framework health and safety directive. The next wave of EU legislation, dating from 1994 onwards, included more general and systematic information and consultation obligations but these apply on a transnational basis within companies operating in a number of EU countries. The adoption of European Works Councils (EWCs) directive in 1994 provided the model for reshaping the employee involvement provisions of the (optional) ECS which was finally adopted in 2001. The 2002 information and consultation directive represented a further, critical stage in the development of the EU's regulatory strategy, establishing a general consultation framework applicable to national undertakings.

Rationales for regulation

Although the Commission's initial employee participation proposals—the ECS and the fifth directive—were rooted in the essentially technocratic company law harmonization programme associated with the early stages of European economic integration, the major impetus behind the drive for an EU-wide framework for employee consultation has been political pressure for the development of a more active EU social policy role. Information and consultation measures emerged as a central element of what has become known as the EU's 'social dimension' or 'social Europe'. Significantly, a number of the information and consultation measures that were successfully adopted had their origins in the social action programmes of 1974 and 1989 that underpinned two key periods of EU-level social policy activism.

Pressure for a more extensive EU social policy role came from left of centre national governments, trade unions, and the European Commission itself, but there was also broad support from Christian democratic governments and political parties. Reflecting the primary focus of the early European Economic Community on market integration, the original Treaty of Rome contained only limited and ambiguous social policy provisions. But by the late 1960s and early 1970s, in the context of the discussion of the Community's next stages of development as well as economic growth, the Brandt-led social democrat government of West Germany was notably influential in raising the priority of EU action in the social field and pressing for the subsequent social action programme. Similarly, in the late 1980s, the central EU project of completing the single market was the catalyst for new moves to develop the EU's social dimension, reflecting in particular the French socialist government's promotion of *l'espace social européen*, resulting in the social action programme of 1989 (Hall, 1994).

The importance of the prevailing political and economic context in terms of the scope for and momentum behind EU employee participation initiatives was also demonstrated by the experience of the first half of the 1980s. The election in 1979 of the Thatcher-led Conservative government in the United Kingdom and subsequently of centre-right governments in several member states including Germany, and the deregulatory thrust (to varying extents) of their labour market policies, contributed to the failure of Commission employee participation measures to progress and an 'impasse' over EU employment law initiatives more generally (Hepple, 1987; Hall, 1990). In particular, the Commission's 1980 'Vredeling' proposal (named after the social affairs Commissioner at the time) for a directive requiring the information and consultation of employees in multinational and multi-establishment enterprises was blocked as a result of strong opposition from international business and some member state governments, principally the United Kingdom. The wider impasse over EU social policy highlighted the ability of member states, notably the Thatcher-led UK government, to 'veto' key legislative proposals. This contributed to growing pressure for treaty changes to provide a clear legal basis for EU social policy intervention and a wider scope for decisions by majority voting that eventually opened the way to the adoption of subsequent EU consultation measures.

Various rationales have been used to justify EU intervention (Gold, 2010), including those relating to 'power-sharing', 'employee rights', and 'efficiency' discussed in Chapter 2. The balance between these has varied over time with 'efficiency' arguments increasingly coming into play. The draft ECS and fifth directive derived from the EU's company law harmonization programme, which was intended to facilitate economic integration. Their stated rationales were consistent with this, referring to employee rights 'only insofar as such rights [were] reflected in the harmonised . . . supervisory board structure being proposed' (Gold, 2010: 15). By the time of the Commission's first social action programme in the mid-1970s, the collective redundancies and transfers of undertakings directives were justified primarily in terms of providing protection and rights for employees. They were also intended to produce a more level playing field by addressing differences in national provision said to have a 'direct effect on the operation of the common market' (an argument tailored to fit the specific treaty base cited). Similar arguments were used in the preamble of the ill-fated 'Vredeling' directive proposed in 1980.

The acceleration of European integration from the mid-1980s, particularly the completion of the single market, generated pressure from trade unions and centre-left governments and political parties for the development of the EU's social dimension (Hall, 1994), of which information and consultation measures were seen as a central element. The 1989 Charter of Fundamental Social Rights of Workers, or 'social charter', referred to the information, consultation, and participation of workers, particularly in international companies, and provided the basis for Commission proposals for the EWCs directive and the revision of the collective redundancies directive. Again, the rationale for these measures was essentially to guarantee employee rights, and in particular to bridge the gap between increasingly transnational corporate decision-making and employees' nationally-defined information and consultation rights (Hall, 1992). The broader political motivation was to promote the 'social acceptability' of the extensive restructuring expected to flow from the completion of the single market (CEC, 1990: 66).

The introduction of explicit references by EU legislators to efficiency rationales to support the case for legislative intervention—in which information and consultation is presented as a 'productive factor' (Gold, 2010: 11)—dates from the EWCs directive. As Gold's analysis underlines, its preamble highlights the consequences of the single market in terms of transnational restructuring and asserts that 'if economic activities are to develop in a harmonious fashion, undertakings . . . must inform and consult the representatives of those of their employees that are affected by their decisions'. By the time the subsequent information and consultation directive was put forward, efficiency or business rationales arguably dominated its preamble. Stronger 'dialogue' was needed to 'promote employee involvement in the operation and future of the undertaking and increase its competitiveness'. Similarly, 'timely information and consultation' was seen as 'a prerequisite for the success of the restructuring and adaptation of undertakings to the new conditions created by globalisation of the economy'. Anna Diamantopoulou, the EU social affairs commissioner at the time of its adoption, presented the directive as a 'modern business tool. Enlightened self-interest is already driving companies to anticipate and manage change. Many businesses already involve employees in this. All businesses should provide a baseline level of involvement' (EWCB, 2002: 2, quoted in Gold, 2010: 19).

Different sources of regulation, different outcomes

The differing rationales advanced in support of successive employee participation measures also reflect the fact that, within the European Commission, which has the responsibility for initiating EU legislation, there have been two distinct sources of legislative proposals, rooted in separate EU policy agendas. Proposals focussing on employee representation at board level derived from the Commission's long-standing company law harmonization programme and were prepared within the Directorate-General responsible for financial institutions and company law. Those focussing on information and consultation developed out of successive social action programmes and were drafted within the Directorate-General for employment and social affairs. These two policy divisions of the Commission pursued notably differing legislative approaches (Hall, 1992; Villiers, 1998).

The 'company law' approach of the Directorate-General for financial institutions and company law tended to be relatively detailed and prescriptive. There were two main strands of its agenda affecting employee participation. The first draft of the ECS—a free-standing, EU-level instrument under which cross-border 'European companies' could be created independently of existing national laws—was put forward in 1970 with an amended text issued in 1975. Based on the 'best practice' German/Dutch models of board-level participation, these proposals provided for both employee representation on the supervisory boards of European companies and the creation of EWCs. The subsequent draft fifth company law directive, launched in 1972, sought to harmonize national provisions in respect of the structure of public limited companies and, again reflecting German/Dutch practice, included a requirement for a two-tier board structure with employee representation on the supervisory board. More flexible arrangements were included in a later (1983) amended proposal. However, both initiatives were seen as unduly prescriptive by member states and discussion within the Council of Ministers stalled. A substantially revised version of the ECS was relaunched in 1989 and eventually adopted in 2001 on the back of the successful adoption of the EWCs directive (see below). The draft fifth directive was formally abandoned in 2004 (Gold, 2010).

A different 'social affairs' (Hall, 1992: 555) or 'labour law' (Villiers, 1998: 188) approach was identifiable in the employment Directorate-General's legislative proposals. These tended to be more pragmatic than the company-law-based, institution-focussed approach to employee participation. Crucially, they sought to promote information and consultation procedures that could utilize member states' existing employee representation arrangements instead of specifying particular models or representative institutions.

The 1974 social action programme—initially envisaged as engaging with the 'social consequences of growth' (Shanks, 1977: 5) but drawn up and implemented in the context of the economic difficulties following the oil crisis of 1973—included proposals for the two earliest EU consultation directives that were adopted. These required employers to undertake consultation procedures with employee representatives, designated in accordance with national practice, over the specific issues of impending collective redundancies (1975) and transfers of undertakings (1977). The 1975 directive required employers who were 'contemplating' collective redundancies to begin consultations with the workers' representatives 'with a view to reaching an agreement'. These consultations were intended to cover 'ways and means of avoiding collective redundancies or reducing the number of workers affected, and mitigating the consequences'. Similarly, the 1977 directive included requirements on both the transferor and the transferee to inform representatives of employees affected by a transfer about the reasons for the transfer and the 'legal, economic, and social implications' for the employees, and consult them 'with a view to seeking agreement' on 'measures envisaged in relation to the employees'. Although narrowly focussed in terms of their subject matter, both directives specified that consultation should be 'with a view to reaching agreement'. While this wording envisaged an advanced form of consultation, its specific meaning is uncertain. For Deakin and Morris (2009: 791, 816), it implies a process 'close to negotiation' but 'ultimately leaves [managerial prerogative] intact', notwithstanding the opinion of the European Court of Justice in its 2005 judgement in *Junk v Kühnel* that the directive '[appeared to impose] an obligation to negotiate'.

At that time there was no specific treaty base on which the Commission could propose EU legislation on employment and labour law matters. This meant that political agreement was necessary within the Council of Ministers to base key measures in the social action programme, including those on redundancies and transfers, on a more general treaty article—Article 100 of the Treaty of Rome—that enabled the 'approximation' of national provisions which 'directly affect the establishment of functioning of the common market'. In practice, as the then director-general for social affairs at the Commission made clear, the content of the 1974 social action programme 'reflected a political judgement of what was thought to be both desirable and possible, rather than a juridical judgement of what were thought to be the social policy implications of the Rome Treaty' (Shanks, 1977: 13).

However, the employment and social affairs Directorate-General's subsequent and much more ambitious 'Vredeling' proposals, focussing on multinational and multi-establishment enterprises, failed to secure adoption during the early 1980s. This also sought to utilize existing national institutions of employee representation (and indeed local management) as the channel for statutory information and consultation procedures. But its provisions, including the annual disclosure of specified company or group information and a thirty-day consultation period for management plans likely to have a substantial effect on employees' interests, were sufficiently wide-ranging to provoke a strong lobbying campaign by international business, prominently including US firms. The UK Conservative government, among others, also resisted the measure.

A revised and substantially less interventionist draft of the directive produced by the Commission in 1983 failed to allay employer and governmental concerns, as did a subsequent 'new approach' attempted by the Irish EU presidency in 1984 (Docksey, 1986). Along with the draft fifth directive, the Vredeling proposal went into 'a kind of European limbo' (Cressey, 1993: 92) and neither was subsequently 'resuscitated'. European trade unions, which had strongly supported EU moves towards more extensive information and consultation, recognized that they had been out-gunned by employers' groups and multinational companies in 'the battle of the Vredeling directive': 'US multinationals poured men and money into Brussels... unions will have to become much more skilled manipulators of the European bureaucracy, while at the same time building up trans-frontier union strength within [multinational companies]' (Rebhan, 1984: 9, quoted in Cressey, 1993: 93).

New approaches to EU regulation

The rejection of the ECS, fifth directive, and Vredeling proposals in the mid-1980s represented the nadir of the Commission's established approaches to legislating for employee participation and consultation. Yet, within a remarkably short period, a series of developments associated with the major strides then being taken towards European integration came together to create substantially more favourable conditions for the revival of the European Commission's and European trade unions' regulatory ambitions in this area. First, the limited progress made within the Council of Ministers not just by employee participation initiatives but by a range of Commission employment law proposals had called into question the viability of the traditional approach of 'upward harmonization'. The Commission, by now led by French socialist politician Jacques Delors, recognized that, in order to develop the 'social dimension' of the single market, a 'more flexible and pragmatic' approach was necessary, proposing a new balance between EU-level and national action and between legislation and collective agreements, under which considerable discretion was to be left to member states and the 'social partners' over the application of broadly framed EU minimum standards (CEC, 1988). This was consistent with the more general emphasis on 'subsidiarity'—regulating at the most decentralized level appropriate—in the discussions about closer European integration and in the eventual Maastricht EU Treaty in 1991.

At the same time, the political basis for a renewed period of EU social policy activism was re-established with the development and adoption, against the UK Conservative government's wishes, of the 1989 social charter. This included reference to the need for information, consultation, and participation for workers to be 'developed', especially in 'companies or groups of companies having establishments in several member states' and in the event of technological change, restructuring, mergers, and redundancies. This approach was amplified in the Commission's accompanying action programme, which included proposals for revising the 1975 collective redundancies directive—primarily to ensure its transnational applicability—as well as for creating a new EU instrument on information, consultation, and participation in 'European-scale' undertakings.

The final piece of the jigsaw was the adoption of the Maastricht social policy agreement in 1991. This established for the first time a clear and comprehensive treaty basis for EU intervention in employment and industrial relations issues, including the 'information and consultation of workers' and, as a separate item, the 'representation and collective defence of the interests of workers and employers, including co-determination'. It also formalized the role of the social partners in the formulation of EU labour law and enabled them jointly to opt to regulate the issue in question by means of a Community-level agreement in preference to EU legislation. Finally, it extended the scope for the adoption of EU legislation by majority voting, including that on information and consultation, providing the means of circumventing the scope for individual member states—in practice often the United Kingdom—to block social policy measures that had broadly-based support elsewhere in the EU. These innovations, together with the UK Conservative government's self-exclusion from the social policy agreement in the shape of its 'opt-out', injected new dynamism into EU social policy developments and, in particular, created the conditions for the adoption of a cluster of 'second generation' EU employee consultation measures.

Revised collective redundancies directive

The first EU consultation measure to be adopted in this new context, in 1992, took the form of a directive revising the original collective redundancies directive. The most significant amendment was to ensure that the obligation to consult applies irrespective of whether the redundancy decision is taken by the direct employer or at a higher level within a corporate group, and that it is no defence to argue that the necessary information has not been provided to the employer by the undertaking which took the decision. In line with the provisions of the social charter, these changes were seen as having particular relevance in cross-border situations. A consolidated EU collective redundancies directive was approved in 1998.

European Works Councils directive

Of much greater significance, in terms of both regulatory and institutional innovation, was the EWCs directive, adopted by the Council in 1994. The central objective of the EWCs directive was to promote the establishment of transnational, European-level information and consultation arrangements in 'Community-scale' companies—that is, those with 1,000 or more employees in the European Economic Area (EEA) (the EU member states plus Norway, Iceland, and Liechtenstein) and operations employing 150 or more in at least two of those countries. It is apparent from the social charter action programme that the Commission had originally envisaged an instrument more closely resembling the earlier Vredeling proposal, that is, with the necessary information and consultation procedures being carried out via local management. However, trade union pressure played an important role in redirecting the Commission's thinking towards the promotion of European-level information and consultation bodies (ETUC, 1989; Hall, 1992). The precedent set by the existence of 'prototype European Works Councils' in (a relative handful of) leading European multinationals, notably French-based companies (Northrop et al., 1988; Gold and Hall, 1992), was 'crucial to the persuasiveness of the trade union case' (Hall, 1992: 551). A focus on the transnational dimension of information and consultation was also beneficial politically: it engaged with an issue beyond the scope of national legislation and tied in with the increase in international corporate mergers and acquisitions associated with the single market project. From a regulatory point of view, it enabled a legislative approach that accommodated and did not override national patterns of employee representation.

The Commission adopted its original proposal for the EWCs directive in December 1990. The legal basis for this proposal (Article 100 of the Treaty of Rome) meant that it required unanimous approval on the part of all twelve member states at that time to become law: the UK government's strenuous opposition was sufficient to block the measure. Its prospects for adoption were transformed by the ratification of the Maastricht Treaty on European Union. The fact that measures adopted under the Maastricht social policy agreement would not be applicable to the United Kingdom opened the way to an EWCs directive restricted to the other eleven member states, circumventing the United Kingdom's veto. Moreover, under the terms of the agreement, directives concerning 'the information and consultation of workers' would be subject to qualified majority voting among the eleven. The Commission decided to initiate the new procedures by consulting the EU social partners. The latter engaged in 'talks about talks', that is, discussions about whether, and if so on what basis, they could agree to undertake negotiations about a possible Community-level agreement on the issue (see Gold and Hall, 1994 for details). These talks broke down in March 1994 and the following month the Commission issued a new proposal for an EWCs directive restricted to the eleven which was finally adopted by the Council in September 1994.

Against the background of the failure of earlier employee participation/consultation proposals, the adoption of the EWCs directive represented a considerable breakthrough as well as an early success for the new EU approach to social policy regulation. Its innovative legislative design established a highly flexible approach to the establishment of EWCs (or alternative transnational information and consultation procedures) and provided a broad model for the employee participation/consultation measures subsequently adopted.

In particular, the EWCs directive placed a strong emphasis on the negotiation of arrangements tailored to the enterprise. Companies which had agreements providing for transnational information and consultation in place at the directive's implementation date (22 September 1996) were exempt from its provisions. In other Community-scale companies, negotiations about establishing EWCs or alternative procedures via a 'special negotiating body' (SNB) could be triggered by either employee representatives or management, providing further scope for the negotiation of organization-specific agreements. Statutory EWCs became enforceable only where management refused to open negotiations despite an employee request, where the negotiations with an SNB did not produce an agreement or where management and the SNB agreed to adopt the statutory model, as set out in the directive's 'subsidiary requirements'. These set out a basic constitution for an EWC, identified the transnational issues on which central management must inform and consult the EWC, and provided for annual meetings between management and the EWC with the scope for additional meetings in 'exceptional circumstances'—essentially in the event of major restructuring.

The framing of the directive reflected the principle of subsidiarity in a range of ways (Hall, 1992). Among other things, this entailed devolving to member states considerable scope for determining important elements of the legal framework for the establishment of EWCs. Thus, the provisions of the EEA member states' national transposition measures were generally 'customized' to reflect national industrial relations traditions and practices (Carley and Hall, 2000: 110). Most notably, however, the directive gave precedence to arrangements negotiated between management and employee representatives: the subsidiary requirements constituted a fall-back model of last resort. Similarly, Müller and Platzer (2003: 58) observe that the novelty of the directive lay in 'its combination of three principles: regulation (procedural rules and an enforceable set of statutory minimum provisions), subsidiarity (adaptability to national and corporate conditions), and the primacy of negotiations (which give the parties . . . considerable leeway in shaping their institutions)'.

An important point to note is that the EWCs directive defined 'consultation' in broad terms as meaning 'the exchange of views and establishment of dialogue' between employee representatives and management. This is a formulation that arguably falls well short of traditional conceptions of consultation—'generally regarded as a right to be informed of planned measures in advance and to have an opportunity to express an opinion prior to implementation' (Budd and Zagelmeyer, 2010: 492). (Only in the—in practice, very rare—event that the directive's subsidiary requirements apply to a company are there more specific procedural requirements enabling EWC representatives to request a meeting and submit an opinion to management, and these apply only in 'exceptional circumstances'.) This broad definition provided a precedent that was carried over into the ECS employee involvement directive and the 2002 information and consultation directive, though in each of these subsequent measures it was buttressed by more detailed procedural requirements applicable generally (ECS) or in the case of the default provisions (information and consultation directive).

In the period since the adoption of the directive, EWCs have become an established feature of the international employment relations landscape. While only a relative handful of pioneering EWCs existed at the time of the directive's adoption, the number grew rapidly during 1996, prompted by the September 1996 deadline for voluntary 'Article 13' agreements, and thereafter more steadily. By 2011, EWCs existed in 917 companies (Jagodzinski and Pass, 2011). Although it remains the case that only a minority (38 per cent) of the approximately 2,400 companies that fall within the scope of the directive have actually established EWCs, those that do have them tend to be the larger and more internationalized multinationals.

The extensive body of research into EWCs indicates that their role and influence vary considerably between companies. Practice ranges from 'symbolic' EWCs whose activity is largely confined to a ritual annual meeting, through more active bodies involving ongoing networking between employee representatives and regular liaison with management, to those (still relatively few) that exert a measure of influence over management decisions or even engage in the negotiation of agreements or joint texts with management (Hall and Marginson, 2005). The most far-reaching of these agreements, typically found in companies whose operations are highly integrated internationally, have established a binding framework for handling aspects of transnational restructuring, with direct consequences for national and local negotiations—confirming EWCs' potential to be a vehicle for European-level collective bargaining. Nevertheless, the existence of an apparently long 'tail' of uninfluential, largely symbolic EWCs fuelled demands from European trade unions and members of the European Parliament for stronger statutory consultation requirements, eventually resulting in the 'recasting' of the EWCs directive in 2009 (considered further below).

European Company Statute and linked employee involvement directive

The ECS, re-launched in more flexible form in 1989 and with its 'employee involvement' provisions now contained in an accompanying Directive, finally reached the EU statute book in 2001. Its failure over the intervening period to gain approval in the Council of Ministers was largely due to continuing disagreement over the employee involvement provisions to apply to European Companies. States such as Germany, with statutory systems providing for strong employee representation at board level, were concerned that a flexible approach to employee involvement, including employee representation and information and consultation arrangements outside the board, would enable companies based or operating in their countries to escape existing national legislation. In countries without legal rules on board-level participation there was resistance to introducing such arrangements. However, following the report of the 'Davignon' group of experts in 1997 on how to break the deadlock, revised legislative proposals achieved wider support among member states. The provisions finally adopted prioritized negotiated solutions to the issue of employee involvement in European Companies, reflecting a recognition that 'the great diversity' of national rules and practices concerning employee representatives' involvement in company decision-making made 'a single European model' for European Companies 'inadvisable' (recital 5). On the model of the EWCs directive, the ECS employee involvement directive enabled management and an SNB of employee representatives to agree EWC-type information and consultation arrangements and/or employee participation at board level, while requiring a two-thirds majority of SNB members to approve any reduction of existing board-level participation rights covering a certain proportion of employees. In the absence of agreement, fall-back statutory provisions apply, again in similar fashion to the EWCs directive.

The impact in practice of the employee involvement aspects of the ECS has been less extensively documented than that of the EWCs directive. At the beginning of 2011, a European Trade Union Institute database of registered European Companies contained some 700 entries, but only about one-quarter constituted 'normal' European Companies having both business operations and employees. By far the largest number of these (85) were in Germany, where European Company status can be used to 'freeze' or circumvent existing German employee participation rights (Stollt and Kluge, 2011: 184). The majority were either 'empty' European Companies with operations but no employees, or 'shelf' European Companies with neither operations nor employees. Of the 169 'normal' European Companies, only 68 had a known arrangement for European-level employee involvement. As with EWCs, there is substantial variation in the quality of agreements. Despite this 'ambiguous picture', Stollt and Kluge (2011: 188) conclude that the establishment of European Companies has 'in many cases... significantly improved the rights of the workforce and has contributed to an extension of the European dimension of employee involvement'.

The road to the information and consultation directive

The story of the 2002 negotiation of the information and consultation directive illustrates the complex dynamics of social policy regulation within the EU, reflecting the various stances of the social partners, EU institutions, and member state governments. The adoption of the (transnational) EWCs directive in 1994 prompted the development of proposals for legislation on information and consultation within national undertakings to 'complete' the EU legislative framework, reflecting the Commission's ambition to achieve a comprehensive settlement in what had been one of the most intractable areas of EU social policy for over a quarter of a century. The European Parliament's employment and social affairs committee also favoured a directive on the right to information and consultation in national undertakings.

Regulation by the social partners?

Initially, developments revolved around whether or not the European private sector employers' organization UNICE (Union of Industrial and Employers' Confederations) (now BusinessEurope) could be persuaded to engage in negotiations about a possible Community-level agreement on the issue with the other EU-level 'social partners'—the European Trade Union Confederation (ETUC) and the public employers' body CEEP (European Centre of Employers and Enterprises providing Public Services). In April 1995, a medium term social action programme published by the Commission proposed consultations with the social partners about potential EU action on the issue of information and consultation in national undertakings. In November 1995, in a communication to the other EU institutions and the social partners, the Commission outlined possible approaches to progress the various outstanding employee participation proposals and canvassed support for a proposed 'Community instrument' on employee information and consultation at national level to complement the EWCs directive's requirements at transnational level. The proposal met with a mixed reaction. The European Parliament again called for a directive on minimum standards for information and consultation. The ETUC expressed strong support for such a move but UNICE vehemently opposed the idea of EU regulation of information and consultation at national level and continued to oppose the measure in principle throughout the subsequent consultative and legislative processes.

The furore over Renault's closure of its Vilvoorde factory in Belgium in early 1997—without observing the necessary procedures for the prior information and consultation of employee representatives (ruled unlawful by court rulings in France and Belgium)—provided further political impetus to the calls for legislation. Similar controversies followed over high-profile restructuring and closures at companies such as Levi Strauss, Goodyear, and Marks and Spencer, contributing to continuing pressure for new EU information and consultation rules.

In June 1997, the Commission began a formal two-stage consultation of the social partners under the Maastricht social policy agreement by first seeking their views on the 'possible direction of Community action' on 'the information and consultation of workers within the national framework'. With the situation of the United Kingdom (and Ireland) apparently in mind, a central argument advanced by the Commission in support of its proposal was that:

> The absence of a general framework for information and consultation nationally results in the provisions of the [collective redundancies and transfer of undertakings] directives having a limited impact. The preventive approach on which they are based is difficult to implement in the context of information and consultation procedures that are isolated, fragmented and limited to cases of imminent collective redundancies and transfers of undertakings, and would be consolidated by the definition of more general and permanent information and consultation procedures. (Commission consultation document quoted in EWCB, 1997: 5)

The ETUC supported the move to strengthen national information and consultation rules while UNICE opposed the idea, arguing that the EU should not intervene in a matter which had 'no transnational implications'. The Commission proceeded with the second stage of consultations in November 1997 on the basis of a more concrete set of proposals. The Commission's stated preference was for the social partners to negotiate a Community-level agreement on employee consultation under the Maastricht social policy procedures, but made it clear that in the absence of such an agreement it would bring forward its own proposals for a directive. While the ETUC and CEEP responded positively to the idea of a possible Community-level agreement, UNICE eventually decided not to enter into negotiations—a position it confirmed in October 1998 when it revisited its stance on the issue following the leak of an unofficial text of a draft directive. Consequently, the Commission published a formal proposal for a directive in November 1998.

Commission proposal

Under the draft directive, all undertakings with at least fifty employees would be required to inform and consult employee representatives about a range of business, employment, and work organization issues. However, member states could allow the social partners, including at undertaking level, to negotiate procedures for implementing information and consultation, including arrangements which differed from the directive's requirements while respecting its general objectives. Controversially, the draft included a provision on sanctions for non-compliance under which the legal effect of restructuring decisions taken by employers in serious breach of their information and consultation obligations would be suspended.

In launching the proposal, the Commission employed a range of arguments stressing the 'employee rights' and 'efficiency' arguments for EU intervention as well as the broader political factors justifying the measure. The explanatory memorandum accompanying the draft directive stated that the proposed framework was 'designed to fill the gaps and counter the shortcomings... in the employee information and consultation provisions currently in force at national and Community levels', with the objective of '[ensuring the] existence of the right to regular information and consultation of employees on economic and strategic developments in the undertaking and on the decisions which affect them'. The social affairs commissioner at the time, Pádraig Flynn, emphasized that the directive would 'help create a more positive and flexible approach [by workers] to reorganisation and change'. More broadly, the Commission saw its initiative as an 'essential step in completing the EU's social dimension' and '[ensuring] that corporate restructuring is done in a socially acceptable way' (EWCB, 1999: 8–9).

Views of the social partners

The Commission's proposal received starkly differing responses from the EU-level social partners. The ETUC gave it a 'warm welcome' and said that, by proposing the draft directive, the Commission had 'given new impetus to Social Europe, even if the [proposal] does not fully meet trade unions' expectations'. The ETUC argued that the legislation should apply to 'all undertakings', not only those with at least fifty employees. UNICE said that the draft directive constituted 'totally unwarranted interference in member states' systems of industrial relations' and could 'paralyze' the decision-making process within companies.

At UK level, similarly divided views were expressed by the Trades Union Congress (TUC) and the Confederation of British Industry (CBI). The TUC said: 'In reality this is a modest measure. It simply requires all companies to do what successful ones do already—tell staff what is going on and listen to what they have to say'. The CBI argued that the directive would constitute a 'completely unacceptable breach of the principle of subsidiarity'.

Position of the UK government

The Blair-led Labour government adopted a strongly negative stance towards the proposed information and consultation directive, justifying this by reference to both voluntarism and subsidiarity. The government stated that it supported employee information and consultation, but it was 'important that such mechanisms reflect the requirements of individual organisations'. The government was 'not persuaded of the need for a directive on information and consultation arrangements within companies operating purely within one member state. Such a Directive would cut across existing practices in member states to no benefit' and was 'difficult to reconcile with subsidiarity' (DTI, 1998). The government also indicated that it had secured the support of the German Social Democrat-led government in seeking to block the proposal in the EU Council. According to the *Financial Times* of 12 November 1998, a 'deal' had been reached between the two governments under which the German government would back the United Kingdom in opposing the draft information and consultation directive. In return, the United Kingdom would support provisions in the ECS to safeguard board-level codetermination in German companies opting to become European Companies.

Legislative process

The European Parliament approved the draft directive at first reading stage in April 1999, proposing thirty-four amendments mostly aimed at toughening the draft's provisions. The EU Economic and Social Committee adopted its opinion on the draft directive—a necessary stage of the legislative process—in June 1999. The opinion was equivocal, reflecting differences of view among the committee's members (representatives of employers, employees, and other interests).

Meanwhile, in May 1999 the legal base of the draft directive was changed. It had originally been proposed by the Commission under Article 2(2) of the Maastricht social policy agreement, but this was changed to Article 137(2) of the EC Treaty, as a result of the entry into force of the Amsterdam treaty (which ended the United Kingdom's social policy 'opt-out' and incorporated the former social policy agreement into the main body of the Treaty). The effect was formally to apply the proposal to the United Kingdom, and make it subject to the 'cooperation procedure' between the Council and the European Parliament, enhancing the latter's influence during the legislative process. Article 137(2) provided for Community action on 'the information and consultation of workers', with adoption on the part of the Council by qualified majority voting. The UK government subsequently argued—unsuccessfully—for the draft directive instead to be based on Article 137(3), which provided for Community action on 'representation and collective defence of the interests of workers and employers, including co-determination', with adoption on the part of the Council unanimous vote (which would have allowed the United Kingdom alone to block the proposal).

The German government avoided discussion of the draft directive within the Council during its EU presidency over the first six months of 1999 and successive EU presidencies kept the issue off the Council agenda until June 2000 when the Portuguese presidency initiated official-level discussion of the proposal at a meeting of the Council's social questions working group just days before handing over the presidency to France.

Under the French presidency, during the second half of 2000, extensive discussion of the draft directive took place, in which the majority of member states adopted a generally positive stance towards the Commission's proposal. However, the United Kingdom, Germany, Ireland, and Denmark each entered a 'general reservation' concerning the proposal, together constituting a potential 'blocking minority' under the qualified majority voting rules applicable to the directive. This prevented a 'common position' being agreed by the Employment and Social Policy Council under the French presidency.

However, once political agreement had been reached on the ECS in December 2000, it became clear that the German government would not continue its opposition to adopting the information and consultation directive beyond the 2001 UK general election. Denmark's and Ireland's main concerns related to their preference for collectively agreed consultation arrangements and were accommodated by revisions to the text. Faced with the disintegration of the blocking minority, the UK government was forced to accept the directive, which it did quickly following its re-election in June 2001, securing eleventh-hour concessions on the timetable for applying the directive to smaller undertakings.

The Council formally adopted a common position in July 2001. The European Parliament subsequently put forward a series of amendments at second reading stage and, as not all of these were acceptable to the Council, under the co-decision procedure the directive was referred to a joint Council-Parliament conciliation committee. Compromise proposals put forward by the Commission were approved at a 'trialogue' meeting between representatives of the three institutions and final agreement on the text of the directive was achieved in December 2001. Formal adoption of the directive took place in March 2002.

During the Council's discussion of the draft directive, the UK government was active in promoting amendments intended to offer member states and the social partners' greater flexibility in terms of its implementation. The final version of the directive (Box 3.1) differed from the Commission's original proposal in a number of important respects. Whereas the original proposal sought to 'establish a general framework for informing and consulting employees', the final version referred to the 'right' to information and consultation and included a new recital (15) stating that the directive was 'without prejudice' to national systems in which the exercise of this right depended on employees indicating their wishes collectively (i.e. via some sort of trigger mechanism as in a number of member states). This meant that employers need not be obliged to inform and consult where employees choose not to exercise their right to initiate such arrangements—a central element of the UK government's flexible approach to implementing the directive as we explain in Chapter 4. The final directive gave member states the choice of whether to apply the directive's requirements at establishment rather than undertaking level, in order to accommodate existing German works council legislation. It also provided wider scope for the social partners to negotiate alternative information and consultation provisions to those specified in the directive, and omitted the Commission's proposed approach to sanctions for non-compliance. The deadline for the national transposition of the directive was extended from two to three years after its formal publication. Transitional arrangements allowed member states without a 'general, permanent and statutory' system of information and consultation or employee representation (effectively the United Kingdom and Ireland, prior to EU enlargement) to phase in the application of the directive to smaller undertakings over a longer period. We review the impact of the directive in Britain in Chapters 4 and 5, and elsewhere in Europe in Chapter 8.

Box 3.1 KEY PROVISIONS OF THE 2002 INFORMATION AND CONSULTATION DIRECTIVE

Object and principles

The purpose of the directive is to establish a general framework setting out minimum requirements for the right to information and consultation of employees in undertakings or establishments within the Community. The practical arrangements for information and consultation are to be defined and implemented by member states in accordance with national law and industrial relations practice in such a way as to ensure their effectiveness (Article 1).

Definitions

'Employees' representatives': those provided for by national laws and/or practices.
'Information': transmission by the employer to the employees' representatives of data in order to enable them to acquaint themselves with the subject matter and to examine it.
'Consultation': the exchange of views and establishment of dialogue between the employees' representatives and the employer.

Scope

The directive's requirements apply, according to the choice made by member states, to:

- undertakings employing at least fifty employees in any one member state; or
- establishments employing at least twenty employees

Practical arrangements for information and consultation

Information and consultation covers:

- information on the recent and probable development of the undertaking's or the establishment's activities and economic situation;
- information and consultation on the situation, structure, and probable development of employment within the undertaking and on any anticipatory measures envisaged, in particular where there is a threat to employment; and
- information and consultation on decisions likely to lead to substantial changes in work organization or in contractual relations, including collective redundancies and transfers of undertakings.

Information shall be given at such time, in such fashion, and with such content as are appropriate to enable employees' representatives to conduct an adequate study and, where necessary, prepare for consultation.

Consultation shall take place:

- while ensuring that the timing, method, and content are appropriate;
- at the relevant level of management and representation, depending on the subject under discussion;

- on the basis of the information supplied by the employer and the opinion which the employees' representatives are entitled to formulate;
- in such a way as to enable employees' representatives to meet with the employer and obtain a response, and the reasons for that response, to any opinion they might formulate;
- with a view to reaching agreement on decisions within the scope of the employers' powers likely to lead to substantial changes in work organization or in contractual relations.

Information and consultation deriving from an agreement

Member states may entrust management and labour, including at undertaking or establishment level, with defining through negotiated agreement the practical arrangements for informing and consulting employees. These may differ from those set out by the directive while respecting the principles set out in Article 1.

Confidentiality

Member states must provide that employee representatives and any experts who assist them are not authorized to disclose any expressly confidential information provided to them, though member states may authorize its disclosure to employees and third parties bound by an obligation of confidentiality. Member states must also provide, in specific cases and within the limits laid down by national legislation, that employers are not obliged to communicate any information or undertake any consultation which would seriously harm the functioning of the undertaking or would be prejudicial to it. Employers' decisions to require confidentiality or withhold prejudicial information must be open to review via administrative or judicial procedures.

Protection of employees' representatives

Member states must ensure that employees' representatives have adequate protection and guarantees to enable them to perform their duties properly.

Enforcement

Member states must provide for appropriate measures in the event of non-compliance by employers or employees' representatives with the provisions of the directive, and ensure in particular that adequate administrative or judicial procedures are available to enable the obligations deriving from the directive to be enforced. Member states must also provide for adequate sanctions to be applicable in the event of infringement of the directive. These must be effective, proportionate, and dissuasive.

Links with other measures

The directive is without prejudice to the specific information and consultation procedures of the EU collective redundancies and transfers of undertakings directives, provisions adopted in accordance with the EWCs directive, and other rights to information, consultation, and participation under national law. Implementation of the directive shall not be sufficient grounds for any regression in relation to the situation which already prevails in each member state and in relation to the general level of protection of workers in the areas to which it applies.

Implementation

Member states were given until 23 March 2005 (three years from the directive's official publication) to adopt the laws, regulations, and administrative provisions necessary to comply with its requirements. Implementation via agreement between management and labour is permissible, in which case member states must be able to guarantee the results required by the directive. However, transitional arrangements enabled member states with no general, permanent, and statutory system of information and consultation or employee representation at the workplace to apply the directive in three phases, covering:

- undertakings with at least 150 employees (or establishments with at least 100 employees) by the March 2005 implementation deadline;
- undertakings with at least 100 employees (or establishments with at least 50 employees) two years later; and
- undertakings with at least 50 employees (or establishments with at least 20 employees) three years later.

Review of the directive

Not later than 23 March 2007 the Commission was required, in consultation with the member states and the social partners at EU level, to review the application of the directive with a view to proposing any necessary amendments.

Subsequent EU measures

EU legislative activity in this area continues. Further subject-specific provisions were included in the 2004 takeover bids directive, giving employees and their representatives information and consultation rights in the event of company takeovers (EWCB, 2004). Further transnational participation requirements, similar to those in the ECS employee involvement directive, featured in the 2005 cross-border mergers directive (EWCB, 2005). Most notably, reflecting 'joint advice' submitted by the EU-level social partners, the EWCs directive was 'recast' in 2009, strengthening the original directive's provisions in a number of important respects (Jagodzinski, 2009). In particular, its definitions of information and consultation were strengthened and made more detailed, drawing on the corresponding provisions in the ECS employee involvement directive and the information and consultation directive. Other innovations included linking and differentiating between information and consultation via EWCs and national employee representation bodies, providing an explicit role for EU-level trade union organizations in SNB negotiations, a right to training for EWC and SNB members, and rules on adapting EWCs where the structure of a company changes.

The cross-fertilization between the three major recent directives illustrates not only the close relationship and strong similarities between them but also the scope for the further 'ratcheting up' of EU information and consultation provisions in the future. As discussed in Chapter 8, the European Commission is expected shortly to announce the outcome of a review of the 2002 information and consultation directive. Given that the rights and facilities of employee representatives under the 2002 directive are limited compared to those contained in the recast EWCs directive, it is possible that EU legislators will look to incorporate similar provisions in any revised information and consultation directive in terms of representatives' rights to paid time off and the necessary financial and material resources to carry out their duties, to undertake training, to call special meetings, to meet separately from management, and to seek external advice. Such measures would arguably encourage and underpin more robust processes of consultation, particularly in those member states with relatively recent statutory information and consultation frameworks (Hall and Purcell, 2011).

Conclusion

The adoption of the 2002 information and consultation directive constituted the final major element of the EU legal framework regulating employee participation and consultation and the culmination of debates dating back almost to the inception of the EU in the 1950s. As well as covering specific issues such as redundancies and business transfers, EU legislation now provides a more general framework of minimum standards governing information and consultation on a range of key business, employment, and restructuring issues within purely national undertakings as well as transnational undertakings or groups and those incorporated as European Companies.

The eventual achievement of this comprehensive EU framework reflected the gradual strengthening of both the legal and political bases for EU-level intervention in this area. Treaty changes in the early 1990s finally established unambiguous EU competence to regulate information and consultation arrangements and also included information and consultation within the widened scope for majority voting within the Council. Although, as this chapter has shown, the political momentum behind EU legislative proposals is heavily dependent on the prevailing political and economic context, the European Commission has sought to entrench information and consultation as a key component of the 'European social model' blending 'competitiveness and solidarity' (CEC, 1994; Bercusson, 2002). This has been reinforced by the inclusion of a 'workers' right to information and consultation within the undertaking' in the 'solidarity' chapter of the Charter of Fundamental Rights of the European Union: 'workers or their representatives must, at the appropriate levels, be guaranteed information and consultation in good time in the cases and under the conditions provided for by Union law and national laws and practices' (Article 27). This charter, originally adopted in 2000 on the basis of political agreement, was given legal enforceability (subject to another UK opt-out) by the Treaty of Lisbon in 2007.

But arguably the key to the eventual success of the post-1980s legislative initiatives discussed in this chapter has been the adoption of a less prescriptive, more flexible approach to EU regulation in the face of successive EU enlargements, each resulting in a wider diversity of national industrial relations regimes within the EU. The early aspirations of EU regulators—to engineer the upward harmonization (in the sense of generalizing best practice) of national employee participation and consultation arrangements—inevitably gave way to a less ambitious, more pragmatic approach. Reflecting the growing significance of the principle of subsidiarity in EU policy debates, this new approach to regulating information and consultation practice and social policy issues more generally sought to introduce minimum standards to underpin national provision while leaving considerable scope for devolved regulation by member states and by national social partners.

Indeed, the three major recent directives discussed above—on EWCs, employee involvement under the ECS, and national information and consultation arrangements—share notably similar legislative approaches, with the emphasis on facilitating flexible implementation. Each enables member states to 'customize' the detailed legislative framework to be applied to reflect the national employment relations context. Each provides extensive scope for employers and employee representatives at company level to negotiate organization-specific information and consultation or participation procedures, while specifying statutory default or fall-back arrangements to apply in the absence of agreed alternative arrangements. Notably, each enables the adoption of negotiated arrangements that fall short of the default standards specified, an approach seemingly at odds with the EU's formal recognition of information and consultation as a 'fundamental right' for workers (Ales, 2009). The three measures have been seen as displaying the characteristics of 'reflexive' employment law (Koukiadaki, 2009), under which 'the preferred mode of intervention is for the law to underpin and encourage autonomous processes of adjustment' by the parties to the employment relationship (Barnard and Deakin, 2000: 341). Under reflexive law, legal regulation provides a procedural framework rather than specifying substantive outcomes (Rogowski and Wilthagen, 1994). More broadly, Marginson and Sisson (2004) argue that the less prescriptive approach to such measures, compared to earlier legislative initiatives, and a growing EU preference for 'softer' forms of regulation, reflect the emergence of a 'multi-level' system of industrial relations governance within the EU in which outcomes are shaped by the interaction between governmental and social partner bodies at supranational, national, sector, and company levels.

Comparative industrial relations analysis has traditionally warned against the assumption that collective institutions and procedures can easily be 'transplanted' from one system of industrial relations to another (Kahn-Freund, 1974: 21)—or, indeed, in the EU context, 'harmonized'. EU regulators have long since ceased basing legislative proposals in this area on perceived 'best practice' national institutional models. However, in the context of the espousal of a 'European social model', contemporary, more flexible approaches to regulation still act as a transmission belt or carrier of broad, essentially Western European patterns of workforce-wide employee consultation. This has meant that the United Kingdom has had to implement 'Community legislation derived from the continental tradition' (Davies and Freedland, 2007: 139), which has brought with it some fundamental challenges to traditional UK patterns of workplace representation and the regulation of industrial relations.

Nevertheless, the fact that the information and consultation directive confines itself to establishing a 'general framework', allowing member states considerable flexibility regarding the practical arrangements for its implementation, means that, more than ever, the impact and outcomes of EU employment law will be dependent on national cultural, economic, and institutional context. The national impacts of the directive will be mediated by national employment relations frameworks and traditions (e.g. the primacy accorded to trade union representation, the extent of social partnership), the key policy choices made by national implementing legislation (e.g. whether the establishment of information and consultation bodies is dependent on employee initiative), and the attitudes of the social partners (with limited interest reported in some countries). The background to and policy debates surrounding the approach to transposing the directive taken in the United Kingdom is a central focus of Chapter 4.

4

Half-Hearted Regulation in the United Kingdom

Historically, employee consultation in the United Kingdom has not been subject to statutory intervention, reflecting its 'voluntarist' industrial relations traditions, and the primacy accorded to collective bargaining. In Chapter 1 we discussed the reasons why governments rejected the use of legal compulsion to promote both the Whitley Committee's proposals for works committees and joint production committees during the Second World War (Dukes, 2008). The UK debate about industrial democracy in the 1970s, focussing on proposals for employee representation on company boards but including consideration of sub-board level participation via consultative committees, also resulted in no legislative intervention. Moreover, the Confederation of British Industry's (CBI) successful campaign against the proposals of the Bullock committee cemented the stance of opposition in principle to statutory consultation mechanisms that the organization has maintained ever since.

Nevertheless, starting in the mid-1970s, there has been a significant growth in statutory provisions requiring employers to inform and consult employee representatives in a range of circumstances. This has been driven primarily by EU regulation rather than domestic policy.[1] The process culminated in the introduction of the Information and Consultation of Employees Regulations 2004—the ICE regulations—which are the central focus of this chapter. Intended to implement the requirements of the 2002 EU information and consultation directive, the regulations represent a radical development in the UK context. They establish, for the first time in the United Kingdom, a general statutory framework giving employees of domestic undertakings the right to be informed and consulted by their employers on a range of key business, employment, and restructuring issues.

Equally significantly, EU law has also driven important legal changes concerning the identity of the employee representatives with whom statutory consultation should take place. Until 1995, statutory consultation rights in the United Kingdom remained the exclusive preserve of trade unions recognized by employers. Since then, the effect of key European Court of Justice (ECJ) rulings has been to require UK law to accommodate the universal, workforce-wide approach to employee information and consultation rights embodied in EU legislation.

The combined effect of these two developments has been to bring about 'a dramatic change in the laws concerning the structures of collective representation at enterprise level in Great Britain' (Davies and Freedland, 2007: 132). However, key policy choices on the specifics of the United Kingdom's legislative response to EU requirements have been shaped by domestic employment relations and political concerns, arguably limiting the extent to which these changes have brought the United Kingdom closer to the European mainstream. The result has been a 'half-hearted' approach to regulating for employee consultation on the part of governments of both main political parties, reflecting among other things entrenched employer opposition to—and trade union ambivalence about—legislative intervention in this area. Despite the ECJ rulings that the United Kingdom's early information and consultation provisions, introduced in response to the collective redundancies and transfers of undertakings directives of the 1970s, were deficient, the United Kingdom's more recent legislation has been 'minimalist' in character and arguably also of doubtful compliance with EU requirements.

Before looking in detail at the factors affecting the introduction and design of the ICE regulations, this chapter reviews the evolution of the United Kingdom's employee consultation legislation in the light of legislative developments at EU level, the (mainly hostile) attitudes adopted by successive UK governments to EU regulation in this area, and the respective policy preferences of the United Kingdom's principal employer and trade union bodies. It also highlights the continuing repercussions of the landmark 1994 rulings of the ECJ for the critical issue of how UK law designates the employee representatives who are to be informed and consulted—in particular the extent to which existing trade union representatives may fulfil this role.

The legacy of the Bullock debate

It is often forgotten that the previous occasion on which a UK government had produced legislative proposals to promote the generalized adoption of consultation machinery was in 1978 in response to the report of the committee of inquiry on industrial democracy chaired by Lord Bullock. The principal focus of the debate surrounding the establishment of the Bullock Committee was employee representation on company boards in the light of the EU's draft fifth directive (see Chapter 3). But the Labour government's 1978 white paper included a proposal to require UK companies employing more than 500 people to consult employee representatives on major business issues before decisions were made. In the absence of agreed arrangements, the proposed statutory fall-back was consultation via a 'joint representation committee' made up of the recognized unions within the company (but with scope for the voluntary inclusion on non-unionists in the process). The white paper also proposed that employees should have the right to representation on company boards. Where voluntary agreement on board-level employee representation could not be reached, joint representation committees in companies with more than 2,000 employees would, after three or four years in existence, have the statutory right to trigger a workforce ballot on the issue. Majority support would entitle employees to one-third of the seats on the policy board in a two-tier board structure.

Significantly, the approach of the white paper owed more to the position of the CBI at that time, and to the minority report submitted by the three employers' representatives on the Bullock committee, than to the proposals supported by the Bullock majority. Inside the CBI, the draft fifth directive had prompted an internal debate over whether a policy of supporting statutory consultative councils should be put forward as an alternative to board-level participation requirements. Such a course was favoured by CBI leaders but was turned down by the CBI council in September 1973 (Elliott, 1978: 215). The CBI subsequently backed the idea of statutory 'participation agreements' to be negotiated by larger companies within a set period, but its objectives 'centred on only communication-style exercises aimed at "promoting understanding" and making employees aware of the reasons for decisions that affect them' (Elliott, 1978: 118). Within the Bullock committee itself, the three employers' representatives signed a minority report proposing statutory company participation councils, potentially as a precursor to minority employee representation on supervisory boards.

The Bullock report and the subsequent white paper proved to be something of a watershed in the UK debate about statutory consultation and participation measures. Any prospect of the white paper's proposals reaching the statute book was extinguished by the election of a Conservative government the following year. The incoming government was fiercely opposed to the principle of industrial democracy. The 'Euro-sceptic' Conservative governments of the 1980s and 1990s resisted successive legislative proposals at EU level, including the draft 'Vredeling' directive, amended proposals for the 'fifth' company law directive and the European Works Councils (EWCs) directive. They regarded proposals for mandatory consultation or participation as 'alien' to the UK tradition of voluntarism and incompatible with British companies' increasingly individualized approaches to employee involvement practice (Hall, 1992). The sharply polarized Bullock debate also shaped union and employer stances towards subsequent, more limited EU proposals concerning the information and consultation of employees. Within the Trades Union Congress (TUC), insistence on 'single channel', trade union-based representation had been central to its proposals for industrial democracy: statutory provisions for board-level worker representation should apply only where there was trade union recognition, and workers' representatives were to be chosen via trade union machinery at company level (TUC,1974). The CBI's attitude was diametrically opposed: it refused to accept 'the imposition of trade union nominated directors' (Elliott, 1978: 244). As we shall see, the TUC's 'unequivocal support for the single channel' at the time of Bullock (Towers, 1997: 207) subsequently underwent something of a reappraisal, most notably in the mid-1990s, but still continues to underpin TUC policy. The CBI's tactical support for statutory consultation measures proved short-lived. Since its vociferous and ultimately successful campaign against the Bullock report, the CBI has essentially maintained a position of opposition in principle to legislative intervention in the area of employee participation and consultation.

Key stages in the evolution of UK consultation legislation

Most contemporary UK employee consultation requirements emanate from EU directives (see note 1 p. 87). As highlighted in Chapter 3, the initial statutory interventions at European level in the mid- to late 1970s were confined to directives requiring issue-specific information and consultation on collective redundancies and transfers of undertakings. These were implemented in the United Kingdom in 1975 and 1981 respectively, but underwent significant amendment in the 1990s in response to infringement proceedings by the European Commission and the resulting ECJ rulings. After a lengthy impasse over EU social policy proposals in general—and employee consultation measures in particular—the next wave of EU legislation, dating from 1994 onwards, included more general and systematic information and consultation obligations but applied on a transnational basis within companies operating in a number of EU countries. The 1994 EWCs Directive was eventually implemented in the United Kingdom, following the reversal of the United Kingdom's social policy opt-out, via the Transnational Information and Consultation of Employees (TICE) Regulations 1999. The European Company Statute (ECS) and the linked employee involvement directive, finally adopted in 2001, led to the European Public Limited Liability Company Regulations 2004 in the United Kingdom. The final key element in the EU legislative framework—the 2002 directive on employee information and consultation in national undertakings—was transposed into British law by the ICE regulations in 2004.[2]

Issue-specific consultation

Statutory provisions on consultation over impending redundancies, now contained in sections 188–198 of the Trade Union and Labour Relations (Consolidation) Act 1992, as amended, were first introduced in the United Kingdom by the Employment Protection Act 1975 drawn up by the Labour government of the day. These were intended to meet the requirements of the EU directive on collective redundancies of the same year. Although the regulation of redundancies was already on the domestic political agenda as a result of pressure from trade unions, the provisions of the Employment Protection Act reflected the approach of the directive rather than more far-reaching proposals put forward by the TUC (Davies and Freedland, 1993: 358).

The 1975 Act required employers to consult recognized unions in advance of any proposed redundancies and laid down minimum consultation periods of up to ninety days dependent on the number of employees involved. Consultation was to be about ways and means of avoiding redundancies, reducing the number of employees affected, and mitigating the consequences of the redundancies. Where the required consultation did not take place, unions could complain to an employment tribunal which could make a 'protective award' requiring the employer to maintain the remuneration of the employees concerned for a 'protected period' related to the minimum consultation periods. Significantly, the duty to consult applied only where an employer recognized a trade union in respect of the employees affected—a key issue discussed in some detail below.

Further issue-specific consultation legislation followed in the shape of the Transfer of Undertakings (Protection of Employment) Regulations 1981 (the TUPE regulations). These were introduced with self-confessed reluctance by the first Conservative administration formed by Prime Minister Margaret Thatcher—and only after the European Commission had begun proceedings against the United Kingdom in the ECJ for non-implementation of the 1977 EU acquired rights directive (Davies and Freedland, 1993: 577). Here, too, the duty to consult applied only where employers recognized unions: the TUPE regulations required both the transferor and transferee to inform and consult union representatives on behalf of the employees affected by the transfer or by measures taken in connection with it.

Infringement proceedings were initiated by the European Commission in 1992 on the grounds that UK implementation of the two directives was deficient. These, together with the revision of the collective redundancies directive in the same year, prompted a series of amendments to the UK legislation, introduced by the Trade Union Reform and Employment Rights Act 1993. The most important change was to specify that redundancy consultation should be 'with a view to reaching agreement'—a requirement of the directive omitted from the original UK legislation. But the central issue in the infringement proceedings concerned UK law's restriction of the obligation to consult to those employers who recognized trade unions.

Workforce-wide consultation rights versus single channel

Faced with having to give effect to successive EU consultation directives, a central policy issue for UK governments of whatever party has been how national transposition legislation should designate the employee representatives who are to be informed and consulted—in particular, the extent to which existing trade union representatives may fulfil this role (Davies and Kilpatrick, 2004).

As we have seen, under the United Kingdom's original statutory requirements on consultation over redundancies, dating from 1975, the obligation to consult employee representatives was restricted to employers who recognized trade unions in respect of the employees concerned. At the time, this approach appeared to be in line with the directive's provision, replicated in subsequent consultation directives, that the employee representatives to be consulted were those 'provided for by national laws and/or practice'. In the context of the widespread trade union recognition that existed at that time, coupled with the introduction of the statutory recognition provisions contained in the same 1975 Act, such a policy choice was obvious and clear-cut. The United Kingdom's TUPE regulations of 1981 followed the same pattern, despite the repeal of the recognition legislation in the meantime.

As we have noted, this approach was challenged by the European Commission, which pursued legal cases against the United Kingdom in the ECJ. In two landmark rulings in 1994, the ECJ ruled that the United Kingdom was in breach of the Collective Redundancies and Transfer of Undertakings directives by failing to provide for the designation of employee representatives for the purposes of the consultation required by the directives where an employer did not recognize unions (Davies, 1994). Thus, for the purposes of implementing EU consultation requirements, the ECJ overturned UK law's traditional reliance on recognized trade unions as the single channel of employee representation. The UK government was therefore faced with the prospect of having to introduce alternative or supplementary mechanisms to apply the directives in the absence of union recognition.

The ECJ rulings also had potentially significant implications for the outcome of a major TUC policy review focusing on representation at work, undertaken in 1994–5, that included consideration of advocating more extensive statutory consultation rights. An interim report (TUC, 1994) outlined proposals for giving employees in establishments without recognized unions the legal right to trigger the formation of statutory 'employee representation committees'

Box 4.1 TUC POLICY ON CONSULTATION RIGHTS AND THE SINGLE CHANNEL

From the late 1980s onwards, TUC policy development concerning the legal regulation of employee representation began to show increasing interest in statutory rights to consultation alongside the reintroduction of a statutory recognition procedure. This reflected both the sharp decline in union membership and collective bargaining that had taken place since 1980 and also the TUC's increasingly positive stance towards the EU, symbolized by Jacques Delors' speech to the TUC's annual conference in 1988. The perception of the EU as an alternative source of individual and collective employment rights during a period of sustained deregulation domestically was a key reason for this change in tone. Union interest in exploring the organizational possibilities of works council-type arrangements also dated from this period. For example, the 1998 Congress supported a resolution which stated that 'future employment law must include triggers to trade union recognition, rather than any attempt to create an alternative and necessarily inferior model of collective organisation'. The same resolution instructed the General Council to 'consult [affiliates] on the principle of elected works councils with the power to activate positive legal rights'.

However, the first major TUC policy document that put forward proposals for enhanced consultation rights—a consultative document reported to the 1991 Congress (TUC, 1991)—did so in the context of a three-stage approach to achieving union recognition. Depending upon the prevailing levels of membership or support within a given bargaining unit, unions would have the right to employer provided facilities (stage 1), the right to be consulted on certain issues (stage 2), or full negotiating rights (stage 3). The document noted that there had been 'growing support for the works council concept in sections of the British trade union movement in recent years' (TUC, 1991: 11). Crucially, however, under the three-stage scheme, consultation rights were to be union-based, reflecting the TUC's traditional 'single channel' policy. This approach was not developed further at that time, 'in part reflecting the outcome of the 1992 general election which removed any immediate prospect of legislation in this area' (TUC, 1994: 12).

Subsequent TUC policy development work continued to reflect an interest in patterns of universal employee representation elsewhere in Europe. A 1991 Congress resolution '[called] on the General Council to examine how features of the Franco-German approach to industrial relations, such as works councils and greater rights to information and consultation, might be adapted to British circumstances and traditions'. This led to a study visit to Germany in 1992 (Hall, 1993). In evidence to the House of Commons Select Committee on Employment in October 1993, the TUC called for changes in the law to give employees the legal right to representation. The TUC stated that it 'would ideally wish to see this take the form of a right to trade union recognition' but that 'there are, of course, other ways of achieving this objective. A right to employee representation through elections to works or company councils is another model. In practice, unions have a role in these systems too.'

In 1994, shortly before the ECJ's ruling on the United Kingdom's implementation of EU consultation directives, the TUC set up a General Council task group on 'representation at work' and launched an eighteen-month consultative exercise on the possible policy options, culminating in the adoption of a final report by the 1995 Congress. An outline proposal for statutory employee representation committees in non-union workplaces, with specific information and consultation rights on a range of business and employment issues, was floated—but not recommended by the task group—in an interim report to the 1994 Congress. However, the possibility of the TUC adopting this wider, universal consultation rights strategy receded during the course of the consultative process. The latter 'revealed considerable unease on the part of most major unions at the prospect of such a radical departure from the traditional pattern of single channel trade union representation. This [reflected] not only ideological qualms but also uncertainty about whether a broader range of universal consultation rights, and the emergence of works council-type structures in the absence of recognised unions, would be an effective vehicle for extending union influence and organisation' (Hall, 1996).

The final proposals adopted (TUC, 1995) included provision for a universal right to consultation over redundancies and transfers, preferably via unions but if necessary with representatives elected by employees specifically for this purpose. However, wider consultation rights were envisaged only as part of a new and more general statutory framework for promoting union-based consultation machinery. The TUC proposed that unions with 10 per cent membership or more within an appropriate work group (analogous to a bargaining unit) should be entitled by law to consultation rights on behalf of their members in respect of 'management proposals involving significant changes in employment numbers or working conditions'. Significantly, then, the final TUC proposals advocated universal consultation rights only insofar as they were strictly required by the redundancies and transfers directives. Statutory consultation on issues other than redundancies and transfers would be through trade union channels only—not through elected representatives or works councils.

which would have a range of information and consultation rights. But these proposals failed to survive the TUC's internal consultative process with affiliated unions (see Box 4.1 for further details). The final proposals adopted by the TUC General Council and the 1995 Congress incorporated provision for a universal right to consultation over redundancies and transfers, if necessary via representatives elected by employees specifically for this purpose, in line with the ECJ rulings. But wider consultation rights were to be union based, applicable where trade unions had at least 10 per cent membership and envisaged as a stepping stone towards union recognition. This outcome demonstrated continuing union unease at the prospect of departing from the traditional pattern of 'single channel' trade union representation (Hall, 1996; Davies and Freedland, 2007).

The then Conservative government's own response to the ECJ rulings proved controversial. In 1995 it introduced amending regulations requiring consultation on redundancies and transfers either with representatives of recognized unions or with other representatives elected by employees, the choice lying with the employer. Election arrangements were a matter for the employer: the regulations did not specify how employee representatives should be elected. Appropriate existing consultative bodies were a permissible channel for the required consultation provided their membership was elected. This approach was strongly criticized, particularly by trade unions and Labour members of the House of Lords, among other things for giving employers the option of 'bypassing' recognized unions and consulting other elected employee representatives instead (Hall and Edwards, 1999). There was criticism, too, of the absence of provisions specifying how employee representatives should be elected and ensuring their independence from the employer. Three trade unions obtained leave to apply for judicial review of the 1995 regulations, but the High Court dismissed their claims in a judgement issued in May 1996 (Skidmore, 1996). However, in December 1996 the European Commission reportedly sent a complaint to the UK government, alleging that the regulations failed properly to implement the ECJ's interpretation of the consultation provisions of the two directives. In particular, the Commission was reported to have questioned whether the regulations adequately reflected the ECJ's views on procedures for designating employee representatives.

Following the change of government in 1997, the view of the incoming Labour administration was that the 1995 regulations 'still [did] not provide a clear and satisfactory framework for the necessary information and consultation' (Hall and Edwards, 1999). In February 1998, the then Department of Trade and Industry (DTI) initiated a public consultation on proposed changes to the legislation which eventually resulted in the Collective Redundancies and Transfer of Undertakings (Protection of Employment) (Amendment) Regulations 1999. These adopted a 'union priority' (Davies and Freedland, 2007: 147) or 'supplemented single channel' (Davies, 1994: 278) approach. The law was changed to prioritize consultation via the representatives of independent trade unions where they were recognized by employers. Otherwise, consultation should take place with appropriate existing elected employee representatives (e.g. a consultative committee) or representatives specially elected by employees under regulated balloting procedures.

A similar approach was taken around this time in a number of other areas subject to EU regulation. The ECJ rulings prompted the introduction of the Health and Safety (Consultation with Employees) Regulations 1996. These supplemented existing legislation by requiring employers to consult employees, either directly or through elected representatives, who were not covered by safety representatives appointed by recognized unions. In response to other EU employment directives, a number of pieces of UK legislation provided for 'workforce agreements' between employers and elected employee representatives, in the absence of recognized unions, to make what Davies and Kilpatrick (2004: 125) call 'bargained adjustments to statutory standards'. The concept of workforce agreements in non-union situations was first used in the Working Time Regulations 1998 and subsequently featured in the Maternity and Parental Leave Regulations 1999 and the Fixed-Term Employees (Prevention of Less Favourable Treatment) Regulations 2002.

Given this broad consistency of approach across a range of regulatory measures, it is all the more striking that the same Labour government abruptly changed course in the face of pressure from employers' groups. For subsequent

EU-inspired consultation legislation, including that on EWCs and information and consultation in national undertakings, the UK Labour government abandoned the union priority or supplemented single channel approach in favour of the direct election of employee representatives by workforce ballot, irrespective of existing union structures.

This alternative policy was first adopted in the 1999 TICE regulations that gave effect to the EWCs directive (for a detailed account of the TICE regulations as a whole, see Carley and Hall, 2000). Rather than guaranteeing a role for recognized unions, the TICE regulations required workforce-wide ballots for selecting UK members of special negotiating bodies (SNBs) except where there is an existing consultative committee representing all UK employees. In the latter case, UK SNB members are to be nominated by the consultative committee. UK members of statutory EWCs must also be elected by workforce-wide ballot unless all UK employees are represented by recognized unions or by other elected or appointed representatives—an unlikely scenario—in which case UK members of statutory EWCs are to be elected or appointed by the existing representatives. A similar approach to the election of UK members of SNBs was taken by the European Public Limited Liability Company Regulations 2004 (EWCB, 2004, 2005), implementing the ECS, although in this case the arrangements for employee representation on the fall-back statutory 'representative body', where applicable, would be designated by the SNB. While the TUC had argued for the 'union priority' or 'supplemented single channel' approach to be maintained for these pieces of legislation too, there was strong employer pressure—and a government preference in terms of 'democratic legitimacy'—for the principle of all-employee ballots (EWCB, 1999). Employers also placed considerable emphasis on keeping potentially enforceable consultation arrangements 'structurally separate' (Davies and Freedland, 2007: 149) from trade union recognition and collective bargaining.

It is not fully clear why the Labour government departed from its initial 'union priority' or 'supplemented single channel' approach to one based on direct election. One explanation is that the policy change reflected the 'greater susceptibility' of 'New Labour', once in office, to lobbying by employer groups rather than unions (Hall, 2010: 59). Davies and Freedland (2007) suggest that the change was partly because of the 'unfortunate' coincidence between the United Kingdom's transposition of the EWCs directive and discussion of the Employment Relations Bill: given its clear commitment to the trade unions to introduce a statutory trade union recognition procedure, the government may have considered that offsetting concessions were necessary to the employers' lobby on the design of the TICE regulations to 'keep business support'. However, it seems likely that an underlying aim of the government was to avoid setting any awkward precedents for the implementation of the—potentially much more far-reaching—draft EU directive on national information and consultation rules (Carley and Hall, 2000: 114). Crucially, whatever the full explanation, the TICE regulations' 'direct election' approach to the designation of employee representatives for statutory consultation purposes was carried over into the subsequent ICE regulations. These specified that, under the default 'standard information and consultation provisions', information and consultation representatives must be elected by employees in a ballot, irrespective of any existing trade union representation within the undertaking. Significantly, this approach did not accord with mainstream UK practice in terms of employee representation on existing consultative committees in unionized or partially unionized workplaces. According to the 2004 Workplace Employment Relations Survey, in workplaces where at least some union representatives were present on site, 52 per cent of consultative committees were 'mixed constituency' or 'hybrid' bodies involving both union and non-union representatives, and 25 per cent were made up wholly of union representatives, compared to 23 per cent that were wholly non-union (Kersley et al., 2006: 131). The United Kingdom's broader approach to the implementation of the information and consultation directive, both procedurally and substantively, is the focus of the next section.

UK implementation of the information and consultation directive

The process of developing domestic legislation to implement the 2002 information and consultation directive involved the extensive consultation of key 'stakeholders' and—unusually—agreement between the government, the CBI, and the TUC on a broad framework for the necessary regulations. The government's first step towards transposing the directive was the publication in July 2002 of a discussion paper (DTI, 2002) intended to highlight some of the main issues raised for the United Kingdom by the directive. Despite the government's earlier opposition to the directive, much of the discussion paper was given over to a review of the role of employee involvement in developing 'high performance workplaces'—essentially an exposition of the 'efficiency' argument for consultation identified in Chapter 2. It also sought views from interested parties on what should be the key features of domestic legislation to implement the directive, while giving certain broad indications of the government's likely approach. The aim would be to 'respect and build on' existing information and consultation practice in the United Kingdom, including direct forms of employee involvement. The new law would 'not be imposed on workforces, but will give those who want it the right to information and consultation'. The emphasis would be on organization-specific voluntary agreements. Where agreement was not reached, however, there would be a 'statutory minimum requirement for formal information and consultation procedures consistent with the arrangements set out in the directive'.

During the first half of 2003, the DTI invited representatives of the CBI and TUC to take part in discussions with ministers about how the United Kingdom should implement the requirements of the directive 'within parameters set by the government'. These specified, among other things, that 'there should be no single, static model for information and consultation', and that the legislative framework should 'create room for the wide diversity of practices that have built over the years, combining both representative and direct forms of participation'. At the same time, the legislation had to be 'fully consistent with the new rights and responsibilities' contained in the information and consultation directive (DTI, 2003: 5).

The outcome of this process was a tripartite agreement on an 'outline scheme' setting out a framework for regulations to implement the directive. This provided the basis for key elements of draft regulations published for consultation, particularly in areas left by the directive to national determination. For example, it set out that the support of at least 10 per cent of employees would be required to trigger negotiations on establishing information and consultation procedures, potentially subject to the endorsement of at least 40 per cent of employees in a ballot where 'pre-existing agreements' (PEAs) were in place. It also outlined default statutory provisions, applicable where no negotiated agreement was reached, involving an 'I&C committee' (though the actual ICE regulations do not specify a representative *body* as such) with representatives elected by employee ballot. While the outline scheme made no explicit reference to enabling direct forms of information and consultation, it did state that 'the parties to a negotiated agreement will be able to agree the information and consultation arrangements that best suit their needs and circumstances. The government will provide guidance and greater clarity on this.'

Procedurally, the agreed framework for the regulations was significant in that the United Kingdom had not in the past approached the implementation of EU employment law directives in this way. The joint CBI/TUC statement that preceded the statutory trade union recognition proposals in the 1999 white paper *Fairness at work* was perhaps the nearest precedent. Davies and Freedland (2007: 150) describe the agreed outline scheme as a 'considerable political coup' for the government, reflecting its strategy of generating a high level of consensus on the implementation of the directive. The TUC, too, saw important political benefit in achieving a national 'social partner'-style framework agreement as the basis for the United Kingdom's transposition legislation (Hall, 2010). Indeed, similar tripartite agreements relating to EU measures have followed, for example that on temporary agency workers in May 2008 which paved the way for the adoption of the EU directive on that subject.

In substantive terms, the aspect of the agreed framework shaped most by the concerns of the CBI and TUC was its provisions on pre-existing agreements. The CBI's primary objective was to protect established company practice. The TUC, too, did not want to 'expose existing agreements, including union agreements, to easy challenge' (TUC committee paper, June 2003) but argued that arrangements that were not based on genuine agreement with the workforce must be capable of being overturned. The upshot of the defensive stances adopted by the two organizations was the provision that, where pre-existing agreements were in place, the support of at least 40 per cent of employees in a ballot would be necessary to trigger negotiations about new information and consultation arrangements.

How employee representatives were to be selected under the default information and consultation provisions was a major issue of contention in the negotiations. The TUC argued that union representatives should represent unionized parts of the workforce whereas the CBI insisted on direct election by all employees. In the light of the precedent set on this point by the TICE regulations, the TUC's preferred outcome was always unlikely to be achievable and the government duly sided with the CBI. However, in view of the importance the TUC attached to demonstrating the value of the 'social partner' route to employment regulation, it did not treat the issue as a deal breaker (Hall, 2010). Although the agreement 'did not contain all the elements which the TUC had wanted', the TUC General Council endorsed it on the basis that 'the proposals were the best which could be achieved' (TUC, 2004: 11). Nevertheless, in subsequent representations on the draft ICE regulations published for consultation by the government, the TUC continued to argue—without success—that, under the default information and consultation provisions, employee representatives from unionized parts of the workforce should be appointed by recognized unions.

The final text of the ICE regulations was approved by Parliament in December 2004. The regulations' main provisions are outlined in Box 4.2. The essential elements of the regulations were, of course, pre-ordained by the requirements of the directive. However, a key government objective was to maximize the flexibility available to organizations in responding to the regulations and in particular to facilitate the adoption or continuation of organization-specific information and consultation arrangements.

Crucially, employees' rights to information and consultation do not apply automatically. Unlike the consultation provisions relating to redundancies and transfers, the ICE regulations do not impose a mandatory requirement on employers to inform and consult unless 10 per cent of their employees trigger statutory procedures intended to lead to 'negotiated agreements' on

Box 4.2 KEY PROVISIONS OF THE ICE REGULATIONS

Coverage and commencement

The regulations came into effect on 6 April 2005, and initially applied to undertakings with at least 150 employees. Undertakings with at least 100 employees were covered from April 2007, and those with at least 50 from April 2008. An 'undertaking' is defined as 'a public or private undertaking carrying out an economic activity, whether or not operating for gain'.

The regulations apply to Great Britain. Separate but similar regulations apply in Northern Ireland. However, the employment thresholds specified relate to the United Kingdom as a whole.

Initiating negotiations

Regulation 7 enables 10 per cent of an undertaking's employees (subject to a minimum of 15 employees and a maximum of 2,500), to trigger negotiations with their employer on an information and consultation agreement, to be conducted according to statutory procedures (see below). Employers may themselves initiate the negotiation process on their own initiative by issuing written notification to employees.

Pre-existing agreements

Where a request for negotiations is made by fewer than 40 per cent of the employees and there is a PEA in place, the employer can ballot the workforce on whether they support the request for new negotiations. If the request is endorsed by at least 40 per cent of the workforce, and the majority of those who vote, negotiations on a new agreement must proceed. If not, no further action is necessary. PEAs are defined as written agreements that cover all the employees of the undertaking, have been approved by the employees, and set out 'how the employer is to give information to the employees or their representatives and to seek their views on such information' (Regulation 8).

Negotiated agreements

Where triggered under the regulations, negotiations on an information and consultation agreement must take place between the employer and representatives elected or appointed by the workforce (Regulation 14). The resulting agreement must cover all employees of the undertaking and set out the circumstances in which employees will be informed and consulted—either through employee representatives or directly (Regulation 16).

Standard information and consultation provisions

Where the employer fails to initiate negotiations following a valid employee request, or where the parties do not reach a negotiated agreement within six months, 'standard information and consultation provisions' specified by the regulations will apply (Regulations 18–20). These require that the employer must inform/consult 'information and consultation representatives' on:

(a) 'the recent and probable development of the undertaking's activities and economic situation' (information only);

(b) 'the situation, structure and probable development of employment within the undertaking and any anticipatory measures envisaged, in particular, where there is a threat to employment within the undertaking' (information and consultation); and

(c) 'decisions likely to lead to substantial changes in work organisation or in contractual relations', including decisions covered by the legislation on collective redundancies and transfers of undertakings (information and consultation 'with a view to reaching agreement').

However, as regards category (c), where employers come under a duty to consult trade union or employee representatives under the existing legislation on collective redundancies and transfers of undertakings, they are not also obliged to consult information and consultation representatives under the ICE regulations provided they notify them accordingly on each occasion.

The standard provisions specify that there should be one information and consultation representative for every fifty employees or part thereof, with a minimum of two representatives and a maximum of twenty-five. Representatives are to be directly elected by workforce-wide secret ballot.

Enforcement and sanctions

Enforcement of negotiated agreements reached under the statutory procedure, or of the standard information and consultation provisions where they apply, is via complaints to the Central Arbitration Committee (CAC), which may order the employer to take the necessary steps to comply with the agreement/standard provisions (Regulation 22).

The Employment Appeal Tribunal will hear appeals and is responsible for issuing penalty notices. The maximum penalty payable by employers for non-compliance is £75,000 (Regulation 23). Where necessary, enforcement of CAC orders may be pursued through the courts.

Confidentiality

Employee representatives and other recipients owe a statutory duty to the employer not to disclose information or documents designated by the employer as confidential. Employers may withhold information or documents the disclosure of which could seriously harm or prejudice the undertaking. Disputes over employers' decisions to impose confidentiality restrictions or withhold information may be referred to the CAC (Regulations 25 and 26).

Employee rights and protections

Information and consultation representatives under negotiated agreements and the default provisions—but not PEAs—have the statutory right to paid time off to perform their functions, and employees are protected from unfair dismissal or detriment for exercising their entitlements under the regulations, enforceable via Employment Tribunals.

information and consultation. Management, too, may trigger the negotiation process on its own initiative. Where triggered under the regulations, negotiations on an information and consultation agreement must take place between the employer and employee representatives elected by the workforce. Such a process is not required by the directive itself and seems to have been modelled on the similarly 'reflexive' provisions pioneered by the EWCs legislation. However various trigger mechanisms are used by some other EU member states (Hall and Purcell, 2011) and this approach is sanctioned by the recital 15 in the directive's preamble.[3] If there is already a voluntary, pre-existing agreement (PEA) in place and employees still try to trigger the regulations' procedures, a higher threshold of 40 per cent support is necessary for negotiations to take place. Both PEAs and negotiated agreements reached via the regulations' procedures offer employers and employees considerable latitude to agree organization-specific information and consultation arrangements, including direct means of informing and consulting employees.

Only in the event that the regulations' procedures are triggered but no agreement is reached are default 'standard information and consultation provisions' enforceable. These require the employer to inform and consult elected employee representatives on business developments (information only), employment trends (information and consultation), and changes in work organization or contractual relations, including redundancies and business transfers (information and consultation 'with a view to reaching agreement'). While the topics covered by these requirements are wide-ranging and potentially include strategic business issues and the management of major organizational change, the default provisions are minimally prescriptive in infrastructural terms. They specify the election arrangements for employee representatives (direct election by workforce-wide secret ballot) and the number to be elected (a sliding scale from 2 to 25 depending on the size of the workforce). However, they do not specify the establishment of a representative body as such. Nor do they regulate issues such as the frequency of meetings or facilities for representatives.

The government also pursued a 'minimalist' approach to UK implementation more generally, reflecting sustained pressure from employers' organizations against any 'gold-plating' of the directive's provisions that would impose additional regulation on businesses. In a number of areas, including the default information and consultation requirements and confidentiality provisions, the government essentially adopted a 'copy-out' approach, reproducing the wording of the directive in the ICE regulations. Other aspects of the regulations followed the precedents set by the provisions of the 1999 TICE regulations, including those concerning ballots to elect statutory information and consultation representatives, employee rights and protections, and enforcement and sanctions.

Assessment of the ICE regulations

The regulations have attracted a range of criticisms, principally focussing on the various ways in which the government sought to maximize employers' flexibility of response. Firstly, although a trigger mechanism is ostensibly allowed by recital 15 of the directive, the UK threshold of 10 per cent of the workforce for requesting statutory negotiations on information and consultation arrangements is 'likely to prove a tough standard to meet in practice', particularly where there is no union presence (Hall, 2006). Moreover, the 10 per cent requirement is subject to a minimum of fifteen and a maximum of 2,500 employees. This means that the threshold of employee support will be higher than 10 per cent in all undertakings employing fewer than 150 employees (Ewing and Truter, 2005). Except in undertakings where significant events, such as redundancies, provide the catalyst, it may prove difficult to find employees prepared or able to take the lead in articulating the case for employee consultation/representation and in organizing an employee request. More generally, the extent to which employees actively seek to trigger the introduction of information and consultation arrangements under the regulations may well be limited by low awareness of their statutory rights and employer hostility, especially in smaller undertakings and those with no tradition of representation. Consequently, relatively few employers appear to expect their employees to trigger negotiations (a point borne out in several surveys of employers and our own case study research—see Chapters 5 and 6). For these reasons, the pressure on employers to adopt agreed information and consultation procedures may not be very strong in practice.

As Ewing and Truter (2005: 630) point out, such problems would have been 'minimized' had recognized unions been able to trigger the negotiating procedure in their own right, but this is not possible under the regulations. Indeed, unions have been 'written out of the script' more generally (Hall, 2006: 460), being unable, as discussed earlier in the chapter, to nominate information and consultation representatives from unionized parts of the workforce under the regulations' default provisions. The regulations do indirectly offer unions or union members a range of potential roles or opportunities to intervene. These include negotiating and approving PEAs, collecting names for an employee request for a negotiated agreement, acting as negotiating representatives (at the employer's discretion), standing as candidates for election to information and consultation bodies and providing expert advice to employee representatives. In the case of both PEAs and negotiated agreements, it is open to the parties to agree that union representatives, and potentially even external full-time officials, can represent unionized sections of the workforce in the information and consultation process. But the fact that the regulations do not accord any specific statutory rights to recognized unions is likely to have contributed to unions' ambivalence towards the legislation.

Another concern expressed relates to the absence of a specific cut-off date for reaching PEAs. Whereas the option of putting in place analogous 'Article 13' agreements under the EWCs directive closed on the specified date on which national implementation of the directive became due, under the ICE regulations PEAs can be introduced at any stage predating an employee request to trigger the regulations' procedures. This provision contributes considerably to employers' freedom of manoeuvre under the legislation. Ewing and Truter (2005: 631) suggest that the directive itself required such agreements to be in force by 23 March 2005—the directive's due transposition date—but the wording of Article 5 on this point is far from clear. Interestingly, Ireland's transposition legislation did specify that the window for putting pre-existing agreements in place closed on the relevant date of the legislation's commencement according to the size of undertaking concerned (EWCB, 2006: 15).

A further criticism is that the substantive content of PEAs and negotiated agreements is largely unregulated. There is no requirement that they should meet the default information and consultation standards that they 'displace' (Davies and Freedland, 2007: 153). This flexibility is allowed by the directive itself (see Chapter 3) but clearly provides the scope for agreed information and consultation arrangements that fall well short of the standards established by the default provisions. In the context of management's likely dominance of the process of drawing up such agreements, especially in non-union situations, the regulation of the processes of employee approval of such agreements provides only limited protection. A related factor is that, unlike the EWCs legislation, the 'minimalist' default provisions do not set out an institutional and operational model for information and consultation that could provide a benchmark or point of reference for those involved in drawing up PEAs and negotiated agreements, particularly employee representatives. Instead, they merely specify the number of information and consultation representatives to be elected and the election procedures to be followed. Again, the Irish legislation that implements the directive provides a contrasting approach.

A number of commentators have questioned the compatibility with the directive of the regulations' provisions allowing PEAs or negotiated agreements to provide for direct forms of information only (including Hall, 2005; Davies and Freedland, 2007). The directive not only defines information and consultation as processes involving employee representatives. It also states that it is 'without prejudice to those systems which provide for the direct involvement of employees', but only 'as long as they are always free to exercise the right to be informed and consulted through their representatives' (recital 16). Under the ICE regulations, a PEA providing for direct information and consultation would mean that a substantially higher (40 per cent) threshold of employee support would be required to trigger negotiations. In the light of recital 16, this could be seen as undermining the unconditional right to information and consultation, via representatives, that the directive guarantees.

A final concern is that, while PEAs enable employers effectively to pre-empt the application of the regulations' statutory procedures, they are exempt from the regulations' enforcement provisions and are unenforceable unless they provide voluntarily for legal enforceability or other dispute resolution procedures. There are hints in the European Commission's initial review of the application of the directive (CEC, 2008) that the ICE regulations' provisions in respect of direct forms of information and consultation and the definition and enforceability of PEAs are potentially problematic areas in terms of compliance with the directive which the Commission intends to examine more closely.

Conclusion

The decision of the Blair-led Labour government not to embrace the information and consultation directive when it was first proposed, nor to prioritize information and consultation among its domestic employment relations policy objectives, remains intriguing. On the face of it, the espousal of universal information and consultation rights—whether in addition to or, more radically, instead of the party's commitment to reintroducing a statutory union recognition procedure—would have been consistent with the modernizing agenda espoused by 'New Labour' and its emphasis on 'partnership' at work. It would have established elementary representation rights for all employees irrespective of union membership and could also have been designed to build in a guaranteed role for recognized unions (Hall, 1996). Yet although Labour's front bench employment spokesman, Stephen Byers, was still considering a possible commitment to introduce consultation rights the year before the 1997 election, the eventual election manifesto was silent on the issue (Hall, 2010).

One factor was no doubt that the party's commitment to union recognition legislation was long-standing and effectively set in stone. Moreover, as we have seen, although TUC policy reviews in the early 1990s flirted with supporting a statutory works council-type model of employee representation and universal consultation rights, the ultimate outcome confirmed unions' long-standing support for the traditional pattern of 'single channel' trade union representation. Crucially, statutory consultation measures were strongly opposed by the CBI. Prioritizing information and consultation was effectively an idea without a constituency.

More generally, New Labour's commitment to reverse the United Kingdom's EU social policy opt-out symbolized the party's broadly 'pro-European' positioning ahead of the 1997 election rather than its industrial relations priorities. Its consequent acceptance of the transnational information and consultation framework provided by the EWCs directive and the ECS did not extend to the national-level focus of the 2002 information and consultation directive. In terms of EU-level politics, the United Kingdom's 'subsidiarity'-based case against the latter measure signalled the limits of New Labour's enthusiasm for the EU's social policy agenda, despite its reversal of the UK opt-out. Domestically, ministers' stand against the directive seemed designed to strengthen New Labour's 'business-friendly' credentials.

In such circumstances, a reluctant, half-hearted approach to the regulation of information and consultation was perhaps inevitable. That the government made maximum use of the substantial flexibilities incorporated in the directive was to be expected, given its own opposition to the measure, pressure from employers and the fact that information and consultation had hitherto remained largely a matter for voluntary determination. Ireland adopted a broadly similar approach in similar circumstances (Doherty, 2008). Whether the United Kingdom went too far in the quest for flexibility to remain compliant with the directive, time and the ECJ will tell.

In view of the 'reflexive' legislative design of the regulations, and the experience of analogous legislation—the EWCs directive and domestic provisions on trade union recognition—it was suggested prior to the commencement of the ICE regulations that their main impact was likely to be 'legislatively prompted voluntarism' (Hall and Terry, 2004: 226), with the new legislation driving the diffusion and reform of organization-specific information and consultation arrangements. Within this process, it was argued that managerial choices and behaviour would largely shape the nature and impact of information and consultation arrangements. The CBI's guide to the regulations identified PEAs as providing 'the greatest level of flexibility to agree arrangements which best suit the structure and the culture of the organisation' (CBI, 2004: 18). Acas (2004), the EEF (2005), and leading law firms also encouraged employers to be 'proactive' and to seek to reach a PEA. But it was also pointed out that employer approaches were 'likely to be influenced by their assessment of employee demand for new or modified information and consultation arrangements and the risk of the regulations' procedures being successfully invoked by at least 10 per cent of the workforce... If employees [found] it difficult to pull the trigger, the scope for unilateral management action—or for doing nothing—[remained] wide'

(Hall, 2006: 460, 470). The next chapter reviews the available evidence on the patterns of implementation emerging in the light of the legislation's regulatory design. The implications for union strategies and legislative reform are addressed in Chapter 8.

Notes

1. Among the exceptions are statutory provisions introduced by the Conservative government in 1980 that require the reporting of employee involvement initiatives in company annual reports. These were introduced in an attempt to reduce pressure at EU level for consultation legislation. The main elements of the United Kingdom's health and safety legislation pre-dated EU regulation on the issue. The 1989 EU framework directive on the working environment initially prompted only minor amendments to UK law to comply with its requirements. However, as a consequence of the 1994 ECJ rulings, discussed later in this chapter, regulations were introduced in 1996 requiring employers to consult employees (directly or through elected representatives) who are not covered by safety representatives appointed by recognized unions (James and Walters, 1997). More recent UK provisions requiring consultation with employee representatives on specific pensions issues and in certain circumstances with recognized unions on training matters were domestically driven and do not reflect EU requirements.
2. The subsequent 2004 takeover bids directive and the 2005 cross-border mergers directive, both of which contain issue-specific information and consultation provisions, were implemented in the United Kingdom via the Companies Act 2006 and the Companies (Cross-Border Mergers) Regulations 2007 respectively.
3. Recital 15 provides that 'This directive is without prejudice to national systems regarding the exercise of this right [to be informed and consulted] in practice where those entitled to exercise it are required to indicate their wishes collectively'.

5

The Take-up and Impact of Statutory Consultation

As highlighted in Chapter 4, the introduction of the Information and Consultation of Employees (ICE) Regulations unquestionably represented an innovation of major significance for UK employment law. Driven by EU legislation reflecting continental European models of workforce-wide consultation, the regulations provided, for the first time in the United Kingdom, a comprehensive statutory framework governing a key area of industrial relations that hitherto had been largely a matter for voluntary determination. In doing so, the regulations established procedures under which employees could initiate negotiations intended to lead to the establishment of agreed information and consultation arrangements, but with enforceable 'standard provisions' as a fall-back providing statutory rights to information and consultation on a range of business, employment, and restructuring issues.

But what is the practical impact of the legislative changes? At a rhetorical level, at least, the introduction of the legislation raised high expectations, particularly on the part of the Labour government and trade unions. As Hall (2005) recorded, for the Trades Union Congress (TUC), the adoption of the directive had been a 'real strategic breakthrough', and the UK regulations 'could lead to the biggest change in workplace relations for a generation'. A Downing Street adviser was quoted as comparing the directive to an 'asteroid' about to hit Britain. The government minister responsible for the regulations described them as 'ground-breaking', while a Labour peer hailed their approval as a 'red letter day in the history of industrial relations' (Hall, 2005: 103). The regulations were widely expected to have the effect of reversing the decline that had taken place since the late 1980s in the incidence of 'joint consultation committees' as measured by the Workplace Employment Relations Surveys (WERS). Yet within a year of the regulations' initial introduction there were suggestions that, in practice, the regulations were proving to be something of a 'damp squib', with little evidence of employees and unions seeking to trigger the statutory procedures or of widespread moves by employers to put voluntary pre-existing agreements (PEAs) in place (Hall, 2006: 457).

This chapter assesses the emerging patterns of implementation of the ICE regulations, highlighting the available survey data on the extent to which the regulations have prompted both increases in the incidence of information and consultation mechanisms and modifications to existing arrangements, as well as the ways in which employers, employees, and trade unions have responded to the changed statutory framework. The chapter includes qualitative data from the authors' own extensive case study research (see the Appendix for details) which, among other things, sheds light on the factors shaping managerial decisions to establish or revamp information and consultation arrangements and identifies the low salience of the regulations' provisions in this respect. It also looks at the extent and key outcomes of enforcement applications under the regulations to the Central Arbitration Committee (CAC) and Employment Appeal Tribunal (EAT). Chapter 7 draws on further evidence from our case studies to analyse the operation and effectiveness of information and consultation bodies established in the context of the regulations.

The WERS 2004 benchmark

The most authoritative data on the extent of information and consultation arrangements derive from the WERS carried out since 1980. Prior to the publication of the findings from WERS 2004, there had been some speculation that moves by organizations to put in place information and consultation arrangements in anticipation of the introduction of the ICE regulations might be reflected in an upturn in the proportion of workplaces covered by joint consultative committees (JCCs). In terms of the 'headline' figures—the proportion of workplaces with ten or more employees that were covered by JCCs—this did not prove to be the case. On the contrary, the previous downward trend continued (Kersley et al., 2006). In 2004, JCCs were present in 14 per cent of workplaces with ten or more employees. A further 25 per cent of workplaces were covered by a JCC which operated at a higher level of the organization (e.g. in multi-site organizations like retail banks). Both figures had declined since 1998, when they stood at 20 and 27 per cent respectively. Thus, whereas in 1998 47 per cent of workplaces were covered by a workplace or higher-level JCCs, by 2004 the proportion stood at 39 per cent.

However, Kersley et al. (2006: 127) report a bigger decline in (workplace-level) JCC in workplaces that did not recognize trade unions (down from 14 to 8 per cent) compared with unionized workplaces where the incidence was largely unchanged (32 per cent in 1998; 29 per cent in 2004). Moreover, the overall figures mask a clear size effect with larger workplaces having a

Table 5.1. Incidence of JCCs in 1998 and 2004 (% of workplaces in different size bands)

Workplace size	1998			2004		
	Workplace-level committee	Higher-level committee only	No committee	Workplace-level committee	Higher-level committee only	No committee
All workplaces with ten or more employees	20	27	53	14	25	62
10–24 employees	–	–	–	4	26	70
25–49 employees	19	29	52	16	24	59
50–99 employees	30	23	47	26	27	47
100–199 employees	41	21	37	47	16	37
200–499 employees	56	16	28	59	13	28
500 or more employees	66	11	23	73	9	18

Source: Cully et al. (1999: 99) and Kersley et al. (2006: 127).

Table 5.2. The incidence of JCCs in the United Kingdom in 2004 by industry sector (% of workplaces with ten or more employees)

Sector	Workplace-level committee	Higher-level committee only	No committee
Private	11	20	69
Public	28	46	26
Industry			
Manufacturing	21	4	75
Electricity, gas, water[a]	52	35	14
Construction	8	5	87
Wholesale and retail	11	31	58
Hotels and restaurants	4	28	68
Transport and communication	16	29	55
Financial services	5	57	38
Other business services	10	16	74
Public administration	42	40	18
Education	30	31	40
Health and social work	13	25	62
Other community services	14	23	62

[a]Fewer than twenty observations, so not a reliable estimate.

Source: Kersley et al. (2006: 127).

markedly higher incidence of JCCs (Table 5.1). In terms of the trend among workplaces corresponding to the size bands (of undertaking) covered by the EU directive/ICE regulations, the incidence of workplace-level JCCs declined between 1998 and 2004 only within the 50–99 employees category. Even here, the proportion of workplaces covered by workplace or higher-level JCCs remained the same at 53 per cent. Among workplaces in the higher size bands, the incidence of workplace JCCs increased. The proportions with workplace or higher-level JCCs were stable except in the largest category (500 or more employees) where the figure increased by 5 percentage points.

In terms of distribution by industry sector, public sector workplaces were more likely to have a JCC than those in the private sector. Across all workplaces with ten or more employees in 2004, 74 per cent of public sector workplaces were covered by workplace or higher-level JCCs compared to 31 per cent of private sector workplaces (Table 5.2). The gap was markedly narrower among workplaces in the size bands covered by the directive/regulations where 45 per cent of public sector workplaces with fifty or more employees had a (workplace-level) JCC compared with 37 per cent in the private sector (Kersley et al., 2006: 126). In only four sectors were a majority of workplaces with ten or more employees covered by workplace or higher-level JCCs. In the utilities (gas, electricity, and water) and public administration, JCCs covered more than 80 per cent of workplaces. In financial services and education, the figure was approximately 60 per cent. In all other sectors, a minority of workplaces were covered by JCCs.

Arguably, the main message from WERS 2004 is that, immediately before the ICE regulations came into force, large parts of the UK economy were not covered by information and consultation arrangements. It is possible that the imminence of the regulations' commencement at the time of the WERS 2004 fieldwork may help account for the halt in the decline in JCCs among workplaces with fifty or more employees and the increase in JCCs among those with 500 or more employees. However, WERS 2004 can best be seen as a pre-ICE regulations 'benchmark' (Kersley et al., 2006: 313) against which subsequent changes in the incidence of information and consultation arrangements in the changed legislative context may be assessed. We will have to await the first findings of the next WERS to do so. In the meantime, there have been indications from smaller, less comprehensive surveys, discussed later in this chapter, of considerable activity in terms of the introduction, review, and reform of information and consultation arrangements in the light of the regulations.

Implications of legislative design

Initial assessments of the likely impact of the ICE regulations were informed, at least in part, by the experience of analogous UK legislation. UK statutory provisions on employee consultation and representation that predated the ICE regulations exemplified two different approaches in terms of their applicability to employers. Those requiring consultation on redundancies, transfers, and health and safety issues impose a duty to consult on all relevant employers that is directly enforceable by employees. In contrast, employees' statutory rights concerning trade union recognition and European Works Councils (EWCs) are indirect in that they depend on employees or trade unions invoking statutory procedures and achieving specified levels of workforce support, and the relevant legislation is 'reflexive' in character, providing extensive scope for agreed, organization-specific arrangements. Given the broad similarities in legislative design, the implementation patterns of the EWCs and union recognition legislation, dating in both cases from 1999, were expected to provide at least a rough guide to the potential impact of the ICE regulations.

Reflexive implementation

The key consequence was expected to be the primacy of voluntary information and consultation agreements rather than the imposition of the statutory default provisions. Under the EWCs legislation, UK-based multinationals had shown a strong predisposition towards reaching pre-emptive 'Article 13' EWC agreements, concluded voluntarily before the directive's implementation date. Even once the window for concluding Article 13 agreements had closed, negotiations under the legislation's statutory procedures still invariably resulted in negotiated 'Article 6' agreements: in no case has a statutory EWC been imposed on a UK-based company in line with the legislation's 'subsidiary requirements'. Similarly, under the United Kingdom's trade union recognition legislation, the indirect or 'shadow of the law' effect of the statutory procedure—prompting voluntary recognition agreements—has been much more significant than its direct effect, that is, union claims to the CAC resulting in recognition (Gall, 2007). Moreover, only a relative handful (19) of the 770 statutory union recognition applications to the end of 2011 have reached the final stage where the CAC determines the method of collective bargaining to be followed, based on the statutory model, because of a failure to agree by the parties. The omission from the ICE regulations of a cut-off date for PEAs (which can be concluded at any point prior to the date an employee request to initiate negotiations is made under the regulations) meant it was less likely that there would be a comparable 'spike' in new or revised PEAs similar to upsurge in pre-emptive voluntary agreements ahead of the introduction of the EWCs and union recognition provisions. Nevertheless, the experience of both these pieces of legislation suggested that there were likely to be relatively few cases where the regulations' 'standard information and consultation provisions' were imposed on employers (Hall and Terry, 2004: 226; Veale, 2005: 28).

The fact that, like those of the EWCs legislation, the ICE regulations' provisions do not become applicable unless proactively 'triggered' by employers or employees was thought likely to limit the impact of the regulations and result in substantially less than comprehensive take-up among eligible undertakings. As we saw in Chapter 3, it is still the case that, more than fifteen years after the implementation date of the EWCs directive, EWCs have been established in only a minority (38 per cent) of all multinationals covered by the legislation. The proportion of UK-based multinationals with EWCs is about the same at 39 per cent (Waddington, 2011: 57). Hall and Terry (2004: 221) expected that the take-up rate of information and consultation arrangements under the ICE regulations was likely to be 'significantly lower than for EWCs, which have been established in large enterprises, in the great majority of cases with an active trade union presence to articulate and develop the rights available'. The 10 per cent level of employee support necessary to trigger negotiations under the ICE regulations is a more onerous requirement than of the EWCs legislation, under which the statutory processes can be triggered by employee representatives on behalf of the requisite number of employees, and, as argued in Chapter 4, is likely to prove a high hurdle to jump, especially in non-union contexts.

This, in turn, is likely to influence employers' propensity to resort to PEAs. The adoption of a substantial number of Article 13 agreements under the EWCs legislation often reflected multinational companies' readiness to signal compliance with EU standards as well as their aim to secure company-specific EWC arrangements. In the context of the ICE regulations too, PEAs were identified as providing the maximum flexibility to agree company-specific information and consultation arrangements and organizations such as the Confederation of British Industry (CBI), Engineering Employers' Federation (EEF), and Advisory, Conciliation and Arbitration Service (Acas) encouraged employers to be 'proactive' in seeking to reach them. At the same time, however, it was argued that 'employer approaches are likely to be influenced by their assessment of employee demand for new or modified information and consultation arrangements and the risk of the regulations' negotiating procedure being successfully invoked by at least 10 per cent of the workforce ... if employees find it difficult to pull the trigger, the scope for unilateral management action—or for doing nothing—remains wide' (Hall, 2006: 460, 470).

Another area of potential divergence from the experience of the EWC legislation concerns the extent to which the statutory fall-back model provides a template for voluntary and negotiated agreements under the ICE regulations (Hall, 2005). Despite considerable variation in the detailed provisions of EWC agreements, the EWC's directive's 'subsidiary requirements' exerted a strong influence on the main constitutional and operational issues—labelled the 'statutory model effect' by Gilman and Marginson (2002: 38). Thus, although the directive allowed for the establishment of a decentralized 'procedure for informing and consulting employees' instead of an EWC, very few agreements have departed from the basic EWC format. The model provided by the subsidiary requirements resulted in broad convergence in key areas such as the limited information and consultation remit of EWCs, the issues to be discussed, the frequency of meetings (and the circumstances in which extraordinary meetings may be required), and the rights of employee representatives (e.g. to expert assistance, to appropriate financial and material resources, to meet separately from management, and to report back to their constituencies) (Carley and Marginson, 2000). However, the ICE regulations' 'standard information and consultation provisions' could not be expected to have the same normative impact—for two main reasons. First, unlike EWCs, information and consultation arrangements do not constitute a new phenomenon. Companies with established information and consultation arrangements could be expected to pursue a 'path-dependent' response and seek to maintain or build upon existing approaches. Elsewhere, there is a wide range of precedents and examples on which companies can draw in establishing new information and consultation arrangements. Second, as already noted in Chapter 4, the ICE regulations' fall-back provisions are extremely 'minimalist' in infrastructural terms and offer little by way of an operational template.

Experience and lessons of directly applicable consultation rights

It is at least arguable that, had the UK government and social partners sought to implement the directive by making its information and consultation rights directly applicable on the model of the redundancies and transfers legislation—that is, obliging all relevant undertakings to inform and consult on the specified issues through recognized unions where present, and otherwise via elected representatives—the impact of the legislation would have been substantially greater. In other words, the traditional 'hard law' approach may have been more likely to lead to employer compliance than the 'reflexive' character of ICE regulations. WERS 2004 recorded a notably high rate of compliance with the statutory redundancy consultation provisions, as reported by management respondents. The survey did not enable a precise focus on redundancy situations where the statutory obligation to consult applied (i.e. where twenty or more redundancies at an establishment are proposed within a ninety-day period). However, in workplaces where twenty or more redundancies had been made over the previous year, the incidence of consultation was 88 per cent (94 per cent where unions were recognized). Moreover, in workplaces where unions were recognized, consultation took place with union representatives—as required by statute—in 88 per cent of cases (Kersley et al., 2006: 203).

A number of factors may explain this high rate of compliance, including the direct applicability—and, potentially, enforceability—of the statutory provisions, union presence, and clear sanctions for failure to consult in the form of a protective award of up to ninety days' pay per employee. Although the adequacy of this sanction has been a matter of debate, in Acas's experience a potential protective award is seen by employers as 'hugely expensive' (Ranieri, 2010: 5). There are indications that the high levels of compliance with the redundancy consultation provisions recorded by WERS 2004 may not have been sustained over subsequent years. Ranieri (2010: 4) noted a sharp rise in the employment tribunal claims in 2008–9 alleging failure to consult over redundancy plans. However, as she commented, it was unclear whether this represented 'a growing failure on the part of employers to consult, or to consult properly', or was a more general reflection of the recession-related surge in the number of redundancy announcements.

In overall terms, irrespective of whether redundancies were of a scale to be subject to the statutory provisions, WERS 2004 found that employers consulted with employees or their representatives in 75 per cent of workplaces where redundancies were made or proposed and in 77 per cent where redundancies actually occurred (Kersley et al., 2006: 202). The use of more than one method of consultation was widespread, but direct consultation with employees was the most widely cited method, even in unionized workplaces.

Consultation was both more likely and was undertaken through union, JCC, or other employee representatives to a much greater extent in unionized workplaces.

WERS 2004 also provided data on the incidence (almost universal) and nature of health and safety consultation arrangements. As we noted in Chapter 4, the 1994 European Court of Justice ruling prompted the introduction of the Health and Safety (Consultation with Employees) Regulations 1996, requiring employers to consult employees who are not covered by union-appointed safety representatives. The 1996 regulations give employers the discretion to consult employees directly or via elected representatives. Since this legislation, WERS figures suggest that direct methods of consultation over health and safety issues have become increasingly prevalent, including in workplaces with union recognition, whereas consultation via representative channels has 'declined markedly' (Kersley et al., 2006: 204).

Two main messages may be derived from the evidence from WERS 2004 on consultation over both redundancies and health and safety matters. First, the findings suggest that the existence of directly applicable statutory provisions has proved to be important in shaping both the incidence and nature of consultation. In particular, redundancy consultation is more likely to take place—and to take place via union representatives as required if union recognition exists—where redundancies are of a sufficient scale to be covered by the statutory requirements. Second, where unregulated or permitted by the statutory procedures, there is a strong preference on the part of many employers for direct consultation with employees rather than through union or elected representatives.

Impact of the ICE regulations—legislatively prompted voluntarism?

Assessing the likely impact of the regulations prior to their introduction, Hall and Terry (2004: 221) argued that the legislation could be expected to lead to an increase in the proportion of UK workplaces and employees with access to a formal system of indirect representation, contributing to a decrease in the 'representation gap'. In line with their 'reflexive' character and the experience of analogous EWCs and union recognition legislation, the regulations were expected to result in 'legislatively prompted voluntarism', with the prospect and introduction of the new legislation driving the spread of voluntary information and consultation agreements, reached either in the 'shadow of the law' or as a consequence of its trigger mechanism being used (Hall and Terry, 2004: 226–7). The extent to which these expectations have been met is far from clear cut. While WERS 2004 provided a comprehensive picture of the extent of information and consultation arrangements prior to the ICE regulations' entry into force, evidence concerning subsequent developments is less systematic. Nevertheless, the findings of a number of smaller, less comprehensive surveys, reviewed below, indicate that the regulations have prompted considerable activity in terms of both the introduction of information and consultation bodies and the modification of existing arrangements. Where such surveys have been repeated, the results suggest that the regulations have resulted in some increase in the overall incidence of information and consultation arrangements.

Quantitative impact

For a number of years, the CBI's annual employment trends surveys provided data on company-level information and consultation arrangements. Its 2006 survey (CBI, 2006) showed that a majority (57 per cent) of member companies responding reported that, as at May 2006, they had permanent mechanisms for informing and consulting employees, such as a staff council. A further 12 per cent said that they intended to introduce such a structure over the following year. Larger companies were more likely to have such arrangements or the intention to introduce them: employers with 5,000 or more employees were most likely to have introduced such mechanisms (85 per cent), compared with 51 per cent of those with 50–199 staff. Figures from previous years' CBI surveys suggested an upward trend in the incidence of such arrangements—rising from 35 per cent in 2002, the year the directive was adopted, to 47 per cent in 2003, 49 per cent in 2004, and 47 per cent in 2005. The CBI's view was that 'clearly firms are stepping up to the challenge posed by the new law' (CBI, 2006: 21). Questions regarding information and consultation arrangements did not feature in later CBI employment trends surveys.

Another survey of employers, conducted among client companies by management consultants ORC Worldwide and law firm Baker & McKenzie to coincide with the commencement of the ICE regulations (ORC Worldwide and Baker & McKenzie, 2005) focussed more specifically on company responses to the new legislative framework. It found that 55 per cent of respondents had no plans to establish new information and consultation arrangements or alter existing ones before the commencement date of the regulations, even though more than half of the respondents (52 per cent) did not currently have standing consultation arrangements in place and only two organizations indicated that their arrangements met the validity criteria for PEAs. Some 85 per cent of respondent companies had reportedly assessed the impact of the regulations on their business and employment relations, and 80 per cent considered the regulations would have 'little impact' or would require 'no significant change'. Most organizations reportedly preferred to rely on existing practice or on a lack of interest on the part of their employees in triggering the new law's procedures.

However, a range of other surveys has suggested more active responses to the regulations on the part of employers. In successive surveys by IRS (2005, 2006, 2008), substantial majorities of employers reported having permanent consultative bodies. Seven in ten (69 per cent) said so in 2008, compared with 55 per cent in 2006 and 68 per cent in the 2005 survey. The same surveys also indicated that the ICE regulations had been influential in prompting employers to establish such bodies. In the 2005 survey, some two-fifths of employers had set one up in the period 2003–5. Nearly half of the respondents (49 per cent) said that they had made changes to their information and consultation arrangements in the previous two years. Of these, 65 per cent said that the changes had been made in order to comply with the ICE regulations or made partially for reasons of compliance. A further 16 per cent of respondents said that changes were planned in the next two years—again, mostly to comply with the regulations or partially for that reason. The 2006 and 2008 IRS surveys produced broadly consistent results. In the 2006 survey, one-third of employers with consultative bodies said they had established these arrangements in 2003 or later. Approaching one-third (31 per cent) of employers had made changes to their information and consultation arrangements in the previous two years, largely in response to the new legal framework. A further one-fifth (22 per cent) planned to make changes in the next two years, again mostly driven by the regulations. In the 2008 survey, two-fifths of employers (41 per cent) set up their consultation body after 2003. Over half had made changes to their information and consultation arrangements in the previous three years, with 45 per cent '[citing] some influence from legislation' (IRS, 2008).

Corroboration of this broad pattern of employer responses is offered by other surveys. An academic survey of UK operations of multinational companies in 2006 found that the ICE regulations had prompted substantial change in arrangements for employee consultation. More than 40 per cent of companies with consultative arrangements reported that they had introduced new or modified arrangements over the previous three years (Marginson et al., 2010: 164). In a 2008 survey of employers by the Chartered Institute of Personnel and Development (CIPD), two-thirds (67 per cent) of respondents reported that their organization had representative arrangements for informing and consulting employees, such as a staff council. Nearly two-fifths (39 per cent) of employers had introduced new information and consultation arrangements since the commencement of the ICE regulations in April 2005. Of these, three-quarters (76 per cent) had 'entered into a voluntary agreement formalising existing arrangements', while 22 per cent had 'introduced new arrangements following negotiation with employee or union representatives'. A survey of trade union representatives conducted by the Labour Research Department (LRD, 2006) also produced comparable results. Over two-thirds of respondents reported that formal information and consultation arrangements were currently in place at their workplace, with almost half of these having been drawn up, amended or reviewed in the light of the ICE regulations. Where new arrangements taking account of the regulations had been established, the initiative had come from the employer in the majority of cases.

Overall, the findings of these surveys indicate that the ICE regulations have stimulated considerable activity in terms of the establishment, formalization, and/or modification of information and consultation arrangements both immediately before and since the introduction of the legislation. It also seems likely that the legislation will have resulted in the increased incidence of information and consultation arrangements, at least in the size band of undertakings (those with at least fifty employees) covered by the legislation, but we will not be able to establish conclusively whether this is the case until the results of the next WERS, the fieldwork for which was carried out in 2011. What can be concluded is that the extent of 'legislatively induced innovation' (Marginson et al., 2010: 164) in the area of information and consultation, while far from universal, does not support the charge that the regulations have been a 'damp squib' with negligible practical impact. The surveys reviewed above suggest that the changed legislative environment has prompted substantial minorities of employers to introduce new or revised information and consultation arrangements. As we now go on to discuss, however, relatively little data are available on the extent and specific patterns of employer, employee, and trade union engagement with the provisions of the regulations.

Patterns of employer, employee, and union engagement with the regulations

There are currently no statistics on the incidence of 'pre-existing agreements' or 'negotiated agreements' as defined by the regulations, nor of the extent to which employees or, indirectly, trade unions have submitted requests under the regulations to trigger negotiations about the introduction of information and consultation arrangements. The only official record of employee requests to negotiate an information and consultation agreement is provided by the CAC in the shape of the list of complaints submitted under the regulations (a valid employee request being a prerequisite for most of the CAC's jurisdictions) and the number of employee requests submitted indirectly to the employer via the CAC. As discussed below, both these figures are notably low, though they do not include employee requests submitted directly to employers that do not result in any reference to the CAC.

Research into employer and trade union approaches to the regulations by Hall (2006) found little evidence of the widespread adoption of formal PEAs, despite the protection they offer against the regulations' statutory procedures being invoked by employees. Interviews with representatives from management consultancies and employer bodies suggested that a 'widespread response' by companies has been to undertake reviews or audits of their current information and consultation practices in the light of the regulations and to assess the prospects of their employees seeking to trigger the statutory procedures. While in some cases initiating the revision of existing arrangements, many companies took the view that employee 'challenges' under the legislation were unlikely, making formal PEAs unnecessary. In other words, their approach was generally one of 'risk assessment' rather than 'compliance' (Hall, 2006: 470).

Such a response is facilitated by unions' general lack of interest in engaging with the legislation and the low take-up of its provisions by employees. A striking finding from the IRS (2005) survey, echoed implicitly by the ORC/ Baker & McKenzie (2005) survey, was the extremely low expectation on the part of employers (3 per cent in the IRS survey) that their employees would request negotiations under the regulations on the establishment of new information and consultation arrangements. A smaller-scale survey of organizations belonging to the West Midlands Employment Relations Forum, reported in Hall (2006), produced the same 3 per cent figure. The authors' case study research, discussed below, also found a similar picture. The consequence of this, given the regulations' legislative design, is that the pressure on employers to adopt agreed information and consultation procedures is in practice not very strong. This helps explain the apparently lower than predicted tendency of employers to pursue formal PEAs as well as the fact that, in some cases, new or revamped information and consultation arrangements are 'management initiatives, intentionally not negotiated or agreed with the workforce', rather than PEAs as such (Hall, 2006: 465). It also supports the suggestion that where companies do move to 'reposition' their information and consultation arrangements, this is 'typically driven by internal employment relations considerations, not compliance-led' (Hall, 2006: 465).

Koukiadaki (2009) interprets the evidence slightly differently. Although she states that 'the majority of [information and consultation] arrangements that have been established or amended in the light of the legislation are in the form of PEAs', she notes concerns on the part of employers' representatives that, 'if tested, a considerable number of PEAs would not satisfy the statutory requirements' (Koukiadaki, 2009: 402). Problem areas she identifies that may undermine their legal validity include meeting the regulations' requirements as to employee approval and coverage of the entire workforce. The 'overriding majority' are reported to be 'designed and signed off by management'. Both authors, therefore, emphasize the employer-led nature of much of the activity in terms of introducing or revising information and consultation arrangements in the light of the regulations, and an apparent absence of concern by some employers with the legal niceties required to achieve a legally watertight PEA.

Notably, however, despite the CBI's insistence on provisions in the regulations that allow compliance strategies based on direct, not representative, forms of information and consultation (see Chapter 4), there has been little employer interest in pursuing this option. Union fears that this could prove to be a widely exploited loophole appear to have been unfounded. Koukiadaki (2009) cites just two companies—Yell/Yellow Pages and mobile phone operator 3—known to have adopted workforce-wide direct information and consultation mechanisms in response to the regulations. At Yell, a 'communications and consultation policy' based on information cascades, team briefings, and electronic communications was introduced with employee approval (via email) but no discussion with recognized unions. The present authors identified two further such cases in their search for case studies but neither agreed to take part in the research. Some other organizations are reported to have introduced or formalized direct methods of information and consultation for particular groups of employees (e.g. head office or management staff) not covered by representative consultation arrangements (Hall, 2006: 466). The limited take-up of the direct information and consultation option may reflect a managerial concern to avoid the 'juridification' of 'business-driven' employee involvement initiatives. In larger organizations, reliance on the use of direct methods only is unlikely to be a realistic option. The EEF's guidance on the regulations warned that 'direct information and consultation with all employees [may be] difficult to organize and operate effectively, except in the smallest undertaking' (EEF, 2005: 66). Koukiadaki (2009: 406) argues that such an approach '[lacks] clear endorsement' from employers' associations because it may be 'legally questionable' in the light of the EU directive.

The largely free hand enjoyed by managers in determining their response to the regulations is to a great extent a reflection of trade unions' general indifference towards and lack of engagement with the legislation and, in non-union organizations, the low likelihood of employees taking the necessary action to trigger the application of the statutory procedures. Despite the TUC's support for and involvement in framing the regulations, and its emphasis on the organizational possibilities they offer unions (see e.g. Brendan Barber's preface to the TUC guide to the regulations—TUC, 2005: 3), the predominant union approach to the legislation has been 'defensive' and 'reactive' (Hall, 2006). Unions have not generally sought to exploit the ICE regulations. As discussed in Chapter 4, this reflects a visceral preference for 'single channel' trade union representation as well as the apparent fear that the introduction of universal, workforce-wide information and consultation arrangements could undermine or marginalize union recognition and collective bargaining. It also suggests that many union officials see little potential for using the regulations as a tool for building trade union organization. While there is some indication that established unions have sought to extend the scope of existing recognition agreements in the light of the regulations to include consultation (Koukiadaki, 2009: 403), only rarely are unions reported to have actively organized their members to trigger the regulations' statutory procedures.

The former Graphical, Paper and Media Union (GPMU), subsequently the graphical, paper and media (GPM) sector of Amicus and now Unite, provides the most notable exception to this approach. Leading officials in this part of Unite have pursued a proactive strategy of seeking use the regulations for organizational purposes. By early 2009, the Unite GPM sector's database of information and consultation agreements listed thirty-nine companies in which agreements had been signed or union campaigns for information and consultation arrangements were at various stages of development. It included seven companies—among them Yell—which, according to the union, had 'imposed' pre-existing agreements.

Speaking at an Institute of Employment Rights seminar in 2010, Unite's then assistant general secretary for the GPM sector, Tony Burke, contrasted the TUC's 'optimism' that the regulations would 'give [unions] a foothold in any company and any sector' with unions' 'disappointing lack of success in securing information and consultation agreements across the board'. The GPMU and then the GPM sector of Amicus and Unite 'saw the potential' of the ICE regulations to help with 're-organizing' the industry following the derecognition suffered by the print unions in the newspaper sector in the 1980s. 'We surmised that, using the regulations, we could establish a base camp where we had members but no formal structures or where we were not able to mount a current CAC claim for recognition... Equally, we surmised that many companies would find it very hard to resist the arguments for greater provision of information to the workforce and wider and more detailed consultation' (Burke, 2010).

The union's most notable success in using the regulations was at Macmillan Publishers. Having successfully pursued a case to the CAC for the disclosure of data on corporate structure and employment levels, it subsequently collected sufficient employee signatures via a campaign page on its website to trigger negotiations over information and consultation arrangements with the company. When the company failed to respond, the union, as discussed further below, successfully pursued cases at the CAC and EAT to ensure that the company met the terms of the regulations' standard provisions. On the back of the petition to establish information and consultation arrangements, the union recruited new members and successfully pursued a union recognition claim at one of the company's warehouses. Unite also claims some 'major successes' elsewhere within the GPM sector, including signing information and consultation agreements with significant companies such as Chesapeake, Communisis, De La Rue, D. A. Smith, Kimberly Clark, Polestar, and Trinity Mirror. The union has also negotiated model information and consultation agreements with three employers' organizations—the British Printing Industries Federation, the Confederation of Paper Industries, and Graphic Enterprise Scotland.

Unite's focus on securing information and consultation agreements in this sector reflects sector-specific circumstances and union organizing traditions, including the former GPMU's long record of active engagement with statutory provisions, and is untypical of union approaches more generally. Instances of unions organizing requests to trigger the introduction of information and consultation arrangements appear to be comparatively rare—as, consequently, do reports of negotiated agreements (Hall, 2006; Koukiadaki, 2009). While this may reflect the widespread union ambivalence towards the regulations identified earlier, Unite's Tony Burke has questioned 'why have we not had more [successes], and why have we not drilled down into smaller companies?' The design of the regulations is seen as a key factor. As demonstrated by Taylor et al.'s study (2009), the mere existence of the ICE regulations provides no readily available rights for unions to exert on behalf of employees. Burke's own assessment is that information and consultation agreements 'take a long time to set up: the regulations are complex [and] cumbersome and it is largely down to workforces to negotiate with their management . . . The reality is that, without a union taking the lead, ordinary members and reps do not have the experience or back-up to find their way through the steps which have to be taken' (Burke, 2010). This highlights the importance—and the resource implications—of unions providing training for activists and representatives and also full-time officer support. His view more generally is that the regulations have been 'underused [and] misunderstood and that unions are missing a chance to get a foothold in companies and sectors that have remained union free'.

Enforcement and case law

The emerging picture of only limited engagement with the regulations by unions and employees is reinforced by the low volume of ICE-related cases received by the CAC—the principal agency for the enforcement of the rights and procedures established by the regulations. In the period from April 2005, when the regulations came into effect, to the end of 2011, only forty applications relating to twenty-two organizations had been received by the CAC—an average of barely six cases per year. The highest annual total was ten in 2009. As at the end of 2011, twenty-two of the forty applications had resulted in decisions by a CAC panel (summarized in Table 5.3). The rest of the cases were

Table 5.3. CAC decisions under the ICE regulations

Case number	Case name	Complaint	Regulation	CAC decision	EAT involvement
IC/03/(2005)	Mr J. Stewart and Moray Council	Invalidity of claimed PEAs	10(1)	Upheld	Appeal dismissed
IC/04/(2005)	Amicus and Macmillan Publishers Ltd	Failure to provide employment data requested	6(1)	Upheld	–
IC/08/(2006)	Amicus and Macmillan Publishers Ltd	Failure to hold elections for I&C representatives where standard provisions apply	19(4)	Upheld	Penalty notice issued (£55,000)
IC/11/(2007)	Ms G. Pye and Partnerships in Care Ltd	Failure to hold elections for I&C representative where standard provisions apply	19(4)	Rejected	–
IC/12/(2007)	Unite the Union and Newsquest (Worcester) Ltd	Failure to inform employees in time of intention to hold endorsement ballot on employee request for I&C arrangements	8(7)	Upheld	–
IC/13/(2007)	Mr J. Stewart and Moray Council	Failure to hold elections for I&C representatives where standard provisions apply	19(4)	Upheld	–
IC/14/(2007)	Mr G. Darnton and Bournemouth University	Failure to provide employment data requested	6(1)	Rejected	Appeal initiated but EAT found no reasonable grounds for appeal
IC/19/(2008)	Mr G. Darnton and Bournemouth University	Failure to hold elections for I&C representative where standard provisions apply	19(4)	Rejected	Appeal dismissed
IC/21/(2008)	Mr K. Selormey and Electronic Data Systems Ltd	Failure to comply with terms of negotiated agreement or standard provisions	22(1)	Rejected	–
IC/22/(2009)	Mr G. Darnton and Bournemouth University	Failure to hold elections for I&C representative where standard provisions apply	19(4)	Upheld	Penalty notice issued (£10,000)
IC/23/(2008)	Mr J. Archibald and Gardner Denver Ltd	Failure to comply with terms of negotiated agreement	22(1)	Rejected	–

IC/24/(2009)	Mr R. Rodriquez and Ocado Ltd	Non-compliance with requirements for election or appointment of negotiating representatives	15(1)	Rejected	–
IC/25/(2009)	Mr G. Darnton and Bournemouth University	Failure to comply with terms of standard provisions	22(1)	Rejected	Appeal initiated but EAT found no reasonable grounds for appeal
IC/27/(2009)	Mr T. Brown and G4 Security	Failure to hold elections for I&C representative where standard provisions apply	19(4)	Upheld	Penalty notice issued (£20,000)
IC/28/(2009)	Mr J. Gale and Bournemouth University	Failure to comply with terms of standard provisions	22(1)	Rejected	–
IC/29/(2009)	Mr G. Darnton and Bournemouth University	Arrangements for ballot to elect I&C representatives defective	19(2)	Rejected	–
IC/32/(2010)	Mr D. Nixon and Freightliner Ltd (Intermodal)/ Freightliner Heavy Haul Ltd	Failure to provide employment data requested	6(1)	Rejected	–
IC/35/(2010)	Mr X and Local Partnerships LLP	Invalidity of employer notification to initiate negotiations	13(2)	Rejected	–
IC/36/(2010)	Mr X and Local Partnerships LLP	Non-compliance with requirements for election or appointment of negotiating representatives	15(1)	Rejected	–
IC/37/(2010)	Mr X and Local Partnerships LLP	Arrangements for ballot to elect I&C representatives defective	19(2)	Rejected	–
IC/38/(2011)	Mr N. Burgar and Wincanton Container Logistics	Failure to hold elections for I&C representative where standard provisions apply	19(4)	Upheld	–
IC/39/(2011)	Mr S. Mitchell and Wincanton Container Logistics	Failure to comply with terms of standard provisions	22(1)	Rejected	–

Source: CAC website; CAC (2006, 2007, 2008, 2009, 2010, 2011).

withdrawn at an earlier stage in the process. These are remarkably low figures, even accounting for the fact that the phased introduction of the regulations meant that they did not apply to undertakings with 100–149 employees until April 2007 and to those with 50–99 employees until April 2008. The limited extent of enforcement activity is even more significant given that some of the leading cases, most notably Amicus and Macmillan Publishers Ltd, demonstrate the potential for employees and unions to use the law highly effectively against defaulting employers. In addition, the regulations allow employees to make a request for the negotiation of information and consultation agreements to the CAC rather than their employer. The CAC passes on to the employer concerned the number of employees making the request without revealing their names. By mid-2011 this process had been used on sixteen occasions (CAC, 2011: 11). In some cases these requests had been organized by trade unions acting as employees' representatives (CAC, 2006: 5).

Notwithstanding the low level of cases received, some CAC decisions and EAT rulings have addressed key aspects of the legislative framework and have had significant implications for both employers and trade unions (Dukes, 2007). In the first ever CAC decision on an application under the ICE regulations, issued in December 2005, the panel determined that union recognition agreements could potentially constitute PEAs but that one of those relied on by Moray Council was 'insufficiently detailed' about the process for informing employees and seeking their views to do so. This decision has considerable implications for employers and unions seeking to rely on such arrangements to fend off employee requests for negotiations on new information and consultation arrangements under the regulations. The CAC chairman, Sir Michael Burton, commented that it was 'perhaps not surprising that the first substantive decision by the CAC was immediately subject to an appeal and cross-appeal to the EAT' (CAC, 2006: 2). The EAT dismissed both appeals and supported the CAC's approach, albeit with some significant clarifications concerning the approval of PEAs (see Box 5.1).

In February 2007, in what was described by the CAC chairman as a 'landmark decision' (CAC, 2007: 4), the CAC upheld a complaint from Amicus, as the employees' representative, that the publishing company Macmillan had failed to respond in accordance with the regulations to an employee request to negotiate an information and consultation agreement. The CAC panel decided that the company was under the obligation to initiate negotiations but had not done so and therefore became subject to the regulations' standard provisions six months after the date of the request. As a consequence the company was obliged to hold a ballot to elect information and consultation representatives but had failed to do that either. The CAC ordered the company to arrange the requisite ballot—the first such decision issued by the CAC. The outcome highlighted the consequences of a failure by an employer to respond effectively to a request from its employees under the regulations. The union pursued the matter to the EAT, which in July 2007 issued the first ever penalty notice under the regulations to Macmillan, setting the penalty at £55,000. The penalty imposed on Macmillan fell short of the £75,000 maximum, which some trade unions and legal experts had already criticized as being too low to constitute an effective sanction, especially in the case of large companies with substantial financial resources. However, if necessary, the enforcement of a CAC order may be pursued through the courts.

Of the total number of complaints that have been the subject of CAC decisions, the largest group (seven) has been applications for the CAC to order the employer to arrange for the election of information and consultation representatives on the grounds that the regulations' standard provisions applied due to the failure of the employer to respond appropriately to an employee request under the regulations or to do so within the requisite timescales. Five of these have been upheld, of which three have been followed up by successful applications to the EAT for a penalty notice to be issued to the employers concerned. Other than in the Macmillan case, the penalties assessed by the EAT have been relatively low. In the Bournemouth University case, the penalty was 'towards the bottom of the available scale' (the Honourable Mr Justice Underhill, UKEAT/0391/09/RN): the CAC and the EAT held that the fact that negotiations over an ICE agreement overran the appropriate period was not 'deliberate' and did not '[result] from a disregard of the university's obligations under the regulations'.

The next largest category—five cases—has concerned the alleged failure by employers to comply with the terms of either a negotiated agreement or the regulations' standard provisions. In none of these cases did the CAC uphold the complaint. In one case (Electronic Data Systems), the CAC found the complaint not well founded because neither a negotiated agreement nor the standard provisions applied. In another (Gardner Denver), the complaint was ruled out of time, while in two others (Darnton/Bournemouth University and Mitchell/Wincanton Container Logistics), the CAC essentially decided that the alleged failures to inform and consult related to decisions which predated the standard provisions becoming applicable. More significantly, in the Gale/Bournemouth University case, the CAC determined that the proposed dismissal of twelve staff could not be regarded as a 'substantial change', and therefore one subject to consultation under the standard provisions, in the context of the university's total number of 1,300 core staff.

The third largest category—three complaints—has concerned the alleged failure by employers to provide employment data requested by an employee or an employees' representative. The CAC rejected two of these on the grounds that the employer had acted consistently with the regulations. But its decision in the Macmillan case—that the company was required to disclose

Box 5.1 KEY CAC AND EAT DECISIONS UNDER THE ICE REGULATIONS

Moray Council—validity of pre-existing agreements

Mr Stewart, an employee of Moray Council, had lodged a petition with the council in which over 500 employees requested negotiations under the ICE regulations to reach an agreement on employee information and consultation arrangements. The council argued that PEAs were in place covering all of the council's employees and therefore that, as provided by the regulations, it was entitled to hold a ballot to ascertain whether the wider workforce endorsed the employees' request.

Under Regulation 8, to be valid, PEAs must be in writing, cover all employees, have been approved by the employees, and set out how the employer is to give information to employees or their representatives and seek their views on such information. The council contended that three documents—the framework local recognition and procedure agreement covering teachers and related staff, the council officer trade union group constitution, and the protocol for consultation with trade unions—constituted PEAs for the purposes of the ICE regulations, and covered all employees regardless of whether they were union members. However, in Mr Stewart's view, these three documents were agreements with trade unions and provided only for consultation via unions, with no provision for informing and consulting non-members. He therefore argued that they did not cover all employees and had not been approved by the employees.

A CAC panel decided that the agreements related to negotiation and consultation for council employees without differentiating between union members and non-members, and that they did in fact cover all employees. It also decided that the agreements' approval by trade union representatives, and the fact that a majority of the workforce belonged to the unions recognized by the council, constituted approval by the employees under the ICE regulations.

However, the panel concluded that one of the three agreements—the framework local recognition and procedure agreement covering teachers and related staff—was insufficiently detailed about how the council was to give information to the employees or their representatives and seek their views on it, and therefore did not fulfil the requirements of Regulation 8(1)(d). Accordingly, the CAC upheld Mr Stewart's complaint that the PEAs relied on by Moray Council did not fulfil the necessary conditions that would entitle the council to proceed with a ballot, and told the council that it must initiate negotiations in response to the employee request received.

On appeal, the EAT supported the CAC's view that the provisions of the teachers' agreement failed to set out adequately how the employer was to give information to the employees and seek their views. The EAT also accepted that it was appropriate to regard employees as being covered by the terms of an information and consultation agreement if they fell within the categories of employees intended to be regulated by that agreement, whether or not they were union members.

However, in relation to the CAC's conclusion that the agreements had been approved by the employees, the EAT commented that the CAC should have satisfied itself that the employees covered by each agreement had given their approval for that particular agreement rather than looking at the matter in aggregate. Where there are a number of agreements, the necessary approval existed only if each of the agreements had been approved by the employees covered by that agreement. The EAT also considered whether the CAC was entitled to find that employee approval for a union-negotiated agreement existed because the majority of employees it covered were union members. Noting that Regulation 8 does not prescribe any particular way in which employee approval needs to be demonstrated, the EAT stated that 'it will usually be legitimate to infer approval if, at the time the agreement was made, the majority of the employees covered by the agreement were members of the union or unions which are party to that agreement'. However, where union members were in a minority, it would be necessary for the employer to be able to establish the relevant approval in some other way.

Macmillan Publishers—application of default 'standard provisions'

Amicus complained to the CAC that Macmillan had failed to initiate negotiations over information and consultation arrangements in response to an employee request under the regulations. The union argued that the regulations' standard information and consultation provisions had therefore become applicable, but that the company had failed to hold a ballot for the election of information and consultation representatives as required. The CAC upheld the union's complaint and ordered the company to proceed to elect information and consultation representatives as required by the standard provisions.

The union also applied to the EAT for a penalty to be imposed on Macmillan. The regulations provide for a penalty of up to £75,000, depending on the gravity of the breach of the regulations. In this case, Macmillan admitted that it was in breach of the legislation. In mitigation, the company said that they had thought it was sufficient to adapt their existing mechanisms to the new legislation, and that they were now actively seeking to carry out their legal obligations. However, the EAT commented that 'it is difficult not to form the impression that [the company] is opposed to these regulations and is seeking to delay their implementation for as long as it reasonably can'. The EAT stated that, although the company's actions did not constitute the most serious breach of the regulations that could be envisaged, they were nonetheless 'a very grave breach affecting many employees' and fixed the penalty at £55,000.

The EAT stressed that 'employers must recognise that [the regulations confer] important rights on workers. The provisions must be complied with. We think it appropriate, in fixing this penalty, to stipulate a sum which, within the limits imposed by the legislation, will deter others from what can only be described as the wholly cavalier attitude to their obligations that has been demonstrated by this company'. However, the union questioned whether 'the level of the fine will act as a sufficient deterrent for a global company of this size in the future'.

data on the establishments, sites, and/or plants that make up the undertaking and the number of employees within each of those units—represented an expansive interpretation of employees' entitlement to data under Regulations 5 and 6 and arguably one that, in complex organizations, is potentially highly useful to unions in terms of developing company-specific organizing strategies. Indeed, as previously noted the union subsequently submitted a successful trade union recognition application to the CAC in respect of Macmillan warehouse workers in Swansea.

A final point of significance concerns the limited extent of union involvement in complaints to the CAC—again illustrating apparent union reluctance to engage with the regulations. Among the complaints to date that have resulted in CAC decisions, only the GPM section of Amicus and then Unite has been active in pursuing cases to the CAC as an employees' representative. The cases concerned were those involving Macmillan Publishers and Newsquest. The union was also behind CAC applications involving Watt Gilchrist and West Ferry Printers. These were withdrawn but in both cases resulted in the establishment of information and consultation arrangements. In one further case—Nixon and Freightliner—the (unsuccessful) complaint was pursued on behalf of the Associated Train Crew Union, a union that had previously sought recognition from the company.

Case study evidence

A final source of evidence concerning the factors affecting the take-up and impact of the statutory consultation rights provided by the ICE regulations is the authors' own case study research in twenty-five organizations (Hall et al., 2010; also see the Appendix). Chapter 7 provides case histories of eight of the organizations studied. All but one of the information and consultation bodies studied had been established, or significantly revamped, around the time that the regulations progressively came into force. The research explored the hypothesis that the regulations had been a major influence. This proved not to be the case.

In none of the organizations was the statutory trigger mechanism initiated by employees. Nor was this considered by management to be a realistic possibility and there was no evidence of broader employee/union pressure for new information and consultation arrangements. Other than the request for union recognition at one organization—the northern housing association—the initiative to establish or relaunch the information and consultation bodies was management's in every case, and most stressed internal employment relations reasons for doing so. Management saw the regulations as having a 'critical' or 'significant' impact on their decision in only four of the larger organizations, three of them multinationals, reflecting a felt need as good corporate citizens to demonstrate compliance with the legal provisions. Eleven organizations saw the regulations more as a 'catalyst', helping to shape the design of the initiative and secure top management support. Elsewhere the regulations were seen as a 'background' factor at most.

Other factors specific to the organizations were more important. Six were in the not-for-profit sector as charities or housing associations where the community service ethos favoured staff participation. Five organizations had come out of the public sector and felt the need to move away from the perceived adversarial traditions of union-based employment relations. Eleven were multi-site organizations and eight were multinational companies. The corporate offices, while rarely directing compliance, did often establish a corporate ethos towards information and consultation. Four of the multinationals already had an EWC. In addition to these structural factors, the experience of organizational change often stretched existing communication channels and prompted reform. In fifteen organizations the adoption of information and consultation was associated with newly appointed senior managers, usually in HR. Their wider remit often revolved around the perceived need to improve employee understanding of and response to organizational change and to build employee commitment. The adoption of information and consultation was one part of a wider programme of communication and engagement.

Union avoidance was a factor in four non-union organizations. In two of these, the information and consultation bodies were explicitly intended as an alternative to union recognition (though in one case union members established a significant presence on the information and consultation structures introduced, illustrating the potential for unions to 'colonize' workforce-wide information and consultation bodies). In two others, there had not been sustained union recruitment activity but the introduction of the information and consultation body was seen as helping maintain the organizations' non-union status. More generally, some other, unionized, organizations, while maintaining collective bargaining arrangements, were seeking to broaden out from a union-based employment relations culture. Workforce-wide information and consultation arrangements were seen as being inclusive and as a means of overcoming the 'disenfranchisement' of non-union employees.

The absence of any attempt by unions or employees to trigger the application of the regulations left the way open for management to design and implement information and consultation arrangements to suit their needs. Management's freedom of action was evident in the choice by eleven organizations to establish information and consultation arrangements unilaterally without employee endorsement and by twelve to base them on a voluntary agreement or PEA that had been signed by employee representatives. In few cases did management regard the latter explicitly as PEAs under the terms of the ICE regulations. Their objective had been to secure broad workforce agreement for the introduction of information and consultation arrangements. In any event, the terms of agreements were usually drafted primarily by management, with only limited input from employee representatives, blurring the distinction between agreed and unilaterally introduced arrangements. In two cases, information and consultation was via union representatives, anchored in a union recognition agreement. In only one case were the information and consultation arrangements accorded the status of a 'negotiated agreement' under the regulations. This was insisted on by national-level union officials to ensure enforceability. Crucially, therefore, in all but one of the cases, the information and consultation arrangements introduced remained outside the statutory framework providing for legal enforceability.

Management's freedom of action did not mean that the regulations had no impact at all. One area where the regulations did appear to have had some considerable influence was the provisions and wording of agreements or constitutions underpinning the information and consultation bodies, particularly among the larger organizations. This was most notable in terms of the subject matter identified for information and consultation (where a majority of the larger organizations we studied echoed the regulations' default provisions by specifying information and consultation on their activities and economic situation, employment developments, and organizational change) but less clear cut in terms of the nature and extent of the consultation process. Among the smaller organizations, the influence of the regulations on constitutional arrangements, though discernible in some cases, was less extensive, reflecting greater informality and more limited HR capacity. In practice, the information and consultation process was often notably less extensive than implied by such provisions but this typically went unchallenged. This underscores the fact that, in almost all of our case studies, the information and consultation arrangements took the form of PEAs or were introduced unilaterally by management, providing no legal avenue for redress. Beyond this, there was little evidence that the regulations shaped managerial approaches to the practice of information and consultation, nor that they were used as point of reference by employee representatives. Significantly, of greater relevance in practice than the ICE regulations were the separate—and directly enforceable—statutory requirements governing information and consultation over redundancies and transfers. As discussed further in Chapter 7, this legislation provided the framework for handling major restructuring exercises at a number of the case study organizations.

Conclusion

The highly flexible, light-touch regulatory approach adopted by the ICE regulations has had important implications for the take-up of information and consultation. Employees' rights to information and consultation under the regulations are not directly applicable and depend on employees (or management) taking the initiative. It seems likely that the legislation will have driven an overall increase in the incidence of information and consultation arrangements. The findings of the next WERS, due shortly, will confirm whether this is the case and to what extent. The evidence currently available suggests that the regulations have prompted considerable voluntary activity in terms of reviewing, modifying, and introducing information and consultation arrangements but this has been largely employer-led. Employees or unions have not been triggering the statutory procedures to any significant extent.

While initial expectations were that employers would favour reaching formal 'pre-existing agreements' to maximize flexibility under the terms of the regulations, union abstentionism and the low use of the regulations by employees has in practice left extensive scope for management unilateralism. Both the small number of enforcement cases dealt with by the CAC and the findings from our own case study research highlight the largely peripheral influence of the legislation on the introduction of information and consultation arrangements and on their practical operation. In this context, internal organizational dynamics, largely unconstrained by the regulatory framework, determine the nature, extent, and impact of information and consultation. Chapter 6 discusses the criteria that can be used to analyse the practice of consultation, and the organizational factors that interact to create the conditions for the type of 'active consultation' implied by the default provisions of the directive and the ICE regulations.

6

The Practice of Consultation

In Chapters 1 and 2 we looked at various ways consultation is defined and how this has changed in different periods. Justifications for consultation, whether to improve organizational efficiency, as a form of power sharing or an employment right, have been given greater or lesser emphasis over time much related to different, and changing, needs of employers, trade unions, and the state. The ebbs and flows of consultation as an employment practice are a constant theme. The ambiguity surrounding consultation has bedevilled its uptake and survival as an important activity in the world of paid employment. It has not been helped by a lack of enthusiasm for the practice from employers, trade unions, and governments.

In theory, much of the ambiguity should have been dispelled with the adoption of the various EU consultation directives. It is clear from the collective redundancies directive, for example, that consultation should take place over impending redundancies. Consultation is also required in respect of business transfers under the transfer of undertakings directive and more generally via European Works Councils (EWCs). The standard, default provisions of the Information and Consultation of Employees (ICE) Regulations, as we showed in Chapter 4, are similarly explicit and specify when and how consultation should take place especially where 'decisions are likely to lead to substantial changes in work organisation or in contractual relations'. The long and tortuous route to the framing of the directives, and the ways these came to be adopted in the United Kingdom, described in Chapters 3 and 4, has led to the very patchy adoption of consultation. In Chapter 5 we used what evidence there is from surveys, cases dealt with by the Central Arbitration Committee (CAC) and the Employment Appeal Tribunal (EAT), and from our own research, to conclude that the ambiguity surrounding consultation remains and many employers are free to side-step the regulations.

Those employers that choose to create a staff council are largely unrestricted in how they structure and practice consultation to suit their needs. After studying the adoption of consultation in four companies, Bull (2010: 290–1) concluded that 'management remain the architects of [information and consultation arrangements] even in the face of EU attempts to legislate for participation. The extent to which employees are increasingly (and meaningfully) involved is contingent on employer goodwill'. This is confirmed by Sarvanidis (2010) in his case studies. Little, it seems, has changed in twenty-five years. Cressey and MacInnes (1984: 20, cited in Marchington, 1989) concluded then that 'it is up to management to determine what information to take to the committee and when, what subjects were proper matters for discussion, what form the discussion should take and finally what would result from the discussion. In practice, management control of participation often extended to unfettered control of the agenda and direction of discussion'. To take this further, we need to understand the component parts of the consultative process and their inter-relationship.

The component characteristics of effective consultation

The purpose of this chapter is to dissect the practice of consultation to enable us to determine how managers, in association with their employees and trade unions, where they are recognized, make participation an embedded and valued practice. There are plenty of examples to draw on, and we will do so from our own research. At the same time we need to determine what makes consultation a weak or marginal activity, and why some staff councils have such a depressing history of dying away after a few years. Again, there are many examples and some case histories are provided to flesh out the bare statistics. Dundon and colleagues (2006: 508) referred to 'high' and 'low' road strategies.

> A "high road" strategy would include a mix of direct and representative mechanisms suited to a given organisational context, encouraging both information and consultation. These mechanisms would be broad in scope and would facilitate employee cooperation as well as the opportunity to question management decisions and shape the agenda for employee voice. In contrast "low road" strategies would focus around a set of disjointed or pseudo participatory processes that, in effect, minimise employee input into decision making while consolidating managerial control.

What do these different strategies entail? Here we indentify six main practices associated with successful consultation. Where any of these are absent or undeveloped, the staff council can become trivialized. These practices do not develop at once at the initiation of a staff council but grow, or wither, over time.

Marchington (2005: 26) suggests four criteria for evaluating participation schemes: the degree of involvement, the scope of decisions, the level of consultation, and the form of involvement and consultation. We add two further factors: the organizing capacity of employee representatives and a culture of cooperation.

- The *degree of involvement* concerns the extent to which employees are able to exert influence on management decisions. Crucial here is the timing of consultation, whether before or after management have made a business decision. Where there is a high level of involvement with consultation taking place before a decision has been taken, it is likely that information will often have to be given in confidence and special meetings of the staff council may be held since decisions of this importance cannot wait until the next scheduled meeting.
- The *scope of decisions* concerns the topics that are open to consultation. We can distinguish between business decisions, HR policy and practice, housekeeping matters, and social affairs. One of the crucial determining factors for the success of the staff council will be the extent to which management places items on the agenda or just relies on representatives to raise matters of concern, having talked to their constituents.
- The *level of consultation* allows for recognition that involvement and participation often takes place at multiple levels, raising questions about the interconnection between each. While most staff council meetings are held at the workplace, in large, multi-site companies there can be company-wide councils with representatives drawn from each location. Multi-national companies (MNCs) with operations in Europe may have an EWC, with representatives coming from one or more sites in each country where they operate. Another way of looking at *level* is to ask who, within management, typically attends consultative meetings? Where there are senior managers involved, it can be expected that the staff council will have more authority, but does the evidence confirm this?
- The *form of involvement and consultation* is the relationship between different types of involvement. One of the crucial features shaping the operation of the staff council is the extent of direct involvement with individual workers through such things as workforce meetings and team briefing sessions held by line managers, as well as participating in problem-solving groups. Do these direct forms of involvement compete with, or complement, the work of the staff council? In those companies which recognize trade unions for collective bargaining, the question of *form* must include the interconnection between collective bargaining and collective consultation. It is not an easy relationship.

- The *organizing capacity of the employee representatives* throws light on how and in what circumstances employee representatives on the staff council create a coherent forum able to represent the interest of their constituents: do they have, in Koukiadaki's term (2010: 384), a 'capability for voice'? In two of her case studies, representatives were 'often uncertain about the nature and purpose of their input to discussions. The employee bodies acted more as a "focus group"' (ibid.: 380). It is rare for representatives to be able to develop an effective capability for voice without the help and support of management and, where possible, trade unions. The law can be important, too, in ensuring that representatives are not discriminated against and in providing access to paid time off and, in some cases, training and facilities.
- A *culture of cooperation* is required if consultation is to be deemed effective by managers and staff council representatives. Summarizing the many studies on the operation of consultative bodies, Wilkinson et al. (2010: 14) 'identified managerial attitudes as key to the existence of highly developed employee participation practices . . . underpinning such practices is a relationship based on a high level of trust between management and employees. In such circumstances, management assumes that employees can be trusted to make important workplace decisions that will result in positive outcomes . . . and employees assume that management can be trusted to share with employees the rewards emanating from these outcomes'. What evidence is there of mutual trust between managers and staff representatives and how does trust, or the lack of it, affect the degree, scope, level, and form of consultation and the organizing capacity of the representatives?

Degree of involvement

It may well be the case that 'many organisations do not involve employees in organisational change initiatives until the later stages of change, that is after management has designed an organisational change initiative and determined how it will be implemented' (Wilkinson et al., 2010: 12) but under the terms of the default provisions of the ICE regulations they should do. How they choose to consult over business decisions is a matter of company policy concerning their 'preferred approach to consultation—whether they are willing to use the ICE body proactively as a forum for providing high-level, strategic information and consulting on proposed business and organisational changes' (Hall et al., forthcoming). The alternative approach is a more limited conception, echoing findings from earlier, pre-directive research that 'employee involvement was typically initiated by management with the intention of improving communications and enhancing employee commitment but it had nothing to do with increasing employee influence' (Delbridge and Whitfield, 2001: 475). Where management want to use the staff council for high-level consultation they must, first, provide information on a regular basis concerning business results and key events and, second, initiate discussions on proposed changes which are likely to have an impact on work organization and employment conditions and contracts.

The authoritative Workplace Employment Relations Survey (WERS) 2004 throws some light on the practice of information provision and the discussion of options for change at consultative meetings (Kersley et al., 2006: 128–9). In those workplaces with a consultative committee, around four-fifths regularly provided information on work organization (81 per cent), future plans (81 per cent), and employment issues (78 per cent). Information on production issues was provided in around 70 per cent of workplaces. Financial results were less often disclosed with only 65 per cent of workplaces doing so. Bryson and Freeman (2007: 75) observed a 'sizable drop [between 1996 and 2004] in the proportion of workplaces disclosing information on many key issues such as investment plans and the financial position of the workplace and the organisation'. This may be because of concerns about the commercially sensitive nature of the financial information. In our case study research, we came across a number of organizations that refused to give information to their staff committee on the grounds that to do so would be in breach of the stock exchange rules. They were misguided here. Government guidance on the ICE regulations (DTI, 2006: para. 77) points out that 'neither the UK Listing Rules, nor the City Code on Takeovers and Mergers, nor US rules prevent a company sharing price-sensitive information with representatives of employees before it is disclosed to the market, as long as those representatives are subject to an obligation of confidentiality'.

According to WERS 2004, of the two-thirds of organizations with staff councils which gave financial information, 60 per cent said they did share commercially sensitive information with representatives while 27 per cent said they did not. Among those that did not provide confidential information, the presumption must be that it was published accounts which were presented to the council to help improve their economic literacy and understanding of the company.

It is self-evident that it is management which provides the information to staff council members. The fundamental difference between those that do and others who only do so grudgingly, if at all, is management's attitude to the role of the council. This was explored in the WERS survey. 'Full information was usually provided in advance of meetings in around 68 per cent of workplaces where representatives considered that managers were supportive of their role, but in only 18 per cent of workplaces where managers were not considered supportive' (Kersley et al., 2006: 165).

Kersley and her colleagues on the WERS team (ibid.: 130) attempted to get a measure of the extent to which consultation took place over the various options management were considering, or would consider, before taking a decision. The management person surveyed was provided with three statements concerning their approach to consultation, if they had staff council (or joint consultative committee (JCC), as WERS termed it). Around two-fifths agreed with the statement that they 'looked to the committee to provide solutions to problems' that is, that management did not go to the council with predetermined policies or plans. A rather larger proportion (45 per cent) said that the JCC examined a range of options put forward by management while, in a further 11 per cent, representatives were only invited to consider management's preferred option, which we can presume to be the decision already taken. In over half of the cases the senior employee representative, who was also interviewed, agreed with the ranking given by management but a quarter felt they had a greater involvement in discussing policy options. The difference in approach was strongly related to the management respondents' perception of the influence of the staff council over management decisions. Of those who said their council 'provided solutions to problems' by discussing a range of options, 35 per cent said the council was 'very influential' and a further half said it was 'fairly influential'. This compared with only 19 per cent saying the staff council was very influential where it was given a list of management's preferences and only 11 per cent when just one policy option was considered.

Union-based and hybrid (mixed union and non-union) staff councils were more likely to be provided with information concerning financial and employment issues than their non-union counterparts. For example, 75 per cent of councils which included union representatives were given financial information compared with 61 per cent of non-union committees (ibid.: 132). But the difference between them ended there. Union-based councils had no greater access to financially sensitive information and were 'just as likely to be treated as a sounding board rather than a problem solving body, and, consequently, were no more influential than non-union committees on average' (ibid.). This goes some way to dispelling the view that union-based staff councils will always be effective while non-union ones are inevitably weak. We need to question Wales and Landsbury's assertion (2010: 580, using data from Gollan, 2006b) that in 'non-union representational arrangements... management usually controlled the structure and agenda at meetings and most non-union representative bodies were only given powers of recommendation to management... and there was a lack of financial, investment and strategic data available to non-union committees'. This is often the case but it can also be a problem for union-based councils. It all depends on what management wish to achieve in consultation.

This is reasonable evidence on which to argue that the degree of involvement through consultation is at its highest when management are prepared to give regular information, some of which will be commercially sensitive, and ask the staff council to discuss proposed changes in advance in such a way that there is a real possibility that employee representatives have a chance to help shape the final outcome. This can be in relation to the decision itself and/or to the way it is to be implemented. It is very likely that active consultative bodies will have rules concerning how confidential information is to be handled. Certainly, this was the case in some of our case study companies which had active consultation and information was often provided in confidence. These staff councils were sometimes convened for special meetings when management tabled proposed plans affecting some or all or the workforce. We provide some illustrations of this in Chapter 7.

Oxenbridge and Brown (2004: 193) found a similar approach in some of the union partnerships they studied. Sometimes 'managers in robust cases informed union representatives about ideas of future plans on an off-the-record basis either during the early stages of the decision making process, or well in advance of their formal announcement, in order to seek representatives' input and advice.... A benefit for management was that representatives often highlighted potential problems or flaws...and gave them advice on how they might position issues or convey messages to gain workforce acceptance'. This can equally apply in well-organized consultative committees, whether union or non-union. We give the illustration in one of our case histories, the mobile phone company, in Chapter 7.

The European Company Survey 2009 (European Foundation, 2010) provides some comparative data on the matters discussed here. These data must be treated with some caution as the UK response rate was low (28 per cent, although this amounted to 1,510 management respondents) and the number of employee representatives interviewed was small (166). What the survey reveals is that British employee representatives were less critical than others on the quality of information provided (figure 47, p. 52). They also had a higher perception than the average (across the twenty-seven member states of the EU) that they were able to exert strategic influence in their organizations. The question focussed on seven HR and employment issues rather than business strategies. Out of a maximum possible score of 21 points, the UK average was just under 12 while across the EU it was just over 10 (figure 63, p. 65). This more optimistic view of British employee representatives was found, too, by Waddington (2006) in his study of EWCs.

Scope of decisions

Consultation is a two-way process with either side able to place items on the agenda. The range of topics often discussed at the staff council fall in four broad categories:

- *Business issues and decisions*. These are nearly always placed on the agenda by management whether before or after a decision has been taken, as discussed above. In some cases, representatives can hear of a development, often through the grapevine, and ask questions about it in the council meeting, or beforehand if it has not been tabled by management. This happened in one of our cases, the news agency, 'where the possible sale of a division prompted numerous questions from employee representatives. Management responded to the extent possible and also said that it would schedule [staff] council meetings immediately before or after the sale, if it proceeded' (Hall et al., 2009: 65). But in this case, management took the view that consultation before a business decision was taken 'was a step too far for us'.
- *HR policies and practices*. These topics are usually raised by management but, again, can be the subject of questions from representatives either to do with the application of policies or requests for new ones. In practice, HR matters often dominate staff council agendas. Although it is often the case that the constitution of a staff council precludes discussions on pay matters, in practice it is often hard to stop representatives raising remuneration questions. In two of our case studies where the staff council was flagging, and it proved difficult to get new representatives, management sought to revive the council by tabling HR matters. In the urban housing association, management had rarely put items on the agenda but a new council chairman asked for a review of sickness policy. Much the same happened in the law firm where, after a bout of bad winter weather, management asked the council to review the absence and lateness policy, a matter of some controversy (Hall et al., 2010: 82, 92).
- *Housekeeping matters*. It is common for topics in this broad area to be raised by employee representatives, often following complaints from employees. This conforms to one of the functions of consultation suggested by Gollan (2010: 225), to be a 'safety valve'. In some of our case studies, the facilities manager had been added as a management member of the staff council in order to field these points. Housekeeping matters can seem trivial, and some are (a broken microwave oven, for example), but they are matters of immediate concern and their resolution can contribute to the credibility of the consultative process if there are also meaty issues to discuss. There are often problems, however. If

management choose not to raise any big items themselves then the whole meeting can be taken over by small, parochial issues. When this happens it is often the case, as in the urban housing association, that there is no pre-meeting of representatives to sort out the agenda and housekeeping items are raised 'around the table'. In the snacks company it was the provision of time for representatives to meet before a meeting which allowed many small housekeeping items to be filtered and to be dealt with directly by appropriate line managers. Perhaps the most deadly effect of a dominance of housekeeping items is that they do not get resolved quickly, if at all, since they are hardly priority items. This means, in the minutes of the next meeting, under 'matters arising' the same problem (the hole in the smoking shed roof, in the snacks company) comes around time and again much to the equal despair of managers and representatives at the meeting, and the employee who raised the matter in the first place who wants an answer.

- *Social issues*. In some, usually quite small, companies the staff council is given responsibility for organizing social functions. In the safety company, with thirty-eight employees, representatives had a budget of £2,000 to spend on social events. They met monthly in the canteen for 20 minutes to discuss ideas but also used this time to filter out trivial items before the next meeting of the council. They also discussed big issues in the council at the behest of the site manager, a passionate supporter of consultation. In the recession, which hit the company hard, the council played a pivotal role in dealing with short-time working and eventually redundancy (Hall et al., 2009: 40; 2010: 92). Another example comes from the rural housing association. Here, efforts to revive the staff council focussed on organizing social activities, which appeared, by the end of the research, to be modestly successful (ibid.: 82). In these cases, one of the functions of the staff council was to help create a sense of community and togetherness.

WERS used a different classification to assess the scope of consultation but it does correspond roughly to the four topics discussed here. What is of interest is that the survey was able to compare management views of how frequently a matter was discussed with those of senior employee representatives, and also to see what difference, if any, there was between union and non-union representatives on the topics covered. These data are summarized in Table 6.1. The first four rows of data roughly equate with business issues, rows 5–10 are HR issues. The bottom row would appear to equate with housekeeping matters. The survey did not ask about social affairs.

Three conclusions can be drawn from these data. The first is that there is general agreement on the topics discussed although management sometimes give a more rosy account than the representatives, for example over work

Table 6.1. Issues discussed at meetings between employee representatives and management[a] (% of response: management, union, and non-union representatives)

	Management	Union representatives	Non-union representatives
Future plans	81	78	84
Financial issues	65	65	53
Work organization	81	76	67
Production issues	71	37	61
Employment issues	78	68	75
Leave and flexible working	68	63	60
Training	79	71	68
Pay issues	66	61	70
Health and safety	80	76	76
Equal opportunities	49	46	44
Government regulations	48	48	53
Welfare services and facilities	77	51	69

[a]Column 2, 'management', covers topics discussed at JCC meetings; Columns 3 and 4 relate to any discussions between management and representatives.

Source: WERS 2004 Kersley et al. (2006: figure 5.1 and table 6.4).

organization and production issues, and this latter issue is discussed in only a minority of cases with union representatives. Second, welfare and facilities, which we equate with 'housekeeping' matters, is much more prevalent in non-union cases, and this conforms to our qualitative research findings. Third, with the exception of 'financial issues' and 'work organization', management generally would appear more prepared to discuss matters in consultation with non-union representatives than with union-based ones. This may be a product of the level of trust between management and the two types of representatives. We return to this later in the chapter.

Two difficulties with fixing the scope of consultation, beyond management preferences, are that there may be no strategic changes to discuss and staff councils can run out of topics, having cleared the pressing issues. The first limitation is described by Clegg and Wall (1984: 439–40, cited by Marchington, 1989: 398) as 'the impediment to participation [being] one of impoverished context'. This is elaborated by Marchington. 'Organisations functioning in a relatively predicable context provide little scope for involvement... Conversely, organisations in a more uncertain environment offer greater scope for involvement because more decisions have to taken and change effected'. We observed this in a few of our case studies, especially in the urban housing association and the hospice, although in neither was this business stability the key factor in the obvious weakness of the consultation process. In both it related more to management reluctance to take issues to their staff councils. We provide case histories of these two organizations in Chapter 7 when we look at the dynamics of consultation.

Miles and Rosenberg (1982, cited in Heller et al., 1998: 60) call the condition where councils run out of useful things to discuss, 'plateauing'. This occurs 'when easy problems have been solved through active participation and some participatory learning has taken place, but the pay-off from further participation is then perceived to decline: frustration and resignation result'. This was evident in a number of our case studies, for example in the regional airport (Hall et al., 2010: 90) and the snacks company. In this latter company of 100 employees, 'relatively few items at the [staff council] are raised by management ("we do not talk about plans") and most are tabled by employees. Once issues of importance had been resolved in the early days of the council, meetings became clogged with housekeeping matters' (ibid.: 93). This 'plateauing' effect is nearly always a reflection of managements' limited conception of the purpose of consultation. Where a council is formed to 'help improve communications', management usually take the view that the staff council is an opportunity for employees to raise items of concern with senior management. What senior managers often hope for, as in the regional airport, is for staff representatives to 'think strategically' and ask questions about bigger issues such as business prospects and strategic objectives. This, all too frequently, turns out to be an unrealistic expectation since representatives do not have the knowledge or experience to engage in such high-level debates unless senior management are prepared to 'talk about plans' and seek views on them. What happens is that the pent up problems, which led to a recognition that better communication was needed, are taken up in the early meetings and the council never moves on to meatier issues.

Level of consultation

Many large companies have quite complex structures of business units, divisions, and national and international corporate offices. The location of consultative committees often mirrors this corporate structure. Edwards et al. (2007: 83) in their large scale study of MNCs operating in the United Kingdom reported that out of the 302 MNCs in the study, 'almost three quarters (73 per cent) held regular information and consultation meetings between management and employee representatives at the level of the UK operation (the top level in the UK). There are regular meetings below the level of the UK operation, covering individual sites, or groups of sites, at 77 per cent of multi-site companies'. This pattern is further complicated by the existence of an EWC in 28 per cent of cases (ibid.: 84). However, 'the presence of an EWC does not necessarily mean that there are consultative arrangements within the UK operation: there are no such structures in one in ten cases with an EWC. Amongst multi-site MNCs, there is complete vertical coverage of representative-based arrangements for employee information and consultation, at European level, UK-level and below UK level, in 22 per cent of cases' (ibid.: 85).

A clear illustration of this complex interweaving of consultative arrangements came from our case study in the diversified technology company. This is a global US-owned company with a commitment to consultation and dialogue with its workforce. In the unionized plant we studied, the union convenor was the key member of the staff council at the site, sitting alongside non-union representatives from the administrative and professional staff. He was also a member of the UK national staff council and was the elected representative on the company's EWC. To add to this, he was also a pension fund trustee. Although the site where he worked only had 450 employees (which dropped to 110 later), he was recognized as being so valuable to the company that he worked full-time on his representative duties. The networks he built up, locally, nationally, and internationally proved invaluable when the site staff council and local management had to deal with a major redundancy exercise.

Multi-level consultative committees were evident initially in the national charity, another of our case studies, but they did not last long. 'By the end of the research, the three business forums, as they were called, had been abolished because of a lack of attendance, problems in finding appropriate business for meetings and growing managerial opinion that formal bureaucratic approaches to employee involvement were not in keeping with the organisation's preferred informal approach' (Hall et al., 2009: 68). It was evident that the business forums had plateaued and management were losing interest in consultation at the local level. The problem in the engineering company, a US-owned MNC, with a multi-level consultation structure was different. Here the EWC was seen to be effective while at plant level the unions had focussed on wide-ranging collective bargaining over many years with good effect. This left the national forum, created in response to the ICE regulations, with not much to talk about beyond developments in HR policy. The value lay less in what happened at the meetings but in the networking it allowed since representatives were drawn from all the UK factories for the first time.

Consultation over collective redundancies and mergers and acquisitions (transfers of undertakings) may be carried out by a staff council, but the fact that recognized unions, where they exist, must, by law, be consulted can create complications. This was the experience in one of our cases, the financial processing company, and both the union and the staff council had to be consulted separately. Sometimes management may wish to create a special consultative body in order to ensure that those affected are fully represented in a focussed committee. This then can lead to questions about the role of the standing staff council and the extent to which it should be involved.

The level of consultation has a wider meaning than the existence of multiple committees in different parts of large companies. What is the level of management taking part in meetings of the staff council? Given the ambiguity surrounding consultation and its weakness in some companies, it could be expected that senior managers would not bother to attend and would not have informal contact with senior representatives outside the formal council meetings. The WERS data, drawn from interviews with representatives, did not show this. Instead 'most (representatives) have access to, and regular contact with, the top level of management in their establishment. The most senior manager was usually the point of contact for almost all of the non-union representatives' (Kersley et al., 2006: 166). This was more often the case in smaller workplaces than in large ones. However, 'even where an HR manager was present at the workplace, or higher level, the majority of representatives still indicated they approached the most senior manager at the workplace' (ibid.). In the twenty-five cases covered in our research, 'top operations managers, including the managing director, or CEO or senior site manager, as appropriate, were in almost all cases regular attendees at information and consultation meetings, often alongside HR managers and, in some cases, a facilities manager to deal with housekeeping issues' (Hall et al., forthcoming). This means that weaknesses and failures in consultation are rarely the product of management neglect but occur, in the main, because senior managers have not envisaged a strategic role for their staff council. Symbolically, their attendance at meetings, often devoted to housekeeping items raised by representatives, is necessary to show continuing commitment to open communication. If they stopped coming, many councils stuck in this communication role would quickly collapse.

The form of consultation and involvement

The two major developments in British employment relations in the last quarter of a century have been the growth in direct forms of employee involvement and the decline in trade unions and especially collective bargaining. These processes, where they exist, can crowd out consultation unless the staff council has a distinctive role and voice.

Marchington (1989: 392), writing at a time when the decline in trade unions and collective bargaining in the private sector had only recently begun, saw consultation exclusively in terms of its relationship with collective bargaining. He painted four scenarios. Consultation could be an 'alternative' to collective bargaining, playing the role of union substitution. This was certainly the case in a few of our case companies and we give a case history of one, the mobile phone company, in Chapter 7. It could be 'marginal', with collective bargaining dominating the relationship between management and employees. In these circumstances it would not last long. Collective bargaining crowded out and marginalized consultation in two of our cases, the professional association and the regional airport. Consultation could be beefed-up to 'compete' with collective bargaining by becoming the forum to debate business strategies forcing unions either to join in or themselves be marginalized. 'There is little doubt that this may be fostered in order to weaken unionism by the back door' (ibid.). This was the experience of unions in the rural housing association. It is also evident in some studies of union partnership arrangements (Oxenbridge and Brown, 2004; Samuel and Bacon, 2010).

Finally, consultation could be an 'adjunct' to collective bargaining. 'Strong workplace organisation may be regarded as a necessary prerequisite for this model' (Marchington, 1989: 392). In the adjunct model the same union representatives would negotiate in the joint negotiating committee and consult in the JCC. Consultation would inform negotiation and also allow focus 'on issues of an integrative character and helps oil the wheels of industry' (ibid.). In their study of union partnerships, Oxenbridge and Brown (2004: 193–4) found that 'managers in four, mostly robust cases, of partnership felt that an important advantage... was the presence of consultative committees or representative bodies which provided employees with a confident "voice" and managers with a formalised mechanism for consultation.... According to managers, union representatives played a crucial role in "smoothing the change process" by providing a gauge for workforce views and by communicating management's change proposals to employees "in their own language"'. This was certainly the experience in the diversified technology company mentioned earlier. The union was confident in its strength with a high level of membership. This enabled the convenor to play such a useful role in consultation and negotiation. The number of such highly unionized workplaces, in the private sector at least, where the adjunct model could apply, has fallen considerably since Marchington provided his analysis. It can no longer serve as an aspirational model, although it might still do so in some parts of the, heavily unionized, public sector.

The contemporary model in many companies which recognize unions is 'hybrid' staff councils where union and non-union representatives sit around the same table while collective bargaining continues via the union on matters concerning the terms and conditions of employment. It is probable that the regulations will have led to an accelerated growth in the number of hybrid councils. Gollan (2010: 231) suggests 'that incorporating a degree of collective bargaining as a complement to, or as part of the non-union collective voice process, could provide more productive outcomes for employers and more just outcomes for employees'. This is an international phenomenon. Freeman et al. (2007: 216) report, on the basis of studies in Anglo-American countries (including the United Kingdom), that 'in unionised workplaces... there is a growing complementarity between union and non-union representative voice systems. Our surveys show that workers regard these systems as providing real benefits rather than being talk fests or management dominated shams'.

The union experience of hybrids can be positive despite concerns about losing influence and membership. For example, 'at the care services company, the union supported the *de facto* merging of the [staff council] and union-based bargaining and, given continuing difficulties with recruitment and input of non-union representatives, was central to the consultation process. The union full-time officer, who was an active participant, argued that the [staff council] offered the union access to senior management and influence over a broader range of topics than collective bargaining' (Hall et al., forthcoming). We will look at why hybrids have a particular advantage later in the chapter when we consider the organizational capability of the representatives. The major limitation to the growth of hybrid staff councils is union ambivalence at national level. In two of our cases the union refused to take up the seats on the council offered to them.

The biggest challenge to the practice of consultation is the now near universal adoption of forms of direct employee involvement, whether work force meetings, team briefing sessions, or problem-solving groups. There has been a remarkable growth in such methods of direct communication in the last twenty-five years (Forth and Millward, 2002, cited in Kersley et al., 2006: 134). The 2004 WERS survey found that 91 per cent of organizations used one or more types of face-to-face communication methods, compared with 85 per cent seven years earlier. Just under two-fifths (38 per cent) held a workforce meeting 'at least on a monthly basis with 10 per cent of the time made available for employee views and questions' (ibid.: 136). Half of employers held monthly team briefing sessions with again at least 10 per cent of the time devoted to employee views and questions. Looking at the topics covered in these meetings, which in the survey were identical to those discussed in staff councils (see Table 6.1), it is clear that future plans and production issues are more often covered in direct communications than in council meetings.

Given that around three-quarters of staff councils meet four times a year but 31 per cent of workforce meetings are monthly (and one in five meet weekly), and just under half of team briefings are weekly (ibid.: figures 5.1 and 5.2), it is obvious that employees are much more likely to get timely information direct from their managers than representatives. If the staff council is only given the same information, it gets 'crowded out' and can never develop a unique voice. This was the experience in the hospice and the electronics company, where the staff council collapsed, in good measure because of management's preference for direct communication (see Chapter 7). If, however, the council has an active role in reviewing and discussing strategic business developments, or even having the opportunity, over a two-hour meeting, of discussing future plans and production issues rather than just listening to management reports, then the council can play a much more meaningful role. Briefing groups and workforce meetings rarely last for longer than 15–30 minutes. In some organizations the link between direct and indirect methods of communication and consultation is emphasized by encouraging employee representatives to report back to their constituents at team briefing sessions after a council meeting.

There is clear evidence that managers prefer to use direct communication methods and have become more reliant on these (ibid.: 139). In the European Company Survey 2009, the management respondent was asked to say if they agreed with the statement 'we would prefer to consult directly with our employees'. Overall, across the EU some 60 per cent agreed, and, of these, one-fifth strongly agreed that this was their preference. In the United Kingdom the preference for direct methods was stronger with around 72 per cent preferring direct communication methods, with just under a quarter saying they 'strongly agreed' (European Foundation, 2010: figure 66). Edwards et al. (2007: 85) found that US and UK MNCs 'display a strong tendency to emphasise direct channels (of communication) especially those in the non-manufacturing and service sectors'.

All this echoes our earlier discussion on the difference between involvement and participation. We provided the evidence in Chapter 2 to show that the combination of direct and indirect methods adds value but it clearly requires an understanding of the different functions each play. At their best, staff councils are complementary to direct methods of communication. Where the two compete over the same issues, the staff council will find it hard to gain a distinctive voice.

The organizing capacity of employee representatives

Employee representatives on staff councils need to have 'participatory competence . . . as well as a preparedness of employees to articulate their interests' (Heller et al., 1998: 50). All too often there can be a 'competence deficit' and Heller and his colleagues are clear that 'relevant competence has to precede effective influence and power sharing' (ibid.: 155). There can be a sort of Catch 22 here. Recently formed staff councils, especially if they are non-union, rarely have members with prior relevant experience, yet are often expected to operate as though they know the ropes: how to communicate with each other between meetings, how to sort out the chaff from important items on the council agenda, how to create some semblance of unity when responding to management proposals, how to tell constituents what happened in meetings, know where and when to go for external advice, how to handle confidential information and know the difference between being a representative and a delegate, and other things too. Koukiadaki (2010: 367) sees this in terms of 'opportunity: the extent to which the actors possess the means, instruments or permissions to pursue what they would like to do; and assess the extent to which they are able to do the things they value doing'.

Building organizing capacity is not simply the responsibility of the representatives themselves since much will depend on what is expected of them by senior managers and how much support they are given. Managers themselves also often have no experience of representative systems and are unclear on what the role entails. For this reason, Heller and his colleagues (1998: 214) believe that 'organisations implementing participation schemes need technical advice; and the successful diffusion of participation through the economy seems to require the services of trusted organisations capable of providing this'. In the United Kingdom this is most often provided by Advisory, Conciliation and Arbitration Service (Acas) but only once the parties have asked for help.

The classic literature on trade unions, but it can apply to staff councils equally, sees the seed bed of organization as processes which lead, first, to interest articulation and then to interest aggregation. Employees come to recognize common goals which blur differences of opinion, and their representatives find the means to group them together. The two processes are not as sequential as implied. The representative is often the person articulate enough to give expression to views, as an opinion leader, and can find common cause among differing employees' needs. Union growth and demands for recognition are often triggered by a particular incident which leads people to believe that they need a union: a 'mobilization' event (Kelly, 1998). Mobilization events rarely happen in generating a demand for consultation.

We showed in Chapter 5 that the staff councils in our case studies were all created by management without any pressure from either employees or trade unions. It can also be that employees show little interest, as Bull (2010: 288) found in her case studies. It is no easy task to create a unified group of employee representatives, but it needs to be done if consultation is to be effective. Management needs an authoritative body to deal with, and employees need to have trust and confidence in their representatives. Hyman (1997: 310) suggests 'the central issues in interest representation may be specified as autonomy, legitimacy and efficacy'. Autonomy means the ability to operate independently, outside of management control. Legitimacy posits the requirement for the union or the staff council to be seen as the legitimate representative system by employees. But also means that managers have to recognize that the union or council acts as the legitimate body and is prepared to work with it. Efficacy refers to the need for the representative body to be organized in such a way as it is seen as competent and trustworthy. The requirements for organization and effectiveness can be quite tough. Gumbrell-McCormick and Hyman (2010: 305) suggest, drawing on Hege and Dufour (1995: 93), that

> First, a coherent employee 'voice' has to be constructed from a multiplicity of interests, aspirations and grievances within the workforce; effective representation must be sufficiently detached to be able to filter and prioritize these, in many cases seeking to align what are at first sight contradictory demands. Second, they need strategic, long-term perspective in order to assess the costs and benefits, risks and opportunities of any course of action.

These authors were writing about the experience of works councils in continental Europe, but the principles remain much the same in the United Kingdom. In our case histories (Chapter 7), we provide an illustration of an effective staff council in the mobile phone company which created a unified group of employee representatives. In another example, the re-launched staff council in the IT services company took great care to build electronic communication networks among representatives and ensure there was adequate time in pre-meetings to try to seek common ground in responding to management items on the agenda. Both of these cases are in large multi-site companies and are non-union, although unions did manage to get candidates elected to both councils. Many non-union staff councils are not as effective as these.

Trade union-based staff councils, including hybrids, do have a number of advantages helping to establish a well-functioning employee side. WERS 2004 showed some significant differences (Kersley et al., 2006: 131–2). Union representatives tended to have longer experience in the role, spent a great deal more time on representative duties, had access to trade union officers outside the workplace, contacted other sources of external advice such as Acas more often, were much more likely to be trained and to hold representative-only meetings (pre-meetings), and were more likely to have been elected to the position or stood unopposed. However, union representatives had no better access to paid time off and facilities such as e-mail.

It is worth recalling that only 11 per cent of the staff councils (JCCs) identified in WERS were union-only bodies while two-thirds were non-union and a further quarter (22 per cent) were hybrids. These proportions changed in workplaces where there was a union representative on site. In these circumstances, a quarter of JCCs were union-only, a similar proportion were non-union, while just around half were hybrids (ibid.: 131). Two-thirds of site-based union representatives worked alone making it difficult to establish a unified employee side to the staff council. In comparison the average number of non-union representatives, in workplaces where they were found, was six. All this points to the advantages that hybrid consultative arrangements can have. There are likely to be a number of representatives able to constitute a functioning committee while union membership means that there is access to external advice and good-quality training. What is more, 'some degree of engagement with employees' representatives over terms and conditions was most common where there were union and non-union representatives on site, although this was more likely to take the form of information and consultation as opposed to negotiation' (ibid.: 195). The scope of issues discussed tends to be wider than in many non-union committees. Dundon and Gollan (2007: 1191) suggest, on the basis of a number of research studies, 'that union and non-union arrangements can develop interdependencies and, over time, become complementary'.

A good example of a successful hybrid staff council comes from the care services company, one of our case studies. As well as giving the union better access to senior managers, as noted earlier, the union provided training for its representatives who became more active in meetings of the staff council, while the full-time officer also attended. The tendency here was for the union to begin to colonize the council. Originally, the union and non-union representatives kept to themselves and at meetings of the staff council, two sets of minutes were produced, one for each group of representatives. This soon ended and an effective staff council emerged (Hall et al., 2009: 69).

The law is not as helpful as it could be in helping to facilitate the organizational capacities of employee representatives. For one thing it is inconsistent. Where UK law provides for employee representatives, they typically have protection against detriment and dismissal while carrying out their duties and access to paid time off. Under Transfer of Undertakings (Protection of Employees) Regulations and the collective redundancy consultation provisions, representatives also have rights to receive training and to be provided with facilities to help them perform their duties. The Acas Code of Practice on time off for trade union duties and activities (Acas, 2010) does what it can to fill in the gaps with advice but the fundamental weakness of the ICE provisions in terms of rights and protections for representatives is clear. Information and consultation representatives only have a right to paid time off and against detriment. There is no mention of training or facilities. But the key weakness is that these rights only apply to information and consultation arrangements established by negotiated agreements or under the standard or default provisions. Pre-existing agreements are exempt. Hall et al. (forthcoming) note that since effective consultation, or 'dialogue',

> can best be achieved where there is an organised and functioning representative body able to articulate employees' interests, the absence of elementary statutory rights for employee representatives to, among other things, hold pre-meetings, undertake training and use office facilities is a notable omission from both the directive and the UK regulations, leaving such practices dependent on management goodwill.

In contrast, the EWC directive and corresponding regulations in the United Kingdom, as amended in 2010, provide representatives with rights to paid time off and the necessary financial and material resources to carry out their duties, to undertake training, to call special meetings, to hold pre-meetings without management being present, and to seek external advice.

A culture of cooperation

The purpose of consultation is dialogue on matters of mutual concern. Cooperation and trust are thus axiomatic and where these fail to develop the staff council will struggle. There has to be a climate of cooperation. 'A major challenge [is] to develop an information and consultation culture in which mutual respect, trust, openness and honesty prevail' (Hall et al., 2002: 55). Much will depend on the expectations managers and representatives have of the consultative process. It is evident from the previous section that management support for representatives is essential if they build organizational capability. This is seen in time off to attend meetings and hold pre-meetings, the provision of facilities, access to training, providing opportunities for representatives to talk and communicate with their constituents and external advisers, the early provision of information, and a willingness to take consultation seriously. Generally, representatives rate the support they get from management quite highly, with just over three-quarters agreeing this happened (Kersley et al., 2006: 169). There is little difference here between union and non-union representatives on staff councils. Representatives also reported that the quality of their relationship with management was high with over three-quarters of union representatives (76 per cent) agreeing it was 'good' or 'very good'. Half of non-union representatives on staff councils said their relationship with management was 'very good' (ibid.: 168).

Trust between the parties has long been recognized as the essential ingredient in collective relationships (Purcell, 1981). Trust, to be effective, needs to be mutual or shared. It has to be earned and allowed to grow through experience as mutual gains, or benefits, are achieved by both parties. This is because trust is a form of risk taking and few people are prepared to trust the other without a feeling that this behaviour will be reciprocated. Dietz and Fortin (2007: 1161) identify 'two sources of trust evidence [that] are expected to influence participants' engagement with the JCC: the trustworthiness of the voice process itself (i.e. the structures and protocols of the JCC)... and the trustworthiness of the committee members'. This means that there is a need for both institutional trust and interpersonal trust.

The level of trust between management and representatives was explored by WERS (Kersley et al., 2006: 171–5). Generally, there was quite a high level of trust. For example, in answer to the statement that 'the other party can be relied upon to live up to the commitments they have made', half of management and union representatives agreed (mutual trust), a quarter of managers said they trusted the union representatives even though trust was not mutual (one-sided trust), while 11 per cent of the representatives said they trusted management even when it was not reciprocated. In 14 per cent of cases there was no trust. This pattern was repeated in the other two scenarios in the survey concerning attempts to understand the other party's point of view and behaving with honesty and integrity. The level of trust, especially mutual trust, was higher with non-union representatives; although not all of these were members of the staff council, so meaningful comparisons cannot be made.

The implications of this trust for the operation of the staff council were clear. 'Where managers and representatives trusted each other, the vast majority of representatives agreed they worked closely with management when changes were being introduced, and that management valued their opinion and gave information without it being asked' (ibid.: 174). The level of trust also influenced management. 'Management was very likely to be supportive, and the quality of the relationship was almost certain to be good, where there was mutual trust' (ibid.: 175). The authors were able to conclude from these data that 'trust contributes to a climate that is conducive to collaboration... yet is not a sufficient condition' (ibid.: 174). What they meant by this was that there were quite a few instances where there was mutual trust but the degree of collaboration in the management of change had not taken root. It is possible to have mutual trust even where the role of the staff council is restricted to being a communication forum and where most items are housekeeping matters raised by the representatives. An effective consultative body has to have a serious diet of issues to discuss and be able to do so in a climate of mutual trust and support. This can only develop over time as experiential learning is crucial for consultation to become a valued and embedded practice. We look at the dynamics of consultation in Chapter 7.

Conclusion

The effective practice of consultation requires six interdependent behaviours or practices to be in place.

- The staff council has to be able to exert some influence over management decisions and this must mean that consultation takes place when these business decisions are still in a formative stage.
- There needs to be a reasonably wide scope of decisions and issues raised in the staff council with both sides bringing matters to the council's

attention. These cover business, HR, and housekeeping items, and in some cases can include social matters helping to reinforce the organization as a community.

- Consultation takes place at all appropriate levels, from the workplace to company level and internationally at least in Europe via an EWC. Whatever the location of consultation senior managers have to attend meetings to give the process legitimacy.
- The work of the staff council has to dovetail with other processes of negotiation and staff involvement. This means that while collective bargaining, in unionized companies, is often a separate process, it is connected to consultation through overlapping membership and some shared topics. The staff council needs to discuss a wider range of items, and in more depth, than are covered in workforce meetings and team briefings, otherwise it will be 'crowded out'.
- Employee representatives, with management support, have to build the organizational capability to express their collective voice. This requires good networks and communication channels with each other and with the constituents, a forum to meet without management being present to work out what approach to take on a particular agenda items, and access to facilities such as e-mail, intranet, and meeting space. Some paid time off from the day job is essential. There is also a need for training and access to external advice. There is a need for leadership to create and sustain a viable employee body.
- Management support is essential but the process has to be conducted in a climate of cooperation if dialogue is to flourish. This means generating mutual trust on an interpersonal level and having faith in the institution itself. This is more likely to come about if there is collaboration on issues such as the management of change.

Chapter 7 uses company-specific case histories from our research to explore how the presence or absence of these six factors have combined, through time and experience, to shape a range of operational behaviours and outcomes of the staff councils. We start by providing four case histories of successful staff councils, all of which had developed 'active' consultative committees. Less successful staff councils, where their role was limited to 'communication', are the subject of three further case histories, while the final case is a story of a staff committee which collapsed after only two years in operation.

7

The Dynamics of Consultation

In this chapter we use case histories in eight organizations with recent experience of consultation through a staff council to show how the practice of consultation can evolve, positively or negatively. Four of these cases can be seen as success stories, where consultation developed as a valued practice and where there was growing 'participatory competence' (Heller et al., 1998: 50). In particular, the employee sides of these councils appear to have been able, with a lot of support from management, to create 'a capacity for voice' (Koukiadaki, 2010: 384). The contrast is with the next three case histories where the practice of consultation had a promising start but seems to have faltered and in each case managerial effort had to be made to keep the council going. The final case history is of a staff council that lasted for only two years before management, in effect, lost interest, claiming the council did not accord with the company culture and no further meetings were called.

In Chapter 6, six key features of the consultative process were identified concerning:

- the degree of involvement in management decisions allowing representatives to exert some influence,
- the scope of decisions covered in consultation (business, HR, housekeeping, and social matters),
- the level at which consultation occurs in large, more complex organizations, and the seniority of managers taking part,
- the extent of direct and indirect involvement and consultation practised in a company and the relationship between the two forms,
- the organizing capacity of the employee representatives to gain a collective voice, and
- the existence of a culture of cooperation supporting the consultative process.

These six process elements combine to create patterns of consultative practice. Many analysts have created classificatory schemes to highlight the differences between types of consultative practice. For example, Dundon et al. (2006) use the terms 'shallow' and 'robust' while Koukiadaki (2010: 379) adapted typologies of European Works Councils (EWCs) developed by Marginson et al. (1998) and Lecher et al. (2001) to evaluate the operation of consultation arrangements as 'symbolic', 'pragmatic', 'dynamic', and 'participative'. Our preference is to use just two terms which focus on management preferences since it is the organization's management which makes the fundamental decision on the purpose of consultation. For some, consultation is an active process where management plans, organizational performance, and strategic decisions which impact on the workforce are presented to the staff council for consideration and debate. This can go so far as being undertaken 'with a view to reaching agreement'. These are the *active consulters*. This proactive approach accords with the Information and Consultation of Employees (ICE) Regulations' default provisions.

The alternative, favoured in a majority of organizations covered in our research (see the Appendix), was for the staff council to be a focal point for communication between top management and employees. We classify these organizations as *communicators*. It was rare for strategic issues to be taken to the staff council by senior management and, in the few cases where they did, it was usually only once the decision had been taken and plans formulated. The crucial purpose of the representatives was then to be a 'communication bridge' with the staff. The role of the representative, in these circumstances, was to explain the decision, gather views and feed them back to senior management at subsequent council meetings. Among both the active consulters and the communicators, one role of the representatives was to raise employees' concerns. These were, in the main, housekeeping matters ranging from broken toilets to bigger issues. Among the communicators these housekeeping items tended to dominate as managers only rarely put items on the agenda. In some cases the council took on the role of organizing social activities. Two of the companies covered in the research allowed their councils to become *defunct*; a third, dormant category.

Case histories in active consultation

A proactive management, willingly initiating discussion on major business policy matters which have organizational and employment consequences, will need to have an effective employee representative group to talk to. The employee side of the staff council is likely to become more effective through experience and growing self-confidence as it gets drawn into considering management proposals. Representatives will need time working in pre-meetings to formulate a response, draft questions, and adopt a position on proposed restructuring or major organizational change. This may require training or development away-days. For example, in one of our cases, a provider of care services to the vulnerable, the chief executive, and the union full-time officer went, with the union and non-union representatives, on such an away-day since there was a felt need to improve the effectiveness of the representatives. One outcome was more time being given for pre-meetings. It was in the organization's interest to have an effective employee body to consult.

In all the cases we studied, where there was active consultation, the organizations had faced major challenges and changes providing a diet of meaty issues for staff council to consider. Heller and his colleagues (1998: 211) observed that 'moderate levels of economic uncertainty are best for cooperation and participation'. What this meant in practice was that regular meetings of the staff council with information updates, reviews on some aspects of HR policy and practice, and housekeeping issues were held as normal but were interspersed with special meetings to consider major policy initiatives that were about to be announced or were in the planning stage. Two notable actions would typically take place around this special meeting. First, it was very likely that informal discussion would take place before hand between the senior staff representative and a senior manager on the staff council. Second, it would be agreed that discussions would be held in confidence with no information leaking out to staff or to the press until it was felt appropriate. This can only happen if there is a high level of mutual trust between the people concerned and in the council as an institution.

The requirement for confidentiality can be difficult for employee representatives who believe it is their duty to report back to their constituents and gain their views. In one case, that of a very small manufacturing company making safety equipment, one representative resigned as she could not face returning to the shop floor after an emergency council meeting where they were discussing the dire effects of the recession. She was asked what was going on and had to say 'sorry lads, but its confidential at the moment. There will be an announcement soon'. She felt she could not cope with the pressure. Subsequently, the site manager held a general staff meeting after these emergency sessions of the council in order to take some pressure off the representatives.

The following four case histories illustrate, in their different ways, the key elements contributing to active consultation. At the *mobile phone company*, the multi-tier staff council started life as a union substitution body but, in an industry that experienced periods of rapid growth, continuous technological development, and extensive merger activity, soon became the vehicle for active consultation over major restructuring programmes. Early experience of consultation led senior management to conclude that real benefits could be achieved through seeking agreement with the staff council(s) over successive redundancy and outsourcing initiatives. With a significant presence of union members on the staff councils and the provision of extensive resources, facilities, and training by management, the employee representatives developed the competence, coordination, and influence to engage in a robust form of consultation over management restructuring plans. This usually involved the formulation of counterproposals by the employee side and the conclusion of a detailed agreement with senior managers on the issues concerned. This approach to consultation was underpinned by agreed constitutional and procedural arrangements, which were periodically updated to formalize evolving practice.

Case history—From union avoidance to highly developed consultation with agreed outcomes: mobile phone company

This UK network of a German-owned telecommunications multinational had some 6,000 employees. It set up a multi-tier staff council structure in 2003 involving a national council and a series of 'local' staff councils covering different business units. In part, this was driven by the perceived need for more structured consultation arrangements, management having previously instituted an ad hoc process for statutory consultation over redundancies stemming from a business review, as well as by the emerging new statutory framework. The move was also a key part of the company's response to pressure for union recognition. The same year, employees voted 2:1 against the recognition of two trade unions. However, although the unions were not recognized for collective bargaining, they provided individual representation.

Operating in a highly competitive sector, the company underwent frequent and extensive restructuring. Under agreed and codified consultation procedures, management consulted and sought agreement with the staff councils on the business case for, as well as the implementation of, major initiatives including restructuring, redundancies, outsourcing, and staff transfers. This approach corresponded closely to the phased consultation process specified in the ICE regulations' default provisions. Consultation was explicitly with a view to reaching agreement. Management routinely informed and consulted the relevant staff council(s) at an early stage about planned changes, typically under a 'non-disclosure agreement', and the employee representatives usually formulated counterproposals. Extensive informal consultation took place between staff council meetings. Management's objective was an 'agreed outcome'. Few proposals went through 'completely unmodified'. In some cases, 'quite major' changes were agreed.

Senior HR managers described this approach as 'effectively negotiation'. The lead employee representative agreed that representatives had the 'ability to influence' management decision-making. Initially, this was driven by management's aim to demonstrate that in-house employee consultation arrangements offered an effective alternative to union recognition, but this 'negative' motive laid the basis for positive managerial commitment to a strong form of consultation and the development of high-trust relationships with employee representatives.

Among the wide range of topics discussed with the staff councils was a series of major restructuring exercises including redundancies and workforce transfers. These included the closure of the London headquarters of part of the company. Intensive discussions with the national staff council resulted in an agreed package of measures to facilitate the move, including relocation support, travel assistance, and severance terms. Further consultations over planned redundancies ensued, in each case resulting in similar agreements on the detailed arrangements and issues such as redundancy selection criteria, often with the national staff council handling the overall framework while local staff councils discussed local implementation issues.

Consultation over a proposed new reward package for customer service staff proved more difficult. Agreement was reached only after the intervention of the lead national employee representative. 'Consultation failures' associated with this issue led to union-instigated employment tribunal claims relating to the changes in customer service staff's pay and bonus arrangements. These were subsequently withdrawn in the context of the adoption of a more formalized consultation framework intended to standardize best practice across the company and ensure consistency between local staff councils.

The outsourcing of aspects the company's activities, involving the transfer of groups of staff to other employers, entailed consultations that were governed by the Transfer of Undertakings (Protection of Employees) (TUPE) Regulations. According to the lead employee representative, these went 'much further' than required by the statutory provisions, involving 'trilateral consultation' between the relevant local staff council and both current and prospective employers.

National staff council meetings were attended by the HR director, senior operations management, and others as appropriate. Management representation on local staff councils included relevant director level or senior managers with HR involvement. Elections for employee representatives were contested in some two-thirds of seats. Employee representatives were well coordinated and resourced. They operated their own formal rules of procedure (under which representatives were occasionally 'deselected', e.g. for breaching confidentiality provisions) and engaged in extensive networking independently of management. Representatives routinely held preparatory meetings and operated their own web pages and e-mail lists. Management helped in this by providing office facilities, regular training, and time off. Improved arrangements were agreed in 2007, including extra time off for handling restructuring issues. The lead national employee representative was effectively full-time in this role and was a pivotal figure in the consultation process at local, national, and EWC levels. Towards the end of our research, the growing consultation agenda prompted employee-side proposals for the secondment of four additional representatives to coordinate the consultation process and carry out representational duties on a full-time basis.

In addition to the staff council structure, the company operated a full panoply of sophisticated HR policies designed to deliver effective performance and foster the commitment of individual employees. Key mechanisms included the company intranet and team briefings. Close attention was paid to the onward communication (to both managers and employees) of the agreed outcomes of key consultations carried out via the staff councils.

Although the information and consultation arrangements were clearly part of a union avoidance strategy by the company—and externally the two unions that had unsuccessfully sought recognition were strongly critical of the staff councils—initially union members secured a significant (30–40 per cent), if uneven, presence among the elected representatives on the staff councils. This 'colonization' approach provided indirect union representation and influence in the information and consultation process. However, by the end of the research, outside the call centres which remained a particular area of union strength, the proportion of employee representatives who were union members had reportedly fallen substantially. This partly reflected transfers of unionized workgroups out of the company but also a decline in union membership attributed by both management and the lead employee representative to the effectiveness of the staff councils.

In the *diversified technology* company, the handling a major restructuring and redundancy exercise provided an illustration of consultation being highly effective when there was a unified, well-led, employee body involved. In the case of the factory in South Wales, the union branch chairman was a well-respected, long-serving activist who attended both the EWC and the UK and Ireland national consultative council. He had a good working relationship with senior managers at the plant and with the non-union staff representatives for the administrative and professional staff. The distinction between consultation and negotiation was difficult to draw and in some sense in this case, at this time, collective bargaining became an adjunct to consultation in the way the restructuring was handled. In contrast, in two other locations the non-union representatives lacked the experience and the capacity to establish a unified employee voice and, as a result, consultation on redundancies was conducted on an individual basis.

An employee satisfaction survey was conducted two years before the massive changes in the South Wales plant, and again afterwards. The results are startling: 'How good are management here at seeking employees' views?' Up from 41 to 79 per cent. 'How good are managers here at keeping their promises?' Up from 37 to 77 per cent. 'How fair are managers?' Up from 50 to 76 per cent. Organizational commitment increased from 70 to 90 per cent. One respondent wrote in the survey form:

> The past 14 months has been a huge challenge to the company and its employees. Levels of consultation and communication reached unprecedented levels following the announced closure of two-thirds of manufacturing operations. Workplace consultation has delivered an amazing result considering the scale of job cuts. Levels of quality, productivity, safety and attendance all exceeded the average run-rate for the previous two years.

Case history—Active consultation over redundancies and restructuring: diversified technology

Diversified technology was an American-owned multi-national company producing a wide range of manufacturing goods in the United Kingdom. Three plants were studied for the research. All were subject to a major restructuring exercise which necessitated substantial redundancies. The company had a long-standing commitment to consultation, with an EWC and a UK national staff council established long before the ICE regulations. Local, site-based councils were established later in 2004 to harmonize with the regulations.

One plant studied, in South Wales, was heavily unionized in the manual working areas and had elected non-union staff representatives who sat with the union representatives on the staff council. This worked well with monthly meetings attended by the plant director and other senior managers, some from UK headquarters. Items for discussion in 'managed consultation' were often raised by the company and representatives, both union and non-union, commented that their 'views were listened to' and consultation was meaningful. Collective bargaining with the manual workers' union took place either at the end of the council meeting or in ad hoc meetings.

Staff councils also existed in the other two, non-union, plants studied and, while senior managers gave regular briefings on business results and prospects, the members of the staff councils attended de facto as individuals and had been unable to find a collective voice. When it came to dealing with the redundancies, management took the view in these plants that consultation had to be undertaken directly with the individuals affected. The staff councils were only informed after the event.

The picture was different in the Welsh plant with the staff council very actively involved from the beginning. This was not simply consultation over the redundancies, but had to deal with a major restructuring of the whole operation to ensure that the plant survived. In January the site manager gave ninety days' notice that 70 per cent of the work would be transferred to Turkey and Poland entailing the loss of around two-thirds of the jobs. The union response was that 'they were not having it' while the staff representatives wanted to explore alternatives. During the ninety-day period, US and UK corporate managers came to meet council representatives in confidence to review options, but employee representatives found it impossible to come up with viable alternatives.

A day after the consultation period expired, 217 redundancies were announced. Representatives objected to the use of compulsory redundancies but, given the paucity of volunteers and the scale of the cutbacks, these were inevitable. There were three challenges which management raised at council meetings. How would the factory be reorganized to preserve future work? How could they 'keep the wheels on the wagon' to ensure that existing customers continued to be supplied? How could they ensure employees assisted in transferring production to Turkey and Poland while reducing head-count?

The staff council decided that monthly meetings were too formal to cope with the intense discussion required. A sub-committee was formed with no minutes taken. Weekly, often day-long, meetings in a nearby hotel evolved. One manager recalled that there was a lot of table thumping while the union chairman said 'there was blood on the carpet; the usual stuff; ours as well as theirs'. Those present recall that there was often no set agenda. Rather 'agreement came around the table. We (management) did not have a definitive plan entering the discussions'. 'We were jointly designing a survival operation for the plant' said the branch chairman.

The design of the new organization centred on the introduction of lean manufacturing principles. New production teams were created with employees required to be flexible reaching the standard of 'a fully effective operator'. Union officers worked intensively with each supervisor to manage the transfers, getting agreement on a person-by-person basis. This involved an exceptional level of cooperation not just in the council but at shop floor level.

The most difficult decision concerned shift work flexibility. Management wanted to be able, at short notice, to run only four shifts, instead of the usual five. An early proposal was for the fifth shift to be manned by agency workers. This was rejected by the union which wanted all jobs for existing staff. It was eventually agreed that when the fifth shift did not run, the workers would lose shift pay, and this could happen for up to thirty-eight weeks in a year. At the same time the redundancies had to be phased to keep production going until the new factories in Poland and Turkey were ready. Overtime was banned. It was necessary to train some Polish and Turkish operatives who came to the plant before the machinery was moved. This was not popular, but agreement was reached with the staff council that there would be advanced notice of any visitors on site. Previously, redundancy selection had been on the 'last-in-first-out' basis, but this now broke age discrimination rules. A new points system was designed by the council after long discussion. This gave points for competence (requiring a new appraisal system), sickness record, timekeeping and discipline, as well as length of service.

The eventual package of measures was taken to a branch meeting for a vote on a Saturday morning. It was rejected. Management had to do something to rescue the deal. They met each employee asking, 'Do you want to work here under the new arrangements?' Virtually everyone did sign. The union chairman praised management for 'doing the drastic thing and not backing off: hats off to them'. Management were equally complimentary to the staff council and the union, recognizing that they could not have managed such a radical change without their active support in the consultative process.

At the *regional charity*, consultation began as a management inspired 'top-down' communication body where council representatives were expected to be 'a sounding board', collating questions and disseminating responses. The experience of dealing with difficult problems of staffing and contracts revealed the limitations of this communication role. On one occasion, direct communication to staff in an e-mail undermined the role of representatives who were in the process of communicating with staff about the issue. The staff council grew into an active consulter, in large part because of staff dissatisfaction with how organizational problems had been dealt with and more assertive representatives demanding time to discuss issues among themselves and limit the role of the chief executive in staff council meetings.

Case history—Active consultation prompted by representatives' growing assertiveness: regional charity

This drugs and alcohol-related charity set up a staff council in 2006 to act as a communications channel between management and its regionally dispersed workforce of around 100 employees, the majority of whom were professional social workers who had moved from the public sector. The ICE regulations were cited as a significant factor behind the establishment of the council, as was the projected growth of the organization. The move was also intended to address tensions between staff's 'public sector'-influenced style of working and the more competitive, performance-oriented environment in which the organization now operated. The charity had previously recognized a union but this arrangement lasted less than two years. Citing poor alignment between the union and the nature of the charity's work and widespread staff dissatisfaction with the representation they received, the charity derecognized the union some months before setting up the staff council.

Initially, the staff council had little impact. Difficulties were experienced in recruiting staff representatives and three of the nine teams within the charity failed to elect one. In practice, most issues were raised by management. Staff representatives were unclear about what issues they could raise and how far their representational role extended. During its first year, the council was used as a 'sounding board' for management proposals to change notice periods and flexitime arrangements. Some minor amendments were made as a result of points raised by representatives. The handling of other major issues underlined the council's limited communications role. Organizational changes involving redundancies and a review of support services were discussed by the council but only after decisions had been made by management. Staff representatives were expected to explain the reasons behind the changes to their constituents. The council became perceived by staff representatives as a 'top-down' communications channel, with the danger that they would be seen as the 'mouthpiece of the chief executive', who chaired the council, unless they developed a more proactive role.

Attempts by the CEO to generate greater staff interest in the council resulted in vacant positions being filled. Constitutional changes increased the term of office of representatives and extended the time available for staff council meetings. However, the council's role remained limited. In the view of senior management, this was 'to collate questions and disseminate responses'. When losses of funding necessitated cost-driven reform of the charity's 'top heavy' structure and working methods, management presented the restructuring plans to the staff council and gave representatives the opportunity to raise issues, but no substantial changes were made as a result of the consultation. Representatives were also asked to undertake a communications role when the restructuring was 'rolled out' within the organization but this was pre-empted by a management e-mail to all staff. Representatives felt that they 'took the flak' from staff members without being able to divulge information earlier.

In the context of staff insecurity and unhappiness resulting from this restructuring, a new CEO conducted a more extensive review of the function and operation of the staff council with a view to developing a more active consultative role for the council. One consequence was the replacement of the CEO as chair with the HR manager. Substantively, further lost contracts and financial difficulties prompted the charity to introduce a performance-related pay system in consultation with the staff council as it could no longer afford to follow NJC pay scales and annual wage settlements. As a result of concerns expressed by the staff council, the introduction of new arrangements was delayed for a year. Management also sought the council's views on the distribution of the pot of money available for pay increases. The suggested alternatives were a flat-rate increase across the board or a percentage increase. However, employee representatives favoured dividing the pot so that those on lower salaries would receive more. Their proposal was adopted by management after a staff vote in which it received a very high positive response. Other significant business issues increasingly featured on the staff council's agenda such as updates on tenders for new work, staff benefits, and stress.

Representatives also became more assertive and influential in terms of the operation of the staff council itself. Some representatives felt there was a conflict between the roles of chair and HR manager and sought the introduction of an elected chairperson. They also proposed that a substantial part of staff council meetings should take the form of 'representatives only' discussion, with the CEO and other management representatives attending only the last half an hour of the meeting, and that staff representatives should have the opportunity to comment on the minutes of staff council meetings before they were circulated to all staff. Management recognized that these developments were a response to the perception that the council had been driven too much by management, but felt that reducing the CEO's input to half an hour would be 'absurd' and allow insufficient opportunity for dialogue. Management's view was that this suggestion had come from a minority of representatives with experience of different types of employee forums in much larger organizations.

Increased confidence among representatives generated by experience and perceived success had led to tensions between management's and (some) representatives' views of the role of the staff council. At an extraordinary meeting to resolve matters, it was agreed that the format for future meetings would include a period of discussion among staff representatives without the CEO being present, that meetings would be more frequent, and that plans for an elected chair should be drawn up. Management reiterated that the role of the council remained dialogue, not decision-making.

Over time the *IT services* company's early experience with consultation under a pre-existing agreement (PEA) became frustrating, leading the employee representatives to give notice of termination of the agreement. Senior management, especially the CEO, wanted the consultative forum to be re-established but as a more effective body. A legally enforceable negotiated agreement under the ICE regulations was signed and the staff council established. Particular care was taken by representatives to ensure they developed excellent communication and discussion mechanisms. This was necessary as the twenty-three representatives were drawn from many locations and occupational groups. Day-long pre-meetings were held before the formal council to ensure issues were fully discussed. The six senior managers who attended council meetings held monthly conference calls to ensure they were fully briefed. The work of the council was not restricted to the formal quarterly meetings since a confidential intranet page allowed for questions and discussion to continue while there was provision for two sorts of emergency meetings to be called at short notice.

Case history—Building an effective consultative body via a negotiated agreement: IT services

The IT services company was a global MNC with around 10,000 employees in the United Kingdom dispersed in a large number of sites.[1] It provided IT services to business clients in the private and public sectors. It had grown in the United Kingdom through acquisitions as client organizations outsourced their IT departments. Two trade unions were recognized in some parts of the organization, one of which was inherited via a TUPE transfer. Elsewhere, the company was non-union.

The company had established a consultative forum as a PEA in 2003. This was originally set up with a genuine desire to improve employee engagement but over a number of years it degenerated into more of a 'tick-box' exercise. Union activists won a significant number of seats on the forum and management disliked the adversarial stance adopted by some of these. Some non-union representatives resigned and by the end of 2009 there were six vacancies. No effort was made to organize by-elections. The demise of the forum came when major employment changes were announced and alternative consultative processes were used which did not involve the forum. At that point the remaining representatives, many of whom were union activists, gave three months notice of termination of the original agreement.

They had hoped to be able to organize sufficient signatures to 'trigger' negotiations for a better staff council. The company pre-empted this by organizing elections for a negotiating committee to establish a staff council under the ICE regulations. The whole-hearted support of the CEO was crucial. As the elected chair of the employee representatives put it, 'the CEO felt that if we are going to have this thing at all we want something that was much more than the legal minimum and which could be used as a sounding board for ideas at a very high level'. It was felt that a negotiated agreement under the regulations provided 'something more vibrant, more useful, more credible'.

It took a long time to get agreement in the negotiating committee set up under the regulations. This was not due to major differences between management and representatives, but because of a need to gain unity among the representatives. The elected employee chair felt it was important to forge a united employee body by ensuring that all decisions on its structure and constitution were taken collectively rather than in subgroups, as preferred by management. One of the key debates centred on whether representatives should take up cases on behalf of individual employees or concentrate on collective issues in management decisions. The emphasis given to the latter was reflected in the constitution which established a broad degree of involvement in management decisions and a wide range of issues subject to consultation.

A big effort was made in the subsequent elections to the newly formed staff council to ensure that the twenty-three seats were contested and a high turnout achieved. This was successful and added to the credibility of the representatives. The two unions nominated candidates and won eight seats. The representatives came from all parts of the company and a wide spectrum of occupations. Despite some training, it was a challenge to forge a united body and great efforts were made to ensure that issues were discussed and agreement reached on how to deal with them. A weekly conference call was held on Friday afternoons for all employee representatives. This discussed progress on some agenda items, checked issues, and allowed representatives to raise matters. It also provided the first filter to ensure that only important matters got to the council. The company intranet provided three 'pages' for the council. One was open for all employees and it was here that the 'update' report issued within two weeks of council meetings was posted. The second level was for all representatives, including the six senior managers who were the company representatives on the council. Here, questions could be posted and answers provided between meetings which ensured a continuing dialogue. The third level was for employee representatives only and this was where ideas for agenda items were generated and papers for future meetings posted. In addition there was a lively e-mail exchange. Finally, the pre-meeting before the council was used to gain unity of purpose. 'If reps start arguing with each other in the main meeting it means we did not do the pre-meeting well enough'.

The strength of the staff council lay in the way it was operated and the organizing capacity of the employee representatives. The council was run by the joint chairs, one from the company representatives and the other from the employees. Two-day regular meetings were held quarterly with the first day devoted to pre-meetings for the representatives. Additional meetings could be held to consider topics which could not be deferred. It was up to the joint chairs to agree this. A third type of meeting could be an ad hoc discussion on topics that needed to be discussed quickly. Only 24 hours' notice was required by the joint chairs and these discussions, which could not lead to a decision and were not minuted, were usually held via video- or teleconferencing. In the first six months of the staff council both sorts of extra meetings were held, one at the request of the employees concerning office closures and the other, a confidential ad hoc discussion, called by management concerning a commercial contract change with substantial employment consequences. There was provision in the twenty-one-page constitution for confidential information and for employee representatives to get external advice, paid for by the company.

It was too early to predict that the council would survive for longer than the original forum but the employee chair was optimistic since 'the attitude of the chief executive and the senior leadership is completely different. That's how I know it is working. It is a level of trust that needs to be protected'.

Consultation limited to communication

The three case histories in this section are of staff councils having a restricted role, being seen by senior managers primarily in terms of a communication bridge with staff. One reason for this may have been that, in two of the three cases, major business issues with consequences for staff have not been experienced. This was recognized by one of the representatives who observed that 'the council needs to deal with meaty issues to prove itself'. However, there were still some potentially important matters that could have been taken to council meetings, but management chose not to and did not regularly brief their councils on financial matters and business results. In one of the cases there was no formal provision for calling special meetings or for handling information confidentially, while in another case there was provision for confidentiality but not of special meetings. In the third case, special meetings could be called. Whatever the formal provision in the constitutions of the staff councils, no special meetings had been called nor confidential information provided. While there usually was provision for pre-meetings of employee representatives, these were not held and pre-meeting papers not produced. In effect, items were raised directly at council meetings which became more like 'focus groups' (Koukiadaki, 2010: 380).

There was clear evidence that the councils were not operating very well since representatives often resigned and it proved very difficult to find replacements. Senior managers often expressed frustration at what they saw was the limited contribution of representatives, especially in raising minor housekeeping matters. Attempts to resuscitate the council often involved more training, a new chairman, and management putting HR matters on the agenda. In another case, that of the rural housing association, one route to reviving the council was to get it closely involved in organizing social and charity events to encourage a sense of community.

At the *urban housing* association, the union opposed the formation of the council and refused to take up the seat it had been provided with, sending an observer instead but it stopped this once it realized the council was an unimportant body. After a promising start dealing with issues of direct interest to staff, such as the office move and a dress code, the council ran out of items as management did not raise matters of any significance on the agenda. Significantly, representatives did not undergo any training and were unclear about the purpose of the council and their role.

Case history—Consultation as a communication bridge with staff: urban housing

The urban housing association had operations across London with around 750 staff and was registered as a charity. Long-standing union recognition was structured through a joint consultation and negotiating committee (JCNC) although relations had been strained in a long running pay and grading dispute. Membership density was in the region of 25 per cent and had been declining for some time. After a crisis concerning financial results, a new board and chief executive were appointed. One aim of the new CEO was to improve communications with staff and plans were made to set up a staff council. This was strongly opposed by the union which feared loss of influence but, after a three-year delay, the new council was instigated in 2006 with the union offered one seat. It refused to take this up although it did send an observer. The JCNC continued to meet every six weeks in the morning with the staff council convened later on the same day.

Early on, management tabled a number of reasonably substantial issues at council meetings and these were subject to extensive discussion over a number of meetings. One issue of particular concern was the move of the head office to a new building in the neighbourhood with discussions ranging from efforts to reduce the environmental impact to office allocations and the design of floor kitchens. Another issue was dress code which triggered a lively debate.

The constitution of the staff council specified that information on business plans, financial performance, and organizational change would be provided. In practice, senior management took the view that strategic business decisions were not to be discussed at the staff council meetings until everything had been finalized. For example, a TUPE transfer of charity shops to the private sector was announced to a joint meeting of the JCNC and the staff council at the same time as a press release was issued. One reason given was the need to abide by what were thought to be the stock exchange rules on information disclosure. A year later a prospective merger with another housing association was widely rumoured. Staff council representatives knew of this but management declined to raise it at a council meeting. They argued that it was premature to do so as no final decision had been taken, and, indeed, the merger did not proceed. But if the merger had proceeded, management thought the role of staff council would have been 'crucial as a catalyst for communication with staff. Representatives will ask staff for their views and concerns and raise them at the next council meeting'. The role of the representatives was 'to test the temperature of staff concerns'. Both the senior managers and the staff representatives saw the function of the staff council to be a 'bridge' between staff and senior management, but representatives were often unclear about their role and lacked the self-confidence to raise strategic items. For example, despite knowing about the planned merger, no employee representative sought to raise the matter at the next council meeting, let alone ask for a special meeting.

One effect of management reluctance to take things to the council until the final decision had been taken, in the context where few such issues had arisen, was that the council was starved of meaty issues. There was a narrow scope for discussion and the degree of involvement was consequently low. Meetings became increasingly dominated by housekeeping matters raised by representatives 'around the table' at the meeting. These then tended to clog up the minutes requiring a note of action taken at the next meeting under 'matters arising'. Many found this frustrating and some people resigned as representatives. It proved hard to find replacements. Pre-meetings of representatives were not held, even though these were explicitly provided for in the constitution, and there was no obvious senior employee representative to build an organizing capability. An attempt by one IT literate representative to set up a confidential intranet group for the exclusive use of representatives quickly fell into disuse. No training for representatives had been organized. Meanwhile, the union no longer bothered to send an observer to meetings as it believed the council was irrelevant.

Following staff changes, a new senior manager took over the chair of the council. He wished to revive it and placed significant HR items on the agenda, unlike his predecessor, such as revisions to the sick pay scheme and the development of a well-being agenda. Management remained committed to the principle of consultation through the staff council but had yet to find the best way to practice it.

The case history of the staff council at the *regional airport* is one of the council being crowded out once unions gained recognition for collective bargaining for some of the staff. In addition, there was strong management emphasis on direct communication especially concerning the major redevelopment of the airport. Representatives had to ask for progress reports to be given to them as well as directly to staff. Management had hoped that council members would want to discuss strategic issues, although they did not put any on the agenda. One of the representatives appeared to have recognized this when she noted that the council 'does not discuss things on a grand scale but is concerned with little things that people are up in arms about'.

Case history—Failing to find a distinctive voice: regional airport

This small commercial airport, part of a larger airports group, had some 120 employees. It established a staff council in 2005, driven primarily by the need to develop more formalized employee involvement mechanisms in the context of the airport's application for Investors in People status and the emphasis placed on communications and consultation by the wider corporate group. The influence of the ICE regulations was peripheral. The staff council operated alongside a range of direct communications mechanisms. These included weekly departmental/team meetings, a monthly group briefing cascading down through different levels of the organization, and a tradition of periodic 'road shows' in each department by the managing director or other senior management figures covering 'big picture' issues. In addition, in 2007, following an application under the statutory trade union recognition provisions, the company recognized a trade union for collective bargaining purposes in respect of air traffic control and engineering staff. This was followed in 2008 by recognition of a second union for fire service crews and the further recognition of the original union for other groups of workers.

Constitutionally, the staff council was a 'hybrid' body comprising employee and trade union representatives from across the business. There were staff representatives from each department, irrespective of union membership, plus a union representative from air traffic control, but no one was designated as formally representing the subsequently recognized second union on the staff council. Management participants were senior operations managers, the airport having no specialist HR staff on site. The manager responsible for engineering became a regular participant, in view of the number of facilities issues raised at council meetings. Staff representatives declined to fill the role of staff council chair, even though this was provided for by its constitution, and in practice meetings were chaired by senior management.

Most agenda items were raised by staff representatives. Reflecting the airport's ageing infrastructure and the technical/specialist nature of many airport employees' jobs, most staff-raised issues concerned facilities or operational issues. Staff benefits queries/suggestions were also raised but representatives generally regarded pay and conditions of employment as being outside the council's remit and as matters for the recognized unions. Management consulted the council, as well as the unions, on successive draft HR policies emanating from group level. The most significant organizational change at the airport—a major redevelopment—was the subject of direct communications initiatives aimed at all staff and featured on the staff council's agenda only to a limited extent. Although the development plan was initially discussed with the council, representatives felt that there had been few updates about subsequent modifications. The relative absence of information from management on the redevelopment project was raised by staff representatives at one council meeting. Management's response was that little information could be communicated pending finalization of redesigned plans but that staff would be briefed directly at that stage. A 'project update' subsequently became a regular item on the council's agenda, but direct mechanisms remained the primary means of communicating with staff on this issue.

While there was little independent networking activity between representatives (e.g. no employee-only preparatory meetings were held), there was a strong emphasis by both management and representatives on effective reporting back to their constituencies. In some parts of the business, staff representatives were given slots in team or departmental meetings to report back to staff on council meetings, though in some departments this was constrained by shift patterns. Issues discussed at the staff council were also sometimes covered in monthly team briefings.

By the end of the research, there was recognition by senior management and, less explicitly, staff representatives that a review of the role and effectiveness of the staff council had become necessary. Management's original intentions for the council, as set out in its constitution, had envisaged a more wide-ranging remit including company performance issues. However, the council's role had been 'squeezed' by management's preference for using direct means of communication with staff to address major airport developments and other issues and the subsequent recognition of two unions on behalf of the majority of airport staff, taking pay and terms and conditions issues firmly outside its remit. This, and the reliance on staff-raised issues to drive the council's agenda, resulted in its increasingly narrow focus, primarily on facilities issues, to the professed disappointment of senior managers who hoped that staff representatives could be encouraged to become more 'proactive'.

The staff council at the *hospice* started well enough with an innovative approach suggested by the HR manager of forming working parties to look at contentious issues. Once these had reported, the council was starved of agenda items as senior management was reluctant to take matters to the council or report on financial and business results. A re-issued and revised constitution which clearly specified that these matters could be the subject of information and consultation appeared to have been ignored by senior management and representatives lacked the confidence to ask about them. Innovations in direct forms of communication, especially a middle management meeting, meant, in the words of the lead employee representative, that the council was 'outside the normal communications channels' and was unable to find a distinctive voice. Management still were committed to the idea of consultation as a communication bridge with staff especially if and when a major change occurred.

Case history—Crowded out and largely irrelevant: the staff council at hospice

The hospice's 160 employees provided palliative care in an urban setting. A consultative forum was established in 1997 but it got bogged down in housekeeping and grievance matters with no items brought to meetings by senior management. The need to consult over pay re-grading (no unions were recognized) and the passing of the ICE regulations led to a revamped staff council being established in 2007. There were four constituencies with three representatives from each, but getting nurses, the largest occupational group, to be active was difficult. Training was provided by Advisory, Conciliation and Arbitration Service (Acas) on two occasions. The chairman of the staff council was an employee representative. Two senior managers attended and the chief executive came to some meetings.

Initially, the council was successful. The HR manager suggested they should break into working groups to explore issues in some depth such as a smoking ban, car parking space, and environmental issues, reporting back to a full meeting of the council. However, in subsequent years the council struggled to find a distinctive role and it proved hard to get people to stand as representatives. As the HR manager observed, 'no one has ever put themselves forward to be a representative so it is obviously not serving the purpose it was set up to do'. Both she and the senior staff representative said that keeping the council going was like 'flogging a dead horse' and that people had to be 'press-ganged' to become representatives. In 2008, at least one meeting was declared inquorate and minutes were not available for another.

Four interconnected reasons were indentified to explain this malaise. First, no major changes in business strategies were required during the two years we were studying the council. The hospice continued to grow slowly and was financially secure. The changes that were introduced were internal matters concerning accommodation, a reorganization of the top management team and the drafting of a three-year strategic plan. These were announced directly to staff with the council excluded, largely as an oversight, according to the HR manager after a representative had asked at a council meeting why they were not asked to contribute. Second, despite changing and re-issuing the constitution of the council, which listed business topics to be discussed, senior management put few items on the agenda and when they did it was only after plans had been finalized. There was no provision for information to be provided on a confidential basis. There was a view that senior managers did not want 'to let go of things' and 'had to cross the Ts and dot the Is' before presenting plans to the council.

Third, substantial management effort had gone into improving internal communications through team briefings, newsletters, and notice boards and a six-weekly meeting held for all middle managers. Three of the eight council representatives were middle managers. Senior management used this meeting to communicate and debate issues for subsequent communication to staff via team briefings, rather than take them to the council. The senior employee representative observed that 'the problem with the staff council is that it is outside the normal communication channels'. It was crowded out and had found nothing distinctive to contribute.

Fourth, the employee representatives did not hold pre-meetings and often did not talk with each other outside the formal meetings. There were complaints that some representatives did not speak with their constituents either before or after meetings especially if they did not work in the same part of the building. Despite training provided by Acas, representatives were unclear on their role. Efforts by the chairman of the council to filter items and eradicate minor issues only relevant to one department had only limited success. Individual representatives still raised seemingly parochial and trivial matters at meetings on the grounds that this was what their constituents asked them to do.

Despite these difficulties and a pervasive feeling that staff would not be bothered if the council failed, senior management made renewed efforts to revitalize it. A new chairman was elected and there was talk of recognizing the work of representatives in performance appraisals. The CEO remained convinced that the council could play 'a transformative role', for example in running focus groups of staff in dealing with major changes.

Failed consultation: a staff council that became defunct

The short and sad life of some consultative committees has been a constant experience since consultation bodies were first set up. Many of the reasons have been alluded to in previous chapters and it was clear in the case of the hospice that the staff council was not operating effectively. But in that case, management were still committed to the principle of consultation and were thinking of new ways to revive it. This did not apply in the case of the *electronics* manufacturing company. Here the council had a rather elaborate constitution and remit, using the default provisions in the ICE regulations as a guide, but the practice of consultation never became embedded. Senior managers had always emphasized direct forms of communication and continued to do so rather than take issues in advance to the staff council. They also did not like representatives raising housekeeping matters so that there was confusion over the purpose of the staff council. The HR manager thought that the council would, in effect, look after itself, needing 'minimum supervision'. Training did not take place and no pre-meetings for representatives were held. Eventually, management lost interest and called no further meetings. Employee representatives, too, were frustrated at the council's ineffectiveness and did not contest management's decision to let the council lapse. In any event, they had no legal means to respond since the council was set up as a PEA.

Case history—A short-lived experiment in collective consultation: electronics company

The electronics company manufactured remote tyre pressure monitoring systems for the automotive industry at two UK plants. It was a wholly-owned subsidiary of a UK-headquartered engineering multinational but operated as part of a US-based corporate group. The company was non-union. Having experienced rapid growth, the workforce stood at 825 in November 2008, by which point the company had begun not replacing employees who left. Its staff council, set up in January 2005, ceased meeting after only two years in existence and became defunct.

The staff council was an HR-driven initiative, motivated primarily by the need to develop more formalized employee involvement mechanisms in the light of workforce expansion. The company had outgrown the managing director's traditional practice of holding workforce-wide canteen meetings about company developments and performance issues, although a strong management emphasis on direct communications via departmental or team meetings continued. As well as being shaped by the provisions of the ICE regulations, the introduction of the staff council to provide a representative channel for putting employee views to management dovetailed with the company's desire to maintain its non-union status despite an influx of new employees from unionized backgrounds and indications of union recruitment activity.

The nature of the discussion at the staff council was much less formal than implied by the terms of its constitution. Initially, its largely management-driven agenda had centred on issues such as the company's expansion plans, the impact of cancelled orders, and delays in planned increases in production. Discussion did not result in any modification of the company's established approaches to these issues. Employee representatives expressed uncertainty about the role they were expected to play (e.g. in terms of generating agenda items, some of which were rejected by management as falling outside the staff council's 'strategic' remit). They undertook no independent networking between council meetings, nor did they hold employee-only preparatory meetings despite the formal constitutional provision permitting these. Representatives were not provided with training to undertake their role, though perceptions varied between management and representatives as to why this failed to materialize.

Subsequently, strategic announcements such as plans to acquire a production facility abroad were announced through management presentations to work groups and discussed with the staff council only later. The eventual decision to buy a plant in the United States was also announced directly to the workforce and not handled via the staff council. By this stage, both management and employee representatives regarded the council as ineffective and it did not meet again.

Management argued that employee representatives made little input and should have been more proactive, taking greater 'ownership' of the council, whereas representatives interviewed felt that they were insufficiently 'empowered' to do so and complained that management controlled the council's agenda. Management eventually concluded that the staff council had not functioned as originally intended and offered no real benefit to the company over and above existing communications mechanisms.

The absence of a shared understanding between management and employee representatives of the role and remit of the staff council, and management's preference for making major announcements directly to the workforce, contributed to management's decision to let the council lapse. In the HR manager's assessment, the staff council proved to be 'a poor fit culturally'. Moreover, although managers accepted that 'there were things we could have done differently', the discontinuation of the council prompted 'no reaction from the shop floor [which] says a great deal. We didn't get buy-in from the employees'.

Conclusion

The distinction between 'active consulters' and 'communicators', with the added category of collapsed or defunct staff councils, builds on much previous research ever since consultation began over 100 years ago. Dundon et al. (2006: 497) categorize consultative bodies as either 'robust' or 'shallow' with the criteria for 'robust' being the 'longevity of the mechanisms for voice as well as the depth of their potential influence'. Our four case histories of active consultation meet these criteria. Although the staff council in IT services had only just begun, it was built on—and crucially had learnt from the problems of—the previous employee forum.

This evolution and learning was clear in the case histories of the active consulters. Developing competence is best seen as a process of experiential learning by *both* the representatives and managers involved. A crucial ingredient is the generation of trust which builds over time. The first step in trust is a willingness to take the risk of sharing information on a confidential basis and a preparedness on the part of senior managers to discuss policy and strategic issues. This was most evident in the case of the mobile phone company and was emerging in the IT services company, for example in the use of special meetings. In the case of the diversified technology's Welsh factory, pre-existing high levels of trust allowed much further cooperation to save the plant. They went further along the cooperative path than either the staff council and union, or the management, envisaged at the outset.

This learning process was just as necessary for managers as it was for representatives. It is nearly always the case that managers, who have taken part in active consultation, or union–management partnerships, are much more positive than those with no experience whose prejudice remains unchallenged. Wills (1999, quoted in Hall and Marginson, 2005: 212) found that managers in companies in Britain that had established EWCs had a much more positive view about the role of EWCs than those in companies without them. This experience helps build an understanding of the work of employee representatives and what is needed to create an effective employee body. It was notable in each of the cases of active consultation how management helped by providing facilities, time off, and access to company media, and encouraged informal contacts with the representatives, especially the senior representative. This support was crucial to enable the representatives to create an autonomous, or semi-autonomous, body and a degree of self-determination. In the regional charity this had to be fought for before being accepted by the CEO. But even here management recognized that it needed a competent 'partner' in the consultation process and not merely a focus group or 'nodding heads'. In the IT services company, considerable attention was devoted to building an effective employee body and putting in place the means by which it could be sustained, for example the weekly conference call for representatives and the day-long pre-meetings.

The most obvious feature of the 'active consulters', in sharp contrast with the 'communicators', was the preparedness of senior management to take big business issues to the staff council and discuss them before a final decision had been announced. In return, there needed to be a reasonably effective employee body able to respond. The one creates the other. It helped that there were important matters to discuss which impacted on work organization and employment. In some cases of redundancy and business transfers, legislation required consultation and the ICE regulations' default provisions specified these types of business decisions as being the proper subject of collective dialogue. In the much smaller regional charity, it was a long run of difficult trading conditions which led to an almost continuous need for staff to adapt. The maturing of the staff council was part of an effort to improve the management of change among the professional staff. It was also the case that union pressure in the mobile phone company and the IT services company led managements to want to show that a union was unnecessary as the staff council was equally effective, confirming Taras and Kaufman's assertion (1999: iii) that 'non-union systems operate best when they exist in the shadow of a viable union threat'.

One of the principle reasons why some staff councils, especially non-union ones, fail to develop an active role is the unwillingness of management to step back from unilateral decision-making and place proposals for change on the staff councils' agenda. This was the case in the three 'communicator' case histories as well as the defunct body in the electronics company. This, however, did not appear to derive from a considered decision to restrict influence but from a perception that the proper purpose of consultation is to listen and respond to the views of staff with the aim of improving communications and, in so doing, to help build staff engagement. This, of course, is at odds with the view 'that the fundamental point of employee participation is to shape *employer* rather than employee attitudes and behaviour' (Hall and Terry, 2004: 216).

The unanticipated consequence of this focus on the upward communication of staff concerns was that staff councils got bogged down in small-scale housekeeping matters much to the frustration of both managers and representatives with the latter sometimes resigning and the company finding it difficult to get replacements. Despite this, senior management remained committed to the idea of consultation and tried to revive it, while still giving strong emphasis to direct communication to the workforce. Efforts to rebuild staff councils usually involved refresher training, searching for ways to filter out the 'tea and toilets' from the agenda and taking more significant items to meetings, usually HR policy matters such as absence or training. It was these types of issue that were seen to be more directly relevant to employees than big strategy questions.

A final conclusion to be drawn from these case histories may be that little has changed in the conduct or scope of consultation despite the implementation of the ICE regulations. Does this mean that consultation will limp on as a neglected feature of British employment relations with islands of good practice in a sea of ambivalence or can, and should, consultative practice be adopted more widely especially in large parts of the private sector where there are no trade unions and no avenues for collective voice? This is considered in the next, and final, chapter.

Note

1. IT services was not part of the original sample of organizations for the main research project. Research was undertaken in spring 2011 with interviews with two managers and the chair of the employee representatives.

8

The Future of Consultation

Consultation has been a feature of UK employment relations for well over 100 years. The paradox is that while it is often seen as a means of creating cooperative and constructive relationships between management and employees, through their representatives, and smoothing the introduction of change—classic 'win-win' outcomes—in practice employers are, for the most part, lukewarm and trade unions ambivalent. This, and the reluctance of governments to regulate consultative practice, has been a regular feature of the largely unhappy history of consultation in the United Kingdom (Chapter 1). Part of the difficulty has been the ambiguity, if not confusion, over the purpose of consultation whether as a means of improving organization performance, as a form of power-sharing, or as an employment right in its own terms (Chapter 2). Regulatory initiatives have been timid. The early ambitions of EU policy makers to harmonize best practice gave way to a minimum standards approach leaving wide scope for flexible application (Chapter 3). Successive UK governments of both major parties resisted EU initiatives and opted for minimal compliance with the EU directives eventually adopted (Chapter 4). Yet by 2008, all undertakings with at least fifty employees were covered by the Information and Consultation of Employees (ICE) Regulations giving employees the legal right to information and consultation on important business, employment, and restructuring developments. The early indications (Chapter 5) were that the advent of the regulations prompted considerable voluntary activity in terms of the introduction, modification, or revival of information and consultation arrangements. The actual extent of this will be measured by the next WERS (Workplace Employment Relations Survey), but it is clear that the process has been largely employer led. Unions' and employees' lack of engagement with the statutory procedures has left wide scope for management unilateralism. The small number of references to the Central Arbitration Committee (CAC), and the findings from our own research, indicate that the regulations' direct influence on the introduction and operation of information and consultation arrangements has been peripheral. Nevertheless, Chapter 6 identified the key behaviours or practices underpinning effective, or active, consultation of the type envisaged by the default provisions of the EU directive and ICE regulations. Chapter 7 used case histories of staff councils in a range of organizations to show how the interaction of such factors determined the character of the consultative process, and the survival, or not, of the consultative committees, and whether the organizations were 'active consulters' or 'communicators'.

In this final chapter (Chapter 8), we ask whether there is scope to improve the take-up and practice of consultation. Does it matter that consultation is not widely practised, at least in its active form, as envisaged by the EU directives and subsequent UK regulations? Does the experience of consultation elsewhere in Europe offer clues to what might be achieved in Britain? What sort of revisions could be made to the ICE regulations to improve the practice of consultation? Taking account of these factors, we end by arguing that there are strong grounds to seeing consultation through staff councils as the last chance for collectivism in a period of relative union weakness and when collective bargaining has become a minority activity especially in the private sector.

Why consultation is important

For much of the twentieth century, consultation was the poor cousin of collective bargaining and the analysis of it often drew unflattering comparisons with strong trade unions bargaining with employers to regulate jobs and determine the economic exchange between effort and reward. Trade unions at that time were central, too, to the efforts of governments to regulate employment relations. Strikes and other forms of conflict expression, including employers' lock-outs, lay behind much of industrial relations whether as a threat or a practice. Not much progress could be made in the theory and practice of industrial relations without an appreciation of power: its sources and forms of expression. Goddard (2011: 299), in his analysis of the substantial decline in strike activity, has suggested that 'it is quite possible that we are at a historical turning point, where the collective manifestations of conflict can be expected to not just return, but to change as well'. Behind this is the flight from collective bargaining and the substantial fall in trade union membership. In 2010, just 16.8 per cent of private sector employees had their terms and conditions fixed through collective bargaining, a drop of 6.7 per cent in ten years. The fall in coverage, at 9.3 per cent, was even higher in the public sector, but even so, two-thirds of employees in that sector remain covered by collective bargaining (Achurn, 2011: 2). Less than a quarter of people in employment now are trade union members, with the density of membership in the private sector down to 14.2 per cent, a decline of 7.2 per cent since 1995. Membership density in the public sector remains just above half (56.3 per cent) but here, too, there has been a 5 per cent decline in fifteen years (ibid.: 1). Most of the working population in employment, who are not union members, have no access to union representation at work. There is little evidence that union recognition legislation and new forms of organizing have made much impact (Wright, 2011). There is a large, and growing, representation gap which trade unions find it increasingly hard to fill. The historical turning point is not just about strikes. It is about the understandable decline in trade unions such that they can no longer claim to be the only channel of communication—or workers' voice, to use modern parlance—between management and employees.

The representation gap is important. Employees want an effective voice at work and in particular want this to be non-confrontational, working cooperatively with management (Freeman et al., 2007: 216–19). While direct forms of involvement through workplace meetings, team briefings, problem solving groups, and, to a much lesser extent, employee attitude surveys can provide some avenues for worker voice, and are very widespread, they do not constitute an institutional basis for dialogue with senior managers on strategic matters and HR policy initiatives. This is where staff councils can help bridge the representation gap. Over half of workplaces (53 per cent) with between fifty and ninety-nine employees had, in 2004, such a committee on site, or at a higher level in multi-site companies. The probability of there being a staff council increased with the size of the establishment. Only 18 per cent of workplaces with 500 or more employees did not have a staff council. What was particularly interesting was that two-thirds of these consultative committees were non-union and only 11 per cent organized exclusively by the recognized union. Around one in five (22 per cent) were 'hybrids' with a mixture of union and non-union representatives working together (Kersley et al., 2006: table 5.6, 131). The incidence of 'hybrid' staff councils is much higher, at 52 per cent, in those workplaces which had a union representative on site.

This search for effective 'voice' is not just to meet the needs of employees, although that is important. We know that the experience of involvement is closely associated with positive worker evaluations of management responsiveness (Bryson et al., 2006: 448–9). This feeds through into productivity. The greater the range of voice systems used the more likely it was that managers reported benefits from increased output to declining absenteeism (Sisson, 2000). Voice systems which combine 'embedded' direct forms of involvement, seen in briefing systems and problem solving groups, with indirect voice via representative bodies, such as trade unions and staff councils, have better performance outcomes than single channels (Purcell and Geogiadis,

2007). The need for such discussions to be held in a spirit of cooperation, as favoured by employees, is reinforced by analysis of the recent European Company Survey which found that firms where managers and employee representatives made 'sincere efforts to solve common problems' had higher than average productivity and experienced increases in productivity. These firms also had, unsurprisingly, a good work climate (Cox et al., 2011: 44–5).

The case for consultation is not that it is a replacement for collective bargaining. It performs a different function and is less dependent on the exercise of power, relying on trust and cooperation, a willingness of senior managers to discuss proposed measures in time to allow employees to express their views and exert some influence, and the creation of an integrated employee 'side'. It can provide an effective representation of employee interests and meet the desire for cooperative working. As we have discussed in earlier chapters, there needs to be 'meaty' issues to deal with where senior managers are grappling with difficult choices and looking for the best means of implementation. The agenda can be too bland when very little, beyond the usual small beer of organizational life, is taking place, and consultation can be overwhelmed when calamity strikes. In the current age of austerity, 'business as usual' is an unlikely option for many organizations. There is a real need for effective consultation, and an appetite for it from employees whose biggest complaint, according to the 2011 CIPD (Chartered Institute of Personnel and Development) representative survey of employees, is the lack of consultation by their 'leaders' regarding important decisions (CIPD, 2011: 6).

Regulating consultation—a story of missed opportunities

It is one thing to assert the need for consultation but quite another to make consultation effective. We have drawn a distinction, based on extensive research, between 'active consulters' and 'communicators'. The crucial difference is the approach of management. In active consultation, management takes a proactive approach, being willing to discuss proposed decisions and implementation plans in advance, allowing employee representatives time to review the information, work through the implications, and discuss them. Representatives can also raise issues of concern. The 'communicators', who constituted the majority of our case study organizations, and probably do so more widely, are led by senior managers who have a different conception of consultation. They want to hear employee views and are open to questions but only once the decision has been taken and implementation plans put in place. They view the staff council as a communication bridge between them and employees with the representatives passing down information and collecting responses. It is hard for their representatives to do this effectively as it is rare for them to meet among themselves to work out a response, and they can come to be seen as management lackeys doing management's bidding without any capacity to influence. In practice, what often happens is that management do not put important items on the agenda, representatives raise often trivial housekeeping matters, and many find the role unfulfilling and step down. Replacements are usually hard to find.

When the staff councils were set up it was common to find that the avowed purpose was to improve communications, help with the management of change, and build employee engagement (Hall et al., 2007: 16–23). The difference between the 'active consulters' and the 'communicators' was how consultation was to be used to contribute to these aims. Is good management just the sharing of information about decisions and being open, or should it be more focussed on achieving consent by tapping into employee views and operational expertise and using the outcome of the consultation to help gain employee commitment to the subsequent decision? The way the ICE regulations were designed meant they provided virtually no advice or instruction on what form consultation should take, except in the standard, or default, provisions—and even here their provisions offer little guidance as to actual practice. The regulations are largely peripheral to management intentions and plans. In contrast, the legislation requiring consultation on large-scale redundancies is widely respected and the penalties for non-compliance are sufficiently strong to achieve this.

The lack of leadership at the national level from employer representatives and union leaders has compounded the confusion on the purpose of consultation, and successive governments have opted, time and again, to delay and weaken EU legislative proposals rather than use them to create a vibrant system of consultation. The social partners at national level, as we showed in Chapter 4, saw proposals for consultation not in terms of potential benefits but through the defensive lens of their own interests. Neither the employers nor the unions at national level were opposed to the practice of consultation; indeed, they often expressed support for it, but not if the implementation of the EU directive compromised what were, to them, more important principles. The Confederation of British Industry (CBI) had tactically proposed a modified works council system at the time of the Bullock report but, with the election of the Thatcher government, retreated to a position of opposition in principle, which it maintains to this day. The principle was, and is, objection to legislation while encouraging company management to develop consultation arrangements on a voluntary basis designed to suit their own preferences. The Trades Union Congress (TUC) similarly flirted with statutory works councils in the 1990s but these never became official policy. The unions retreated to the defence of the 'single channel' found in the declining number of workplaces where they were established and sought recognition elsewhere, but not with much success. The government's primary concern was the 'minimalist' implementation of the EU directive rather than the effective promotion of active consultation. The legislative design chosen took a different path from that adopted by most other EU member states by excluding any direct role for recognized unions in the statutory procedures or guaranteed union participation in consultation, unlike in the collective redundancy and transfer of undertakings consultation provisions. This had the effect of reinforcing union scepticism and gave employers a largely free hand. Labour governments were reluctant to act in the absence of consensus between the CBI and the TUC. It is a sad tale of missed opportunities and fudged outcomes.

What lessons can be learnt from consultation practices in other countries?

> 'Look how much better the Lilliputians do it' is a tempting cry, but the more one looks into it the more one finds that the Lilliputians aren't a fair comparison with us: they haven't got our antiquated industries [or] our legal system, and they are less than six inches tall. (Kahn-Freund and Hepple, 1972: 1)

It is very hard, and often misleading, to make international comparisons on the operation of seemingly similar institutions and practices. Frege and Goddard (2010: 533) observed in their attempts at comparisons that 'cross-national variations in representational rights reflect deeply embedded historical trajectories . . . and deeply held institutional norms that can be traced to formative economic, social and political discourses around them'. Variations can be traced to broad social and economic movements concerning varieties of capitalism (Hall and Soskice, 2001), to different conceptions of the role of law in regulating participatory practices (Heller et al., 1998: 167), or to different historical trajectories especially concerning the role of unions and the changing location of collective bargaining (Gumbrell-McCormick and Hyman, 2006: 488).

One seemingly obvious comparison that can be made concerns the role of law. 'Regulatory rules and laws encourage or force certain behaviours that would otherwise have not taken place' (Gollan: 2010: 221). The crucial distinction is between *de jure* and *de facto* participation. Summarizing a major longitudinal study in twelve countries, Heller and his colleagues (1998: 49–50) concluded that 'the intensity of prescribed participation proved the strongest predictor of *de facto* participation'. This led them to conclude that 'participation is to a significant extent the result of socio-political will' (ibid.). Our conclusion in previous paragraphs was that this 'socio-political will' has been marked by its absence in Britain and this can explain, in part at least, the patchy state of consultation in the United Kingdom.

The EU directive, on which the ICE regulations were based, applies to all EU member states and to the other European countries that belong to the European Economic Area (EEA) (i.e. are part of the single market). Not surprisingly, its impact has varied considerably between EU/EEA member states, reflecting the differing nature and extent of their existing information and consultation provisions and the diverse industrial relations systems within which they are embedded (Carley and Hall, 2008; Hall and Purcell, 2011).

A number of countries, particularly those with 'mature', long-standing works council or trade union-based systems of workplace representation, were largely unaffected by the adoption of the directive. This group includes Austria, Belgium, France, Germany, Italy, and the Netherlands. It also includes Denmark, Norway, and Sweden, whose information and consultation arrangements are based largely on centralized collective agreements and trade union representation. Despite legal changes being required in a number of cases, information and consultation practice in these countries cannot be said to have been significantly shaped by implementation of the directive.

Its impact elsewhere has been much more far-reaching. At the time the directive was adopted—by the pre-enlargement EU 15—the countries for which it had the most significant implications in terms of driving regulatory reform were the United Kingdom and Ireland with their 'voluntarist' industrial relations traditions. However, with the accession of ten new member states in 2004, a number of them in central eastern Europe and most having traditionally relied on trade union-based systems of workplace representation, the directive's potential impact became much wider. (Indeed, it is arguable that, had they been party to the legislative process, some new member states might well have had considerable sympathy with UK concerns about the case for regulation.)

Any analysis of the impact of the directive and of existing patterns of consultation must distinguish between these groups of countries. We look first at the nations with mature consultative practices, paying particular attention to Germany, for years the bellwether of effective consultation via its system of works councils, and then at those countries where the directive has required more extensive regulatory and institutional adaptation.

Countries with long-established consultation arrangements: the example of Germany

The countries with mature systems of consultation have works council arrangements, each with their own idiosyncrasies, which often date back for sixty or more years. Similarly, in the Nordic countries, long-established arrangements are based on centralized, or inter-sectoral, collective agreements and trade union representation. In one sense the directive was irrelevant since all the necessary ingredients were in place, but of greater importance is 'a strong cultural acceptance of the value of partnership and participation' (Hall and Purcell, 2011: 29).

Works councils in Germany have, for many years, been held up as exemplars of workers' participation: 'the most prominent, widespread and powerful form of industrial democracy' (Frege, 2002: 221). At the time when the EU began to consider legislation to extend works councils to all member states, the German and the Dutch works council systems were seen as the benchmark. The level playing field was to be achieved by upgrading arrangements elsewhere to meet this standard. As we saw in Chapter 3, this optimism did not last long. It is instructive to look briefly at the German system if only to explore what makes it relatively successful through a combination of factors which do not, and could not, apply in the United Kingdom. The historical antecedents, or path dependency, of the German system are very different. They are a combination of long-standing, and more prescriptive, laws establishing works councils, first in 1920, then in 1952 and subsequently amended, multi-employer collective bargaining at sectoral levels, and, despite initial opposition, with strong support from trade unions.

Works councils are not mandatory in establishments with five or more workers, but they are much easier to set up than British consultation bodies under the ICE regulations. A trade union with members in the establishment, or three employees, can call for elections to a works council if the employer has failed to initiate one, and can complain to a labour court if needs be (Hyman, 1996: 70). The works council is composed of directly elected employee representatives who meet appropriate managers on a regular basis. While the law specifies a requirement 'to work together in trustful cooperation in the interests of employees and the firm', works councils have significant powers. The type of information that must be provided and the topics for consultation are clearly specified, unlike in Britain. More significantly, certain matters such as pay/skill categories, working time, quality control, recruitment, and dismissals are subject to codetermination. This means that an agreement has to be reached on management's proposals, although the employer can seek to overturn a veto in the courts. This means that the great majority of works councils have formal workplace agreements on these matters (Müller-Jentsch and Seitz, 1998, cited in Frege, 2002). Works councils 'wield considerable ability to restrain managements' autonomous ability to hire and fire' and 'can make life well-nigh intolerable for a management that insists too arrogantly on its own formal rights' (Hyman, 1996: 71–2).

Union support is crucial in establishing the works councils and in providing external advice and support 'often to the displeasure of employers' (Rigby et al., 2009, see also Gumbrell-McCormick and Hyman, 2006). Traditionally, collective bargaining by trade unions has been with employers' associations outside the workplace covering sectors and regions. This gives the works councils a clear hand in dealing with workforce issues in the establishment. In practice, the strong connections between works councils and trade unions and the clear union role in advice and training means that there is a strong union influence. External union representatives can take part in meetings of the works council if a quarter of the members request it (Goerke and Pannenberg, 2007).

The conduct and effects of works councils vary, as would be expected. Kotthoff (1994, cited in Frege, 2002: 226–7) found that only a fifth of the works councils he studied were 'respected as an autonomous interest representative' with the remainder being, to varying degrees, more dependent on management. There are many claims of positive outcomes including promoting innovation (Allen and Funk, 2008) where works councils were 'increasingly being included as "co-managers" in decisions in new areas such as technological change and organizational restructuring' (Frege, 2002: 232–3). In a comparative study of call centres in Germany and the United States, Doellgast (2010: 390) found that in Germany 'unions and works councils use their stronger participation rights to encourage management to adopt a high-involvement approach to work organisation and performance management'. American union-based workplace-level consultation committees were unable to achieve this. Part of the outcome effects is promoting employment growth (Jirjahn, 2010).

The German works council system continues to evolve. A growing trend has been for a decentralization of bargaining to establishment and enterprise levels involving works councils and this has increased their role, especially in manufacturing, in dealing with work organization changes. There is some evidence that workers are more likely to request a council in these circumstances especially when the establishment is facing difficulties or crisis (Jirjahn, 2010). Getting involved in these more advanced types of consultation tends to increase the professionalism of both the managers and representatives involved through a mutual learning process (Gumbrell-McCormick and Hyman, 2006: 77–8).

Works councils are by no means widespread in Germany, especially in the old East Germany. As in Britain, it is the service sector, new firms, and small enterprises that are least likely to have a works council. One of the key contextual changes has been the rapid collapse of trade union membership. Membership density is now around 20 per cent and lower even than in the United Kingdom. The dominant union federation, the Confederation of

German Trade Unions (DGB), has lost almost half of its membership (48 per cent) since 1991. Since the union role in work councils is so important, this is likely to have a profound effect. For example, the proportion of works councillors who are union members has fallen from two-thirds (68 per cent) in 2001 to between 50 and 57 per cent in 2010 (Stettes, 2011). This still means, however, that works councillors are much more likely to be union members than their constituents and continues to point to the way unions can serve a non-union workforce. But it also implies that a future challenge will be to continue the works council movement in workplaces with few or no union members.

Responses to the directive elsewhere in the EU

In a second group of countries, statutory information and consultation systems are more recent, having been introduced ahead of EU accession or in direct response to the directive. This group includes many of the newer EU member states, including countries in central eastern Europe (though works council-type arrangements have existed in Hungary and Slovenia since the 1990s—Tóth, 1997; Stanojević, 2003), as well as the United Kingdom and Ireland. Broadly speaking, in most of these countries the directive prompted reforms to existing information and consultation legislation and, in some cases, the introduction of a comprehensive statutory framework for the first time.

As we saw in Chapter 3, the directive established only a 'general framework' for informing and consulting employees and allowed member states considerable flexibility regarding the practical arrangements for implementing its provisions. Most notably, member states had the discretion to make the establishment of information and consultation arrangements dependent on employee or trade union initiative and to enable agreement-based derogation from the information and consultation provisions of the directive. These flexibilities are widely reflected in the national legislation adopted by the newer member states as well as the United Kingdom and Ireland (Hall and Purcell, 2011).

For example, while in some countries with mature works council systems (though not Germany), information and consultation bodies are technically mandatory, in many of the newer member states their establishment requires trade unions or employees to take prescribed steps to initiate them. In contrast to the United Kingdom and Ireland, however, information and consultation bodies, where they exist, are typically established at the behest of trade unions, and only rarely by employers. In countries enabling specific proportions of employees to initiate such arrangements (including Bulgaria, Estonia, Poland, and Portugal, alongside Ireland and the United Kingdom), there is little indication of the widespread uptake of information and consultation via this route.

A key factor affecting the take-up of information and consultation arrangements among most of these countries is that workplace representation has traditionally been via trade unions. Unions remain the primary designated vehicle for employees' statutory information and consultation rights in a number of countries. In the Czech Republic and Lithuania, employee/works councils may only exist in undertakings without a trade union presence, and a similar rule applied in Slovakia until 2003. Nevertheless, implementation of the directive has created the scope for greater institutional diversity in terms of the types of employee representatives designated as the channel for statutory information and consultation and, in some countries, the creation of a secondary, works council-type channel of employee representation alongside trade unions. Consequently, in some of these countries, echoing the United Kingdom's experience, there has been some reluctance on the part of trade unions to engage with the national information and consultation legislation driven by the directive, for fear of undermining their own representational role and influence. But this has begun to diminish in Poland, where unions have begun to view works councils as 'potentially useful as an institution providing more extensive rights to information', and supportive union attitudes towards information and consultation procedures are reported in Estonia, Lithuania, Slovakia, and Slovenia (Hall and Purcell, 2011). Growing support is apparent among employer bodies too for implementing information and consultation arrangements, in some cases overcoming earlier scepticism.

In terms of the scope for agreement-based information and consultation provision, it is notable that most of the countries with newer legal frameworks enable company-level agreements to supplement the statutory requirements. This contrasts with the position in countries with mature systems which tend to rely principally on statutory regulation or, in the Nordic countries, central collective agreements to determine the constitutional provisions governing information and consultation arrangements. In the Czech Republic, most company-level collective agreements include provisions on information (69 per cent) and consultation (60 per cent) but the proportion going beyond the statutory requirements is lower (22 and 12 per cent respectively). In Poland, organization-specific agreements regulating issues left open by the law are reported in 36 per cent of enterprises with works councils. In Hungary too, such agreements are reported to be important for the effective operation of works councils.

A crucial point is that, in most countries, company-level agreements may only elaborate on, not derogate from, the minimum 'floor' of employee rights provided by law: the United Kingdom and Ireland are the principal exceptions to this approach. Similarly, the United Kingdom is unusual in exempting company-level pre-existing agreements (PEAs) from the ICE regulations' enforcement procedures. Elsewhere in the EU, enforcement of agreement-based ICE provisions is typically via complaints to a labour inspectorate or labour court on the basis of national legislation on information and consultation or on the application of collective agreements (Hall and Purcell, 2011).

Little systematic data is available on the practice, subject matter, and outcomes of information and consultation in the countries with newer legislative frameworks, but the broad indications, reviewed by Hall and Purcell (2011), are that information provision is more prevalent than consultation, and that information and consultation tends to be less concerned with company strategy and performance issues than with work-related issues closer to employees' immediate concerns. Similarly, employee representatives are most likely to influence management decisions relating to work organization and working conditions rather than restructuring.

Lessons from European experience

What lessons can we draw from the operation of information and consultation legislation in Germany and elsewhere in continental Europe, while recognizing the differences in socio-political culture and practice? One broad conclusion from our recent comparative analysis is that the directive's flexible regulatory approach, coupled with the absence of active promotion of information and consultation by the social partners in a number of countries, appears to have limited its impact in driving the diffusion of information and consultation arrangements and in establishing clear standards for information and consultation practice (Hall and Purcell, 2011).

Legal regulation is necessary but not sufficient to ensure the spread of consultative practice. The crucial need is for a socio-political will both at national level and, more importantly, at the place of work in establishments and enterprises. Even supposedly mandatory requirements for information and consultation are ineffective without the active engagement of the parties. Nevertheless, it is a widely applied principle that, where allowed by national regulatory frameworks, agreement-based information and consultation provision should still respect minimum standards set by legislation. The United Kingdom and Ireland are among the few countries that do not stipulate this.

Trade unions can play an important role in the establishment and operation of consultative bodies and this is usually underpinned by the relevant national legislation, unlike in the United Kingdom. In a number of countries, unions, like their UK counterparts, are reluctant to seek the establishment of consultative arrangements for fear of losing influence and representational rights. This was true of the German unions at the start of the works councils in the 1950s but they adapted and now find works councils a crucial route for influence. There are signs of a similar change of heart in some central eastern European countries.

The incidence and coverage of information and consultation bodies falls well short of being comprehensive throughout Europe. Although the data available, reviewed by Hall and Purcell (2011), is patchy, it is apparent that the countries with a higher coverage of information and consultation bodies, particularly among larger enterprises, tend to be those with mature and embedded systems. There is a marked size effect in all countries: larger enterprises are much more likely to have an information and consultation body, whereas the non-implementation of information and consultation arrangements is particularly notable in small establishments or undertakings. This means that a sizable majority of employees work in companies with employee representatives engaging in consultation. There are no other collective voice systems, whether union or non-union, with anything like this coverage.

Finally, while the directive places emphasis on information provision and consultation on strategic business issues, in practice the most usual topics of consultation concern work organization and matters affecting employment and employment relations which have direct relevance to the workforce. Crucially, these include the implementation plans flowing from major business decisions.

Reforming the regulations: an agenda for promoting active consultation

In the light of the experience of the UK ICE regulations, and the impact of the directive and pre-existing national regimes in other EU/EEA countries, the focus of the final sections of this book is on exploring how the take-up and practice of consultation could be improved in the United Kingdom. One obvious starting point, given the importance of law in helping shape practice in this area, is to examine possible changes to the regulations themselves, and, if need be, to the directive. In Chapter 4 we identified a range of criticisms of the highly flexible, light-touch legislative design of the United Kingdom's ICE regulations. Chapter 5 reviewed the available evidence concerning the impact of the statutory provisions. This suggests only limited take-up by employees and unions of the rights and procedures established by the regulations. Instead, the apparently considerable voluntary activity prompted indirectly by the new legal framework—in terms of the introduction, modification, or revival of information and consultation arrangements—has been largely employer-led. The small number of references to the CAC, and the findings from our own research, similarly suggest that the regulations' direct influence on the introduction and operation of information and consultation arrangements has been peripheral. Arguably, key aspects of the regulations' provisions are acting as barriers to the legislation's effective implementation. In the light of these findings, what regulatory reforms can be proposed with the objective of more effectively promoting the type of active consultation envisaged by the directive's—and the regulations'—default provisions? We identify a number of key changes below. Ewing and Truter's comprehensive (2005) critique of the ICE regulations suggests others. Secondly, what are the prospects for such legislative changes in the current political and economic context at both national and EU level?

We have already argued that the required support of 10 per cent of the workforce to trigger statutory negotiations is a high hurdle to jump in order to secure what is supposed to be the fundamental, unconditional right to information and consultation (Ales, 2009). This is reflected in the low numbers of known cases in which employee-initiated negotiations have taken place. The ICE regulations, in contrast to the TICE regulations that implement the European Works Councils (EWCs) directive, do not provide that employee representatives may make the request on behalf of the required number of employees. Specifying a lower proportion of employees—the liberal think tank CentreForum recently suggested 5 per cent (Briône and Nicholson, 2012)—and enabling recognized unions and other existing (non-union) employee representatives to initiate statutory negotiations where they represent the required number of employees might be feasible reforms here. Without a more realistic possibility that employees can trigger the regulations' procedures, the prospect of the genuinely 'reflexive' implementation of the right to information and consultation remains remote and the initiative will continue to come from employers, if at all.

Recognized unions should also be formally integrated into the legal framework for information and consultation more generally. As well as enabling recognized unions to activate the regulations' statutory rights and enforcement procedures, the law should guarantee them a representative role in the event that the default standard information and consultation provisions become applicable, as is the case under the Irish legislation implementing the directive. This would mean enabling union-nominated representatives to represent those parts of the workforce covered by union recognition arrangements in the consultation body established, alongside elected representatives from elsewhere in the organization. It would entail reverting to a 'union priority' or 'supplemented single channel' approach instead of requiring all-employee ballots for the election of information and consultation representatives under the default provisions. The aim would be to reverse what two leading academic lawyers have described as 'an almost complete divorce between the rules on consultation and the rules and practices of collective bargaining' (Davies and Freedland, 2007: 156). Such an approach would be consistent with WERS findings as well as those of our own research that 'hybrid' union/non-union arrangements are the mainstream format for information and consultation in unionized organizations. An alternative approach would be to adopt the German practice of allowing trade unions openly to nominate candidates to stand in elections under the union banner and to campaign on their behalf. Interestingly, this did apply for a few years in Britain during the Second World War in joint production committees with the proviso that the candidate should be a union member.

A number of changes are needed to promote the type of active consultation envisaged by the directive's/regulations' default provisions. First, although allowed by the directive itself, it seems odd and inappropriate that agreement-based information and consultation provisions need not conform with the 'minimum requirements for the right to information and consultation' set out in Article 4 of the directive. These lay down the subject matter and basic requirements of the information and consultation process and are effectively 'copied out' by the ICE regulations' own default 'standard information and consultation provisions' (Regulation 20). Specifying that both PEAs and negotiated agreements cannot derogate from this minimum 'floor' of rights would be consistent with the approach of most other EU countries. It would still provide employers and employee representatives with substantial scope to agree organization-specific information and consultation arrangements but, in conjunction with stronger enforcement procedures, discussed below, would help avoid the limited and ineffectual information and consultation practices found in some of our case study organizations.

Second, the regulations should also be amended to include a basic constitution for a staff council, applicable in the event that the default standard information and consultation provisions become enforceable. This might be similar to the model included in Acas's guidance (2004), establishing elementary arrangements concerning its composition, role and remit, meeting arrangements, information and consultation procedures, election arrangements and facilities for representatives, and perform a similar function to the Trade Union Recognition (Method of Collective Bargaining) Order 2000 applicable in the context of the statutory trade union recognition procedure. Not only would this provide a workable template for operationalizing the default provisions, it could also prove to be an influential point of reference or benchmark for the provisions of PEAs and negotiated agreements, similar to the 'statutory model effect' identified by Gilman and Marginson (2002: 38) in their analysis of the content of EWC agreements, and contribute to avoiding sub-standard agreement-based information and consultation arrangements. Again, the Irish legislation provides more detailed default constitutional provisions than the United Kingdom's (currently highly minimalist) approach.

Third, there are strong arguments (see Ewing and Truter, 2005: 634–8) that the regulations' arrangements in respect of the enforcement of both the standard and agreement-based information and consultation provisions are inadequate. The CAC may order employers found to have breached the terms of a negotiated agreement or the standard provisions to take such steps as are necessary to ensure compliance, but the CAC's powers do not extend to suspending the implementation of employer decisions taken in breach of the duty to inform and consult. A financial penalty, payable to the Treasury and not to employees as compensation, is the only available means of redress and, with an upper limit of £75,000, is widely seen as being an inadequate sanction, especially in the case of large organizations. It would seem to be at odds with directive's requirement that sanctions must be 'effective, proportionate and dissuasive'. Koukiadaki (2009: 413) suggests an increase in the level of financial sanctions. More radically, if the regulations' enforcement machinery is to be effective, the case for requiring employers who fail to inform and consult properly on an issue to revert to the status quo ante appears strong, despite the exclusion of European Commission and European Parliament proposals to this effect from the final version of the directive.

Another key weakness in the regulations' enforcement regime is that it does not apply to PEAs, even though PEAs 'displace' (Davies and Freedland, 2007: 153) the statutory provisions; nor are PEAs required to be legally enforceable. The European Commission's review (2008) of the application of the directive suggested that the unenforceability of PEAs may be problematic in terms of compliance (Hall, 2010: 62). Echoing the view of the TUC (Hall, 2005: 117) and other commentators, including Koukiadaki (2009), we would favour extending the regulations' enforcement regime to embrace PEAs. As well as ensuring compliance with the directive, such a move would provide a potential means of redress for employees who find that, as in a number of our case study organizations, information and consultation proves less extensive in practice than implied by the terms of the PEA.

Research concerning the operation of staff councils in practice suggests that the subject matter for information and consultation specified by the regulations should be reviewed and extended. There is clear evidence from our case studies that the inclusion of HR policies and practices as topics for consultation is beneficial although they are not currently covered by the regulations. These were not only staple agenda items for many staff councils we studied but were often the issues that generated the most interest among employee representatives since they were of immediate concern to, and had a direct impact on, employees. It was also no coincidence that, in two organizations where the staff council was perceived to be on the verge of failure, management tabled HR policies for discussion in the hope of reinvigorating the information and consultation process. As well as the existing topics for information and consultation listed by the regulations' default provisions, relating to business and economic developments, employment developments, and organizational change and restructuring, there is a case for extending the right to consultation to include HR issues such as grievance and disciplinary procedures, pensions, payment systems, diversity policies and equal opportunities, training, working hours and holidays, and flexible working arrangements. Such topics are widely covered by information and consultation requirements in other EU countries.

A further reform to help promote active consultation concerns measures to support the development of employee representatives' competence and coordination. Our research highlights the correlation between active consultation and the existence of an organized and functioning representative body able to articulate employees' interests. The regulations provide employee representatives with the right to paid time off to perform their functions and protection from dismissal or detriment for exercising their entitlements but go no further, while representatives operating under a PEA have no statutory rights at all. These rights and protections compare poorly with those accorded to employee representatives under earlier UK legislation relating to consultation over redundancies and transfers. This provides the right to training, access to employees and appropriate (office) accommodation and other facilities. A broader range of rights is contained in the 'recast' EWCs directive, providing EWC representatives with rights to paid time off and the necessary financial and material resources to carry out their duties, to undertake training, to call special meetings of the EWC, to hold pre-meetings without management being present, and to seek external advice. The absence of most of these rights from both the information and consultation directive and the UK regulations effectively leaves such practices dependent on management good will. Incorporating similar rights and facilities in the ICE regulations would provide further support for the objective of active consultation.

Finally, a brief comment is necessary concerning the scope under the regulations for PEAs and negotiated agreements to provide for direct forms of information only. As we argued in Chapter 4, this seems unlikely to be regarded as compatible with the directive, which defines information and consultation as processes involving employee representatives. It has already been earmarked by the European Commission (2008) as requiring scrutiny. As predicted, the indications are that the scope for relying on direct forms of information and consultation has proved to be 'more symbolic than practical' (Hall, 2005: 126), with few reported cases of agreements providing only for direct methods (Koukiadaki, 2009: 406). Despite being the dog that appears not to have barked, this provision will at some stage require amendment to ensure compliance with the directive. Interestingly, the Irish legislation enables 10 per cent of the employees covered by direct-only arrangements to seek to exercise the right to information and consultation through employee representatives. This request is then subject to approval by a majority of the employees concerned in a ballot. This is arguably more in line with the provisions of the directive than the United Kingdom's approach.

Taken together, the various elements of this reform package should go some way towards encouraging greater employee and union engagement with the ICE regulations' provisions and more effectively promoting active consultation. It may be argued that some of these suggested amendments would go beyond what is strictly required to conform with the directive, thereby 'gold-plating' its provisions—a persistent charge levelled by employers' groups and Conservative politicians against domestic legislation that transposes EU legislation. But if, as we strongly believe it should be, the objective is the effective implementation of employee rights to information and consultation in the UK context, the preferred government approach of 'minimalist' compliance with EU directives is always likely to be inadequate. A sufficiently detailed legislative framework, taking account of the range of workplace environments—unionized, partially unionized, and non-union—that will be affected by its provisions, needs to be developed in order to achieve this objective.

It has to be recognized that the TUC and individual trade unions do not seem to be actively advocating such legislative reforms. In any event, voluntary moves to strengthen the ICE regulations by the present UK coalition government are highly improbable. Indeed, the deregulatory tenor of its continuing review of employment legislation, and its hostility to EU-inspired regulation in particular, suggest the opposite approach is more likely. However, the fact that the regulations are underpinned by binding EU legislation will constrain ministers' deregulatory ambitions in this area. This, and the evidence that the regulations have in practice posed little threat to employers, is likely to mean that the area of information and consultation will not be a priority for review.

Aspects of the ICE regulations that are of questionable compatibility with the directive's provisions may ultimately be referred to the European Court of Justice as a result of litigation or a Commission referral. But it is the current EU-level 'fitness check' of the information and consultation directives that seems most likely to provide the necessary impetus for regulatory reform. Conclusions from the exercise are expected in 2012. Its purpose is to assess whether the EU legislation is 'fit for purpose'. The aim is not deregulation but rather 'smart regulation' and proposals for the amendment of the information and consultation directive are among the possible outcomes. If it is established that there is a widespread implementation gap across the EU between the directive's minimum standards and company-level information and practice, the efficacy of the directive's reflexive approach to promoting information and consultation may be called into question.

The future of consultation

It is easy to be disparaging about consultation. Throughout the long history of establishing and practicing consultation there have been examples of staff councils fading away as early enthusiasm produced very little of worth to either management or employees, and often councils had a limited role being cast as a communication tool. We gave case histories in Chapter 7 of a failed council and of other staff councils with a limited remit. Yet there were other cases where active consultation flourished. In comparison with union partnership agreements or fully functioning collective bargaining, consultation can look tame. But there are few workplaces where this type of active industrial relations still operate. If we use the lens of collective bargaining in its full extent of job regulation, as was often the case in earlier analyses of consultation, we fail to make adjustments to the current conditions. The valid comparison is no longer with the heyday of collective bargaining but with large parts of the contemporary private sector where there is no collective bargaining and no role for unions: even where such arrangements still exist, they are often a pale shadow of their former vigour. Collectivism can no longer be claimed to be a union preserve. Consultation involving employee representatives, whether union-based or non-union, is the last chance for collectivism. When combined with direct forms of employee voice on the shop and office floor, it performs better than any other forms of employee involvement both in terms of worker well-being and organizational performance. Totterdill et al. (2011), in their review of the evidence from around the world, argue that it is effective representative systems engaged in social dialogue which tend to drive direct participation.

The future health of consultation in Britain cannot be assured. We have suggested that changes are needed to the ICE regulations to allow trade unions to play a more active role and to support the creation of an effective body of integrated employee representatives. The European Commission may suggest reforms in the light of its current fitness check of relevant directives. We have to look to the state to take the most significant institutional initiatives (Howell and Givan, 2011: 251). This may seem unlikely at present but future political developments and searches for social cohesion and productivity growth in an age of austerity could well lead to supporting consultation as an active intervention in the world of work.

The backing of trade unions would be necessary and this would involve them in shifting away from their long held position that collective bargaining is the only means of achieving their goals of representing working people. They need to find new ways of working with those who are not members. The growth of hybrid staff councils is encouraging and could be actively embraced. This call for unions to embrace the opportunities of consultation is backed by a growing number of commentators. Heery (2010: 555) argues that 'integrating employer-sponsored and statutory systems [of employee participation] with trade unionism ... is likely to be central to the necessary task of revitalising unions in the years ahead'. Similarly Brewster et al. (2007: 70–1), on the basis of an international study, argue that 'increasingly, unions' appeal depends on their capacity to address the needs of all employees ... and to integrate non-union representatives into their approaches'. Willman et al. (2007: 1332) endorse this approach, arguing that, in terms of union revitalization strategies, unions will 'have to work at becoming part of effective dual channel voice regimes'.

Even more important is the active support of management since it is they who have to decide to enter into dialogue with employee representatives concerning major decisions with employment implications and work through the most effective ways of implementing them. This may be a pious wish since 'most organisations are non-participative, so participation exists in a hostile environment' (Heller et al., 1998: 212). This is why effective government regulation is so important but, even without it in the immediate future, economic self-interest and concern for employee engagement should lead management to adopt consultative practices, or integrated forms of employee voice systems.

Ultimately, however, the debate about the future of consultation cannot ignore the political philosophy issue of worker participation as a fundamental right. It helps that there is very little evidence anywhere that the exercise of this right is damaging to the interests of the firm and its owners or, indeed, the employees. It would be surprising if there was, since the whole purpose of consultation is for management and employees to engage in cooperative dialogue to maximize their joint interests. The challenge for the future is to find the best way to achieve this in as many workplaces as possible.

APPENDIX:

IRRU-Led Research Project on the Impact of the ICE Regulations

The project was funded by the Department for Business, Innovation and Skills (BIS), the Advisory, Conciliation and Arbitration Service (Acas), and the Chartered Institute of Personnel and Development (CIPD). Research took place over four years—from 2006 to 2010. The research team comprised Mark Hall, John Purcell, and Michael Terry at IRRU, Sue Hutchinson at the University of the West of England and, until her departure from IRRU in 2008, Jane Parker, now at Massey University. Freelance researcher Jill Smith also undertook some fieldwork. The research programme was overseen by an advisory group consisting of representatives of the three funding organizations. The final report from the project (Hall et al., 2010) was published in December 2010 in the BIS employment relations research series.

The project investigated organizational responses to the Information and Consultation of Employees (ICE) Regulations via longitudinal case studies in twenty-five organizations. Reflecting the phased implementation of the ICE regulations based on workforce size, the research involved three 'waves' of case studies. Case studies begun in 2006 in thirteen organizations with 150 or more employees were completed in early 2009. A second wave of case studies began in 2007 in eight organizations with 100–150 employees, and a third and final wave of four case studies started during 2008 in organizations with 50–100 employees. These were concluded in early 2008.

Developments in 'wave 1' and 'wave 2' organizations were tracked over a two-year period. An initial research visit was made to each organization and repeated two years later, with telephone updates in the interim. In-depth semi-structured interviews were held with managers, employee representatives, and trade unions (where present) at each stage, supplemented by documentary analysis (agreements or constitutions underpinning information and consultation (I&C) bodies, minutes of meetings, etc.). For the 'wave 3' case study organizations, a shorter, two-stage research programme was undertaken: the initial research visit was followed by a final update one year later.

Table A.1 summarizes the key features of the twenty-five case study organizations, all of which had recently introduced or relaunched I&C bodies. Identification of potential cases was primarily via Acas and the CIPD as co-sponsors of the research—see Hall et al. (2010) for more details. All the participating organizations were from the private and voluntary sectors, though some had recently left the public sector. Workforce size (at the start of the fieldwork) ranged from over 6,200 in the largest organization to forty in the smallest. Fourteen of the case study organizations recognized trade unions for the purposes of collective representation in at least some parts of the organization.

The most common type of I&C arrangement—established in fourteen organizations—was that of I&C bodies elected by all employees. Eleven of the unionized organizations had 'hybrid' I&C bodies involving both union and non-union representatives—the most common type of consultative body in workplaces with at least some union representatives present (Kersley et al., 2006: 131)—and two informed and consulted via recognized trade unions. Two organizations used different types of I&C arrangement at different sites.

In terms of the basis/status of the I&C arrangements, the largest group (twelve, eight of which were larger, wave 1 organizations) comprised those with a voluntary agreement or 'pre-existing' agreement under the terms of the regulations that had been signed by employee representatives, closely followed by eleven where the I&C arrangements had been introduced unilaterally by management. In two cases, I&C was based on a union recognition agreement. There was only one example of a 'negotiated agreement' reached under the regulations' procedures.

Key findings from the research included the following:

- Assessed against the ICE regulations' default provisions that require I&C concerning strategic business issues and major organizational change, a substantial minority of participating organizations were categorized as 'active consulters' while a majority were 'communicators'. In two organizations, the I&C bodies became defunct after only two or three years in existence.
- The differing trajectories of I&C primarily reflected internal organizational dynamics, particularly management's approach to consultation. The research underlined that management is the dominant player and it was their choices that determined the nature and extent of I&C—whether I&C was in practice 'active' or largely limited to 'communication'.

- The degree of organization among employee representatives was strongly influenced by management's approach to I&C. 'Active consultation' required the development of representatives' competence and coordination. In contrast, among the 'communicators', there was no imperative for a coordinated input from employee representatives and, as a result, little opportunity for representatives to develop the necessary cohesion to press for more effective consultation.
- The extent of trade union engagement influenced the trajectory of I&C in a number of cases—both positively, where full-time officers played a key role at two of the 'active consulters', and negatively, where recognized unions sought to limit the remit of I&C bodies. Union concerns that the operation of I&C bodies could weaken their bargaining role and organization proved largely unrealized. In some cases, involvement in I&C bodies enabled unions to engage with a wider range of issues and afforded regular access to senior management.
- The longitudinal design of the research captured the dynamic nature of I&C. Initial problems experienced by some organizations eventually categorized as 'active consulters' were overcome by a change of ownership/management or by employee representatives growing into their role. Conversely, early signs of effective consultation were not sustained in some of the eventual 'communicators'.
- Beyond being a catalyst for managerial moves to introduce I&C, and influencing the provisions and wording of some agreements or constitutions underpinning I&C bodies, the statutory framework proved largely peripheral. There was little evidence that the regulations shaped managerial I&C practice, nor that they were used as a point of reference by employee representatives who, in any case, had no avenue for legal redress under 'pre-existing agreements' or I&C arrangements introduced unilaterally by management.

Table A.1. Key characteristics of the case study organizations and their I&C arrangements

Case study wave	Organization/ sector	Workforce size (at start of fieldwork)	Union recognition	Date I&C arrangement set up	Type of I&C arrangement			Basis/status of I&C arrangements			
					I&C bodies elected by all employees	'Hybrid' I&C bodies (involving both union and non-union reps)	I&C via trade unions	Voluntary agreement/ PEA	Negotiated agreement under the regulations	Introduced unilaterally by management	Union recognition agreement
1	Engineering company	4,500	✓	2005		✓			✓ (draft)		
	Infrastructure contractor[a]	2,500	✓	2005		✓		✓			
	Electronics company[a]	620		2005	✓			✓			
	News agency	1,700		2003	✓			✓			
	Urban housing association	750	✓	2006		✓ (but union seat left vacant)				✓	
	Rural housing association	275	✓	2004		✓				✓	
	Seaside housing association	240		2003	✓					✓	
	Mobile phone company	6,200		2003	✓			✓			
	National charity	3,500		2005 (relaunch)	✓			✓			
	Care services company	500	✓	2006		✓		✓			
	Cosmetics company[b]	1,300	✓ (at one of two sites)	2006 (relaunch)	✓ (non-union site)		✓ (unionized site)			✓ (non-union site)	✓ (unionized site)
	Financial processing company	2,000	✓	2005	✓			✓			

(*continued*)

Table A.1. Continued

Case study wave	Organization/ sector	Workforce size (at start of fieldwork)	Union recognition	Date I&C arrangement set up	Type of I&C arrangement			Basis/status of I&C arrangements			
					I&C bodies elected by all employees	'Hybrid' I&C bodies (involving both union and non-union reps)	I&C via trade unions	Voluntary agreement/ PEA	Negotiated agreement under the regulations	Introduced unilaterally by management	Union recognition agreement
	Diversified technology company	3,500	✓ (at some sites)	2003–4	✓ (at two sites researched)	✓ (at one site researched)		✓			
2	Bathroom manufacturer[b]	160 (plus 20 sub-contract workers)	✓	2003		✓				✓	
	Hospice	150		2007 (relaunch)	✓					✓	
	Law firm	130		2007	✓			✓			
	Northern housing association	170	✓	2007			✓				✓
	Pharmaceuticals company[b]	160 (one site researched. Two further sites acquired subsequently)	✓ (for consultation purposes)	2006 (relaunch)		✓				✓ (but employee input to redraft of constitution)	
	Professional association	150	✓	2007		✓ (but union seat left vacant)		✓ (but no detailed constitution)			
	Regional airport	125	✓	2005		✓				✓	
	Regional charity	100		2006	✓			✓			

3	Theatre	60 (+150 casual staff)	✓	2006		✓				✓	
	Safety company	40		2000–1	✓					✓	
	Snacks company	100		2007	✓			✓			
	Marine services[b]	70		2007	✓ (employee members of employee benefit trust)					✓	

[a]I&C body became defunct.
[b]Dropped out of research after initial phase.

References

Achurn, J. (2011) *Trade Union Membership 2010*. A national statistics publication. London: Department of Business, Innovation and Skills.

Adler, P., Goldolftas, B. and Levine, D. (1999) 'Flexibility versus efficiency? A case study of model changeovers with Toyota Production System'. *Organizational Science* 10 (1): 43–68.

Advisory, Conciliation and Arbitration Service (Acas) (2004) *Information and Consultation: Good Practice Advice*. http://www.acas.org.uk/index.aspx?articleid=383

—— (2010) *Non-union Representation in the Workplace*. Booklet. London: Acas.

—— (2010) *Time off for Trade Union Duties and Activities*. Code of Practice 3. London: Acas.

Ales, E. (2009) 'Information and consultation within the undertaking: employees' right or employer's duty?' In T. Blanke, E. Rose, H. Voogsgeerd and M. Zondag (eds) *Recasting Worker Involvement?* Deventer: Kluwer, 7–21.

Allen, M. and Funk, L. (2008) 'Institutions and innovation: the role of German works councils in supporting radical change'. Paper given at the Entrepreneurship and Innovation—Organizations, Institutions, Systems and Regions conference, Denmark, June.

Bain, G. and Price, R. (1983) 'Union growth: dimensions, determinants, and destiny'. In G. Bain (ed.) *Industrial Relations in Britain*. Oxford: Blackwell, 3–34.

Barnard, C. and Deakin, S. (2000) 'In search of coherence: social policy, the single market and fundamental rights'. *Industrial Relations Journal* 31 (4): 331–45.

Baruch, Y. and Hind, P. (2000) 'Survivor syndrome—a management myth?' *Journal of Managerial Psychology* 15 (1): 29–45.

Batstone, E., Ferner, A. and Terry, M. (1983) *Unions on the Board*. Oxford: Blackwell.

Beardwell, I. and Holden, L. (1994) *Human Resource Management: A Contemporary Perspective*. London: Pitman Publishing.

Bellace, J. (1994) 'The role of law in supporting employee representation systems'. *Comparative Labour Law Journal* 15: 441–60.

Bercusson, B. (2002) 'The European social model comes to Britain'. *Industrial Law Journal* 31 (3): 209–44.

Boxall, P. (2008) 'Trade union strategy'. In P. Blyton, N. Bacon, J. Fiorito and E. Heery (eds) *The SAGE Handbook of Industrial Relations*. London: Sage, 209–24.

—— Purcell, J. (2010) 'An HRM perspective on employee participation'. In A. Wilkinson, P. Golan, M. Marchington and D. Lewin (eds) *The Oxford Handbook of Participation in Organisations*. Oxford: Oxford University Press, 29–51.

——— (2011) *Strategy and Human Resource Management*, third edition. Basingstoke, Palgrave.

—— Haynes, P. and Freeman, R. (2007) 'Conclusion: what workers say in the Anglo-American world'. In R. Freeman, P. Boxall and P. Haynes (eds) *What Workers Say: Employee Voice in the Anglo-American Workplace*. Ithaca, NY: ILR Press, 206–21.

Brannen, P. (1983) *Authority and Participation in Industry*. London: Batsford.

—— Batstone, E., Fatchett, D. and White, P. (1976) *The Worker Directors: A Sociology of Participation*. London: Hutchinson.

Bratton, J. and Gold, J. (1999) *Human Resource Management: Theory and Practice*, second edition. Basingstoke: Macmillan Business.

Brewster, C., Wood, G. and Brookes, M. (2007) 'Are works councils and joint consultative committees a threat to trade unions? A comparative analysis'. *Economic and Industrial Democracy* 28: 49–77.

Briône, P. and Nicholson, C. (2012) *Employee Empowerment: Towards Greater Workplace Democracy*. London: Centreforum.

Brown, W. (1981) *The Changing Contours of British Industrial Relations*. Oxford: Basil Blackwell.

—— Bryson, A. and Forth, J. (2009) 'Competition and the retreat from collective bargaining'. In W. Brown, A. Bryson, J. Forth and K. Whitfield (eds) *The Evolution of the Modern Workplace*. Cambridge: Cambridge University Press, 22–47.

Bryson, A. (2004) 'Managerial responsiveness to union and non-union worker voice in Britain'. *Industrial Relations* 43 (1): 213–41.

—— Freeman, R. (2007) 'What voice do British workers want?' In R. Freeman, P. Boxall and P. Haynes (eds) *What Workers Say: Employee Voice in the Anglo-American Workplace*. Ithaca, NY: ILR Press, 72–96.

—— Charlwood, A. and Forth, J. (2006) 'Worker voice, managerial response and labour productivity: an empirical investigation'. *Industrial Relations Journal* 37 (5): 438–55.

Budd, J. and Zagelmeyer, S. (2010) 'Public policy and employee participation'. In A. Wilkinson, P. Golan, M. Marchington and D. Lewin (eds) *The Oxford Handbook of Participation in Organisations*. Oxford: Oxford University Press, 476–503.

Bull, E. (2010) *The Impact of the Information and Consultation of Employees Regulations on Medium Sized Firms*. Unpublished PhD thesis, Kent Business School, University of Kent.

Bullock, L. (1977) 'Committee of inquiry on industrial democracy'. *Report*. Cmnd 6706. London: HMSO.

Burke, T. (2010) 'Information and consultation: the good, the bad and the ugly'. Speech to Institute of Employment Rights seminar.

Carley, M. and Hall, M. (2000) 'The implementation of the European Works Councils Directive'. *Industrial Law Journal* 29 (2): 103–24.

——— (2008) *Impact of the Information and Consultation Directive on Industrial Relations*. European Industrial Relations Observatory. http://www.eurofound.europa.eu/eiro/studies/tn0710029s/tn0710029s.htm

—— Marginson, P. (2000) *Negotiating European Works Councils: A Comparative Study of Article 6 and Article 13 Agreements*. Luxembourg: Office for Official publications of the

European Communities/European Foundation for the Improvement of Living and Working Conditions.
Central Arbitration Committee (CAC) (2006) *Annual Report 2005–6.*
——(2007) *Annual Report 2006–7.*
——(2008) *Annual Report 2007–8.*
——(2009) *Annual Report 2008–9.*
——(2010) *Annual Report 2009–10.*
——(2011) *Annual Report 2010–11.*
Chartered Institute of Personnel and Development (CIPD) (2004) *Information and Consultation: A Guide*. London: CIPD.
——(2008) *Employment Relations Survey Report September 2008*. London: CIPD.
Chartered Institute of Personnel and Development (CIPD) (2011) *Employee Outlook 2011*. London: CIPD.
Clegg, H.A. (1960) *A New Approach to Industrial Democracy*. Oxford: Basil Blackwell.
——Chester, T.E. (1954) 'Joint consultation'. In A. Flanders and H.A. Clegg (eds) *The System of Industrial Relations in Great Britain*. Oxford: Basil Blackwell, 323–64.
Clegg, C. and Wall, T. (1984) 'The lateral dimensions to employee participation'. *Journal of Management Studies* 21 (4): 429–42.
Commission of the European Communities (CEC) (1988) 'The social dimension of the internal market'. *Social Europe* (special edition). Luxembourg: Office for Official Publications of the European Communities.
——(1990) 'Action programme relating to the implementation of the Community charter of basic social rights for workers'. *Social Europe* 1/90: 51–76. Luxembourg: Office for Official Publications of the European Communities.
——(1994) *European Social Policy—A Way Forward for the Union*. COM (94) 333 final.
——(2008) *Communication on the Review of the Application of Directive 2002/14/EC in the EU*. COM (2008) 146 final, 17 March.
Confederation of British Industry (CBI) (2004) *Employers' Guide to the Law on Informing and Consulting Employees*. London: CBI.
——(2006) *Employment Trends Survey 2006*. London: CBI.
Cox, A., Zagelmeyer, S. and Marchington, M. (2006) 'Embedding employee involvement and participation at work'. *Human Resource Management Journal* 16 (3): 250–67.
——Higgins, T. and Speckesser, S. (2011) *Management Practices and Sustainable Organisational Performance: An Analysis of the European Company Survey 2009*. Dublin: European Foundation for the Improvement of Living and Working Conditions.
Cressey, P. (1993) 'Employee participation'. In M. Gold (ed) *The Social Dimension: Employment Policy in the European Community*. Basingstoke: Macmillan, 85–104.
——MacInnes, J. (1984) 'The relationship between economic recession and industrial democracy'. Glasgow: Centre for Research in Industrial Democracy and Participation, University of Glasgow. Unpublished paper.
——Williams, R. (1990) *Participation in Change: New Technology and the Role of Employee Involvement*. Dublin: European Foundation for the Improvement of Living and Working Conditions.
——Eldridge, J. and MacInnes, J. (1985) *Just Managing: Authority and Democracy in Industry*. Milton Keynes: Open University Press.

Cully, M., Woodland, S., O'Reilly, A. and Dix, G. (1999) *Britain at Work*. London: Routledge.

Cutcher-Gershenfeld, J. and Verma, A. (1994) 'Joint governance in North American workplaces: a glimpse of the future or the end of an era'. *International Journal of Human Resource Management* 5: 547–80.

Daniel, W. and Millward, N. (1983) *Workplace Industrial Relations in Britain: The DE/PSI/SSRC Survey*. London: Heinemann Educational Books.

Davies, P. (1994) 'A challenge to single channel'. *Industrial Law Journal* 23 (3): 272–85.

——Freedland, M. (1993) *Labour Legislation and Public Policy: A Contemporary History*. Oxford: Clarendon Press.

————(2007) *Towards a Flexible Labour Market: Labour Legislation and Regulation since the 1990s*. Oxford: Oxford University Press.

——Kilpatrick, C. (2004) 'UK worker representation after single channel'. *Industrial Law Journal* 33 (2): 121–51.

Deakin, S. and Morris, G. (2009) *Labour Law*, fifth edition. Oxford: Hart Publishing.

Delbridge, R. and Whitfield, K. (2001) 'Employee perceptions of job influence and organisational participation'. *Industrial Relations* 40: 472–88.

Department of Trade and Industry (DTI) (1998) *Memorandum to House of Commons Trade and Industry Committee*, 19 November. London: DTI.

——(2002) *High Performance Workplaces: The Role of Employee Involvement in a Modern Economy*. London: DTI.

——(2003) *High Performance Workplaces—Informing and Consulting Employees*. London: DTI.

——(2006) *The Information and Consultation of Employees Regulations 2004: DTI Guidance*. London: DTI. http://webarchive.nationalarchives.gov.uk/+/http://www.bis.gov.uk/files

Dietz, G. and Fortin, M. (2007) 'Trust and justice in the formation of joint consultative committees'. *International Journal of Human Resource Management* 18 (7): 1159–81.

——Wilkinson, A. and Redman, T. (2008) 'Involvement and participation'. In A. Wilkinson, N. Bacon, T. Redman and S. Snell (eds) *The SAGE Handbook of Human Resource Management*. London: Sage, 245–68.

Dix, G. and Oxenbridge, S. (2003) *Information and Consultation at Work: From Challenges to Good Practice*. Research Paper 03/03. London, Acas.

Docksey, C. (1986) 'Information and consultation of employees: the United Kingdom and the Vredeling directive'. *Modern Law Review* 19: 281–313.

Doellgast, V. (2010) 'Collective voice under decentralised bargaining: a comparative study of work reorganisation in US and German call centres'. *British Journal of Industrial Relations* 48 (2): 375–99.

Doherty, M. (2008) 'Hard law, soft edge? Information, consultation and partnership'. *Employee Relations* 30 (6): 608–22.

Donaldson, T. and Preston, L. (1995) 'The stakeholder theory of the corporation: concepts, evidence and implications'. *Academy of Management Review* 20 (1): 65–91.

Dukes, R. (2007) 'The ICE Regulations: pre-existing agreements and standard provisions—a warning to employers'. *Industrial Law Journal* 36 (3): 329–40.

——(2008) 'Voluntarism and the single channel: the development of single-channel worker representation in the UK'. *The International Journal of Comparative Labour Law and Industrial Relations* 24 (1): 87–121.

Dundon, T. and Gollan, P. (2007) 'Re-conceptualising voice in the non-union workplace'. *International Journal of Human Resource Management* 18 (7): 1182–98.

——Lurran, D., Ryan, P. and Maloney, M. (2006) 'Conceptualising the dynamics of employee information and consultation: evidence from the Republic of Ireland'. *Industrial Relations Journal* 37 (5): 492–512.

Edwards, P. (1983) 'The pattern of collective action'. In G. Bain (ed) *Industrial Relations in Britain*. Oxford: Basil Blackwell, 209–36.

——Edwards, T., Ferner, A., Marginson, P. and Tregaskis, O. (2007) *Employment Practices of MNCs in Organisational Context: A Large-scale Survey*. http://www2.warwick.ac.uk/fac/soc/wbs/projects/mncemployment

EIRR (1991) 'The EWCs Directive and previous participation initiatives'. *European Industrial Relations Review* 207 (April): 23–7.

Elliott, J. (1978) *Conflict or Cooperation? The Growth of Industrial Democracy*. London: Kogan Page.

Engineering Employers' Federation (EEF) (2005) *Information and Consultation: A Practical Guide to the Law*. London: EEF.

European Foundation (2010) *European Company Survey 2009*. Dublin: European Foundation for the Improvement of Living and Working Conditions.

European Trade Union Confederation (ETUC) (1989) *ETUC Proposals for the Action Programme*. Brussels: ETUC, 14 November.

EWCB (1997) 'Commission targets national consultation rules'. *European Works Councils Bulletin* 10 (July/August): 5–7.

——(1999) 'Draft Directive on employee consultation'. *European Works Councils Bulletin* 19 (January/February): 8–12.

——(1999) 'Proposals for implementing the EWCs Directive in the UK'. *European Works Councils Bulletin* 22 (July/August): 4–9.

——(2002) 'Final text of EU employee consultation directive agreed'. *European Works Councils Bulletin* 37 (January/February): 1–2.

——(2004) 'Takeovers Directive adopted'. *European Works Councils Bulletin* 52 (July/August): 14–15.

——(2004) 'ECS implemented in the UK—part one'. *European Works Councils Bulletin* 54 (November/December): 7–10.

——(2005) 'Cross-border mergers Directive'. *European Works Councils Bulletin* 60 (November/December): 12–17.

——(2005) 'ECS implemented in the UK—part two'. *European Works Councils Bulletin* 55 (January/February): 12–17.

——(2006) 'Irish information and consultation Act finalised'. *European Works Councils Bulletin* 63 (May/June): 13–16.

Ewing, K. and Truter, G. (2005) 'The Information and Consultation of Employees Regulations: voluntarism's bitter legacy'. *Modern Law Review* 68 (4): 626–41.

Flanders, A. (1951) 'Editorial, "The right to be consulted"'. *Socialist Commentary* 15 (7): 150.

—— (1964) *The Fawley Productivity Agreements: A Case Study of Management and Collective Bargaining*. London: Faber and Faber.

Folger, R. and Cropanzano, R. (1998) *Organizational Justice and Human Resource Management*. Thousand Oaks, CA: Sage.

Forth, J. and Millward, N. (2002) *The Growth of Direct Communication*. London: Chartered Institute of Personnel and Development.

Fox, A. (1974) *Beyond Contract: Work, Power and Trust Relations*. London: Faber and Faber.

Freeman, R. and Lazear, E. (1995) 'An economic analysis of works councils'. In J. Rogers and E. Streeck (eds) *Works Councils*. Chicago, IL: University of Chicago Press, 49–94.

—— Rogers, J. (1993) 'Who speaks for us? Employee representation in non-union labour markets'. In B. Kaufman and M. Kleiner (eds) *Employee Representation: Alternatives and Future Directions*. Madison, WI: Industrial Relations Research Association.

—— Boxall, P. and Haynes, P. (2007) *What Workers Say: Employee Voice in the Anglo-American Workplace*. Ithaca, NY: ILR Press.

Frege, C. (2002) 'A critical assessment of the theoretical and empirical research on German Works Councils'. *British Journal of Industrial Relations* 40 (2): 221–48.

—— Goddard, J. (2010) 'Cross-national variation in representational rights and governance at work'. In A. Wilkinson, P. Golan, M. Marchington and D. Lewin (eds) *The Oxford Handbook of Participation in Organisations*. Oxford: Oxford University Press, 526–51.

Fröhlich, D. and Krieger, H. (1990) 'Technological change and worker participation in Europe'. *New Technology, Work and Employment* 5 (2).

Gall, G. (2007) 'Trade union recognition in Britain: an emerging crisis for trade unions?' *Economic and Industrial Democracy* 28 (1): 78–109.

Gallie, D. and White, M. (1993) *Employee Commitment and the Skills Revolution*. London: Policy Studies Institute.

Gilman, M. and Marginson, P. (2002) Negotiating European Works Councils: contours of constrained choice. *Industrial Relations Journal* 33 (1): 36–51.

Goddard, J. (2011) 'What has happened to strikes?' *British Journal of Industrial Relations* 49 (2): 282–305.

Goerke, L. and Pannenberg, M. (2007) *Trade Union Membership and Works Councils in West Germany*. IZA Discussion Paper No. 2635. Bonn: Forschungsinstitut zur Zukunft der Arbeit.

Gold, M. (2010) 'Employee participation in the EU: the long and winding road to legislation'. *Economic and Industrial Democracy* 31 (4S): 9–23.

—— Hall, M. (1992) *European-level Information and Consultation in Multinational Companies: An Evaluation of Practice*. Luxembourg: Office for Official Publications of the European Communities/European Foundation for the Improvement of Living and Working Conditions.

—— —— (1994) 'Statutory European Works Councils: the final countdown?' *Industrial Relations Journal* 25 (3): 177–86.

Gollan, P. (2006a) 'Twin-tracks: employee representation at Eurotunnel revisited'. *Industrial Relations* 45 (4): 606–49.

Golan, P. (2006b) 'The changing dynamics of employee voice and union and non-union representation in the new workplace'. *Industrial Relations Journal* 37 (5): 428–37.
——(2010) 'Employer strategies toward non-union collective voice'. In A. Wilkinson, P. Golan, M. Marchington and D. Lewin (eds) *The Oxford Handbook of Participation in Organisations*. Oxford: Oxford University Press, 212–36.
Gomez, R., Bryson, A. and Willman, P. (2010) 'Voice in the Wilderness'? The shift from union to non-union voice in Britain'. In A. Wilkinson, P. Golan, M. Marchington and D. Lewin (eds) *The Oxford Handbook of Participation in Organisations*. Oxford: Oxford University Press, 383–406.
Goodrich, C. (1975) 'Foreword to the 1975 edition'. in R. Hyman (ed.) *The Frontier of Control: A Study of Workshop Politics*. London: Pluto Press.
Gospel, H. (1992) *Markets, Firms and the Management of Labour in Modern Britain*. Cambridge: Cambridge University Press.
——Pendleton, A. (2003) 'Finance, corporate governance and the management of labour: a conceptual and comparative analysis'. *British Journal of Industrial Relations* 42 (3): 557–82.
Green, F. (2001) 'It's been a hard day's night: the concentration and intensification of work in late twentieth-century Britain'. *British Journal of Industrial Relations* 39 (1): 53–80.
——(2006) *Demanding Work: The Paradox of Job Quality in the Affluent Economy*. Princeton, NJ: Princeton University Press.
Gumbrell-McCormick, R. and Hyman, R. (2006) 'Embedded collectivism? Workplace representation in France and Germany'. *Industrial Relations Journal* 37 (5): 473–91.
————(2010) 'Works councils: the European model of industrial democracy'. In A. Wilkinson, P. Golan, M. Marchington and D. Lewin (eds) *The Oxford Handbook of Participation in Organisations*. Oxford: Oxford University Press, 286–314.
Hale, D. (2010) 'Labour disputes in 2009'. *Economic and Labour Market Review* 4 (6): 47–59.
Hall, M. (1990) 'UK employment practices after the social charter'. *Personnel Management* 22 (3): 32–5.
——(1992) 'Behind the European Works Councils Directive: the European Commission's legislative strategy'. *British Journal of Industrial Relations* 30 (4): 547–66.
——(1993) *Works Councils for the UK? Lessons from the German System*. Warwick Papers in Industrial Relations 46.
——(1994) 'Industrial relations and the social dimension of European integration'. In R. Hyman and A. Ferner (eds) *New Frontiers in European Industrial Relations*. Oxford: Blackwell, 281–311.
——(1996) 'Beyond recognition? Employee representation and EU law'. *Industrial Law Journal* 25 (1): 15–27.
——(2005) 'Assessing the Information and Consultation of Employees Regulations'. *Industrial Law Journal* 34 (2): 103–26.
——(2006) 'A cool response to the ICE Regulations? Employer and trade union approaches to the new legal framework for information and consultation'. *Industrial Relations Journal* 37 (5): 456–72.

——(2010) 'EU regulation and the UK employee consultation framework'. *Economic and Industrial Democracy* 31 (4S): 55–69.

——Edwards, P. (1999) 'Reforming the statutory redundancy consultation procedure'. *Industrial Law Journal* 28 (4): 299–318.

——Marginson, P. (2005) ' Trojan Horses or paper tigers? Assessing the significance of European Works Councils'. In B. Harley, J. Hyman and P. Thompson (eds) *Participation and Democracy at Work: Essays in Honour of Harvie Ramsay*. London: Routledge, 204–21.

——Purcell, J. (2011) *Information and Consultation Practice Across Europe Five Years after the EU Directive*. Dublin: European Industrial Relations Observatory. http://www.eurofound.eu/eiro/studies/tn1009029s/tn1009029s.htm

——Terry, M. (2004) 'The emerging system of statutory worker representation'. In G. Healy, E. Heery, P. Taylor and W. Brown (eds) *The Future of Worker Representation*. Basingstoke: Palgrave, 207–28.

——Broughton, A., Carley, M. and Sisson, K. (2002) *Assessing the Impact of the EU Employee Consultation Directive*. London, Eclipse Group, Warwick, Industrial Relations Research Unit.

——Hutchinson, S., Parker, J., Purcell, J. and Terry, M. (2007) *Implementing Information and Consultation: Early Experience under the ICE Regulations*. Employment Relations Research Series No. 88. London: Department for Business, Enterprise and Regulatory Reform.

—————————— (2009) *Implementing Information and Consultation: Evidence from Longitudinal Case Studies in Organisations with 150 or More Employees*. Employment Relations Research Series No. 105. London: Department of Business, Innovation and Skills.

—————————— (2010) *Information and Consultation under the ICE Regulations: Evidence from Longitudinal Case Studies*. Employment Relations Research Series No. 117. London: Department of Business, Innovation and Skills. http://www.bis.gov.uk/assets/biscore/employment-matters/docs/i/10-1380-information-consultation-ice-regulations

—————————— (forthcoming) 'Promoting effective consultation? Assessing the impact of the ICE Regulations'. *British Journal of Industrial Relations*.

Hall, P. and Soskice, D. (2001) *Varieties of Capitalism: The Institutional Foundations of Comparative Advantage*. Oxford: Oxford University Press.

Heery, E. (2010) 'Worker representation in a multiform system: a framework for evaluation'. *Journal of Industrial Relations* 52 (5): 543–59.

——Noon, M. (2001) *A Dictionary of Human Resource Management*. Oxford: Oxford University Press.

Hege, A. and Dufour, C. (1995) 'Decentralisation and legitimacy in employee representation: a Franco-German comparison'. *European Journal on Industrial Relations* 1 (1): 83–99.

Heller, F., Pusic, E., Strauss, G. and Wilpert, B. (1998) *Organization Participation: Myth and Reality*. Oxford: Oxford University Press.

Hendry, C. (1995) *Human Resource Management: A Strategic Approach*. Oxford: Butterfield.

Hepple, B. (1987) 'The crisis in EEC labour law'. *Industrial Law Journal* 16 (2): 77–87.

Hinton, J. (1994) *Shop Floor Citizens: Engineering Democracy in the 1940s Britain*. Cheltenham: Edward Elgar.

Howell, C. and Givan, R. (2011) 'Rethinking institutions and institutional change in European industrial relations'. *British Journal of Industrial Relations* 49 (2): 231–55.

Hyman, R. (1975) 'Forward to the 1975 edition'. In C. Goodrich (ed) *The Frontier of Control: A Study in British Workshop Politics*. London: Pluto Press.

——(1996) 'Is there a case for statutory works councils in Britain'. In A. McColgan (ed) *The Future of Labour Law*. London: Cassell, 64–84.

——(1997) 'The future of employee representation'. *British Journal of Industrial Relations* 35 (3): 309–31.

Industrial Relations Services (IRS) (2005) 'High on the agenda: employee information and consultation'. *IRS Employment Review* 809: 11–17.

——(2006) 'A two-way process: informing and consulting employees'. *IRS Employment Review* 859: 8–15.

——(2008) 'Survey: employee communications'. IRS Employment Review 903. http://www.xperthr.co.uk/article/87582/survey-span-span-classhighlightemployee-span-span-classhighlightcommunications.aspx?searchwords=Survey%3a+employee+communications

Jacoby, S. (1983) 'Union-management cooperation in the United States: lessons from the 1920s'. *Industrial and Labor Relations Review* 37 (1): 18–33.

——(2005) *The Embedded Corporation: Corporate Governance and Employment Relations in Japan and the United States*. Princeton, NJ: Princeton University Press.

Jagodzinski, R. (2009) 'Recast directive on European Works Councils: cosmetic surgery or substantial progress?' *Industrial Relations Journal* 40 (6): 534–45.

——Pass, I. (2011) *The EWC Landscape on the Eve of the Transposition Deadline of the Recast Directive 2009/38/EC: Evidence from the ETUI Database of European Works Councils*. Brussels: European Trade Union Institute.

James, P. and Walters, D. (1997) 'Non-union rights of involvement: the case of health and safety at work'. *Industrial Law Journal* 26 (1): 35–50.

Jenkins, J. and Blyton, P. (2009) 'Works Councils'. In P. Blyton, N. Bacon, J. Fiorito and E. Heery (eds) *The SAGE Handbook of Industrial Relations*. London: Sage Publications, 346–57.

Jirjahn, U. (2010) 'Works councils and employment growth in German establishments'. *Cambridge Journal of Economics* 34 (3): 475–500.

——Smith, S. (2006) 'What factors lead management to support or oppose employee participation—with or without works councils? Hypothesis and evidence from Germany'. *Industrial Relations* 45 (4): 650–82.

Kahn-Freund, O. (1974) 'On uses and misuses of comparative law'. *Modern Law Review* 37 (1): 1–27.

——Hepple, B. (1972) *Law against Strikes*. London: Fabian Research Series.

Kaufman, B. (2000) 'Accomplishments and shortcomings of non-union employee representation in the pre-Wagner Act years'. In B. Kaufman and D. Taras (eds) *Non-union Employee Representation: History, Contemporary Practice, and Policy*. Armonk, NY: M.E. Sharpe, 21–60.

——Tarras, D. (2010) 'Employee participation through non-union forms of employee representation'. In A. Wilkinson, P. Golan, M. Marchington and D. Lewin (eds) *The Oxford Handbook of Participation in Organisations*. Oxford: Oxford University Press, 258–85.

Kelly, J. (1998) *Rethinking Industrial Relations: Mobilization, Collectivism and Long Waves*. London: Routledge.

——(2010) *Ethical Socialism and the Trade Unions: Allan Flanders and British Industrial Relations Reform*. Abingdon: Routledge.

Kersley, B., Carmen, A., Forth, J., Bryson, A., Bewley, H., Dix, G. and Oxenbridge, S. (2006) *Inside the Workplace: Findings from the 2004 Workplace Employment Relations Survey*. London: Routledge.

Klare, K. (1988) 'Workplace democracy and market reconstruction: an agenda for legal reform'. *Catholic University Law Review* 38: 1–68.

Kotthoff, H. (1994) *Betriebsräte und Bürgerstatus: Wandel und Kontinuität betrieblicher Mitbestimmung*. Munich and Mering: Rainer Hampp Verlag.

Koukiadaki, A. (2009) 'Reflexive law and the reformulation of EC-level employee consultation norms in the British systems of labour law and industrial relations'. *International Journal of Law in Context* 5 (4): 393–416.

——(2010) 'The establishment and operation of information and consultation of employees' arrangements in a capacity-based framework'. *Economic and Industrial Democracy* 31 (3): 365–88.

Kynaston, D. (2007) *Austerity Britain 1945–51*. London: Bloomsbury.

Labour Research Department (LRD) (2006) 'Information and consultation regulations make their mark'. *Workplace Report* 35: 15–17.

Lecher, W., Platzer, H-W., Rub, S. and Weiner, K-P. (2001) *European Works Councils: Developments, Types and Networking*. Aldershot: Gower.

Looise, J. and de Lange, F. (1987) *Ondernemingsraden, Bestuurders en Besluitvorming*. Nijmeigen: Institut voor Togepaste Socilogie.

Lower, M. (2010) *Employee Participation in Governance: A Legal and Ethical Analysis*. Cambridge: Cambridge University Press.

MacInnes, J. (1985) 'Conjuring up consultation: the role and extent of joint consultation in post-war private manufacturing industry'. *British Journal of Industrial Relations* 23 (1): 93–113.

MacLeod, D. and Clarke, N. (2009) *Engaging for Success: Enhancing Performance through Employee Engagement*. A report to Government. London: Department for Business, Innovation and Skills.

Marchington, M. (1987) 'A review and critique of research in developments in joint consultation'. *British Journal of Industrial Relations* 25 (3): 339–52.

——(1989) 'Joint consultation in practice'. In K. Sisson (ed) *Personnel Management in Britain*. Oxford: Basil Blackwell, 378–402.

——(2005) 'Employee involvement: patterns and explanations'. In B. Harley, J. Hyman and P. Thompson (eds) *Participation and Democracy at Work: Essays in Honour of Harvie Ramsay*. Basingstoke: Palgrave Macmillan, 38–54.

Marchington, M. (2007) 'Employee voice systems'. In P. Boxall, J. Purcell and P. Wright (eds) *The Oxford Handbook of Human Resource Management*. Oxford: Oxford University Press, 231–50.

——Wilkinson, A. (2002) *People Management and Development: Human Resource Management at Work*. London: CIPD.

Marchington, M., Ackers, P. and Dundon, T. (2001) *Management Choice and Employee Voice*. London: CIPD.

——Goodman, J., Wilkinson, A. and Ackers, P. (1992) *New Developments in Employee Involvement*. Research Series No. 2. London: Employment Department.

Marginson, P. and Meardi, G. (2010) 'Multinational companies: transforming national industrial relations'. In T. Colling and M. Terry (eds) *Industrial Relations: Theory and Practice*, third edition. Chichester: Wiley, 207–31.

——Sisson, K. (2004) *European Integration and Industrial Relations: Multi-level Governance in the Making*. Basingstoke: Palgrave Macmillan.

——Gillman, M., Jacobi, O. and Krieger, H. (1998) *Negotiating European Works Councils: An Analysis of Agreements under Article 13*. Luxembourg: Office of Official Publications of the European Communities/European Foundation for the Improvement of Living and Working Conditions.

——Edwards, P., Edwards, T., Ferner, A. and Tregaskis, O. (2010) 'Employee representation and consultative voice in multinational companies operating in Britain'. *British Journal of Industrial Relations* 48 (1): 151–80.

Marsh, A. and Coker, E. (1963) 'Shop steward organisation in the engineering industry'. *British Journal of Industrial Relations* 1 (2).

——Evans, E. (1973) *The Dictionary of Industrial Relations*. London: Hutchinson.

Martinez Lucio, M. (2010) 'Labour process and Marxist perspectives on employee participation'. In A. Wilkinson, P. Golan, M. Marchington and D. Lewin (eds) *The Oxford Handbook of Participation in Organisations*. Oxford: Oxford University Press, 105–30.

McCarthy, W. (1966) *The Role of Shop Stewards in British Industrial Relations*. Research Paper 1. Royal Commission on Trade Unions and Employers' Associations. London: HMSO.

——(1988) *The Future of Industrial Democracy*. Fabian Tract 526. London: Fabian Society.

McKersie, R. and Hunter, L. (1973) *Pay, Productivity and Collective Bargaining*. London: Macmillan.

Miles, R. and Rosenberg, H. (1982) 'The human resources approach to management—second generation issues'. *Organizational Dynamics* 10 (3): 26–41.

Millward, N. and Stevens, M. (1986) *British Workplace Industrial Relations 1980–1984: The DE/ESRC/PSI/ACAS Surveys*. Aldershot: Gower.

——Bryson, A. and Forth, J. (2000) *All Change at Work? British Employment Relations 1980–1998, as Portrayed by the Workplace Industrial Relations Survey Series*. London: Routledge.

Müller, T. and Platzer, H-W. (2003) 'European Works Councils'. In B. Keller and H-W. Platzer (eds) *Industrial Relations and European Integration*. Aldershot: Ashgate, 53–84.

Müller-Jentsch, W. and Seitz, B. (1998) 'Betriebsrate gewinnen Konturen. Ergebnisse einer Betriebsratebefragung in Maschenbau'. *Industrielle Beziehungen* 5: 361–87.

Nightingale, D. (1982) *Workplace Democracy*. Toronto: University of Toronto Press.

Northrop, H., Campbell, D. and Slowinski, B. (1988) 'Multinational union-management consultation in Europe: resurgence in the 1980s?' *International Labour Review* 127: 525–43.

ORC Worldwide and Baker & McKenzie (2005) *The Information and Consultation of Employees Regulations 2004: Survey of Company Preparations*.

Oxenbridge, S. and Brown, W. (2004) 'A poisoned chalice? Trade union representatives in partnership and co-operative employer-union relationships'. In G. Healy, E. Heery, P. Taylor and W. Brown (eds) *The Future of Worker Representation*. Basingstoke: Palgrave Macmillan, 186–206.

Phelps Brown, H. (1983) *The Origins of Trade Union Power*. Oxford: Oxford University Press.

Purcell, J. (1981) *Good Industrial Relations: Theory and Practice*. Basingstoke: Macmillan.

——(1995) 'Ideology and the end of institutional industrial relations: evidence from the UK'. In C. Crouch and F. Traxler (eds) *Organized Industrial Relations in Europe: What Future?* Aldershot: Avebury, 101–19.

——Geogiadis, K. (2007) 'Why should employers bother with worker voice?' In R. Freeman, P. Boxall and P. Haynes (eds) *What Workers Say: Employee Voice in the Anglo-American Workplace*. Ithaca, NY: ILR press, 181–97.

——Kinnie, N. (2007) 'HRM and business performance'. In P. Boxall, J. Purcell and P. Wright (eds) *The Oxford Handbook of Human Resource Management*. Oxford: Oxford University Press, 533–51.

——Sisson, K. (1983) 'Strategies and practice in the management of industrial relations'. In G. Bain (ed) *Industrial Relations in Britain*. Oxford: Basil Blackwell, 95–120.

Ramsay, H. (1977) 'Cycles of control: worker participation in sociological and historical perspective'. *Sociology* 11 (3): 481–506.

Ranieri, N. (2010) *Collective Consultation on Redundancies*. Acas Policy Discussion Papers.

Rebhan, H. (1984) 'Commentary'. *Multi-National Information*, No. 5. Geneva: Institute for Research and Information on Multinationals (June).

Rigby, M., Contrepois, S. and O'Brien-Smith, F. (2009) 'The establishment of enterprise works councils: process and problems'. *European Journal of Industrial Relations* 15 (1): 71–90.

Roeber, J. (1975) *Social Change at Work: The ICE Weekly Staff Agreement*. London: Duckworth.

Rogowski, R. and Wilthagen, T. (eds) (1994) *Reflexive Labour Law*. Deventer: Kluwer.

Samuel, P. and Bacon, N. (2010) 'The contents of partnership agreements in Britain 1990–2007'. *Work, Employment and Society* 24 (3): 430–48.

Sandbrook, D. (2010) *State of Emergency: The Way We Were: Britain 1970–1974*. London: Penguin Books.

Sarvanidis, S. (2010) *The Implementation of Information and Consultation of Employees Regulations in Great Britain*. Unpublished PhD thesis, University of Bath.

Scott, W. (2008) *Institutions and Organizations: Ideas and Interests*, third edition. Los Angeles: Sage.

Shanks, M. (1977) *European Social Policy, Today and Tomorrow*. Oxford: Pergamon.

Sisson, K. (2000) *Direct Participation and the Modernisation of Work Organisation*. Dublin: European Foundation for the Improvement of Living and Working Conditions.

——Purcell, J. (2010) 'Management: caught between competing views'. In T. Colling and M. Terry (eds) *Industrial Relations: Theory and Practice*, third edition. Chichester: Wiley, 83–106.

Skidmore, P. (1996) 'Worker rights—a Euro-litigation strategy?' *Industrial Law Journal* 25 (3): 225–30.

Smith, S. and Harwood, P. (2011) 'Social media and its impact on employers and trade unions'. *Employment Relations Comment*. London: Acas.

Spreitzer, G. and Mishra, A. (1999) 'Giving up without losing control: trust and its substitutes' effects on managers' involving employees in decision making'. *Group and Organization Management* 24 (2): 155–87.

Standing, G. (2011) *The Precariat: The New Dangerous Class*. London: Bloomsbury Academic.

Stanojević, M. (2003) 'Workers' power in transition economies: the cases of Serbia and Slovenia'. *European Journal of Industrial Relations* 9 (3): 283–301.

Stettes, O. (2011) *Works Council Elections 2010—Survey Results*. European industrial relations on line (eironline): http://www.eurofound.europa.eu/eiro/2011/02/articles/de1102039i.htm

Stollt, M. and Kluge, N. (2011) 'The potential of employee involvement in the SE to foster the Europeanisation of labour relations'. *Transfer* 17 (2): 181–91.

Taras, D. and Kaufman, B. (1999) 'What do non-unions do? What should we do about them?' Task force Working Paper WP14. Conference on "Symposium on Changing Employment Relations and new Institutions of Representation", September, Washington, DC.

Taylor, P., Baldry, C., Danford, A. and Stewart, P. (2009) 'An umbrella full of holes? Corporate restructuring, redundancy and the effectiveness of the ICE Regulations'. *Relations Industrielles* 60 (1): 27–49.

Terry, M. (1983) 'Shop stewards through expansion and recession'. *Industrial Relations Journal* 14 (3): 49–58.

——(1999) 'Systems of collective employee representation in non-union firms in the UK'. *Industrial Relations Journal* 30 (1): 16–30.

Tomlinson, J. (1996) 'Productivity, joint consultation and human relations in post-war Britain: the Atlee Government and the workplace'. In J. Melling and A. McKinlay (eds) *Management, Labour and Industrial Politics in Modern Europe: The Quest for Productivity Growth in the Twentieth Century*. Cheltenham: Edward Elgar.

Tóth, A. (1997) 'The invention of works councils in Hungary'. *European Journal of Industrial Relations* 3 (2): 161–81.

Totterdill, P., Cressey, P. and Exton, R. (2011) *Workplace Social Dialogue as a Driver of Direct Participation?* Nottingham: UKWON.

Towers, B. (1997) *The Representation Gap: Change and Reform in the British and American Workplace*. Oxford: Oxford University Press.

Trades Union Congress (TUC) (1974) *Industrial Democracy: Report by the TUC General Council to the 1974 Trades Union Congress*.

——(1991) *Trade Union Recognition: A TUC Consultative Document Reported to the 1991 Congress*.

——(1994) *Representation at Work: Interim Report to the 1994 Congress*.

——(1995) *Your Voice at Work: TUC Proposals for Rights to Representation at Work*.

——(2004) *General Council Report 2004*.

——(2005) *TUC Guide to the Information and Consultation of Employees Regulations 2004*.

Veale, S. (2005) 'Information and consultation: a TUC perspective on the key issues'. In J. Storey (ed) *Adding Value through Information and Consultation*. Basingstoke: Palgrave Macmillan, 21–8.

Villiers, C. (1998) *European Company Law—Towards Democracy*. Aldershot: Dartmouth.

Visser, J. (1995) 'The Netherlands: from paternalism to participation'. In J. Rogers and W. Streeck (eds) *Works Councils, Consultation, Representation and Co-operation in Industrial Relations*. Chicago: University of Chicago Press.

Waddington, J. (2006) 'The performance of EWCs in engineering: perspectives of employee representatives'. *Industrial Relations* 45 (4): 681–708.

——(2011) *European Works Councils: A Transnational Industrial Relations Institution in the Making*. London: Routledge.

Wales, N. and Landsbury, R. (2010) 'International and comparative perspectives on employee participation'. In A. Wilkinson, P. Golan, M. Marchington and D. Lewin (eds) *The Oxford Handbook of Participation in Organisations*. Oxford: Oxford University Press, 570–89.

Walton, R. and McKersie, R. (1965) *A Behavioural Theory of Labor Negotiations*. New York: McGraw-Hill.

——Cutcher-Gershenfeld, J. and McKersie, R. (1994) *Strategic Negotiations: A Theory of Change in Labor-Management Relations*. Boston, MA: Harvard Business School Press.

Wilkinson, A., Dundon, T., Marchington, M. and Ackers, P. (2004) 'Changing patterns of employee voice'. *Journal of Industrial Relations* 46 (3): 298–322.

——Gollan, P., Marchington, M. and Lewin, D. (2010) 'Conceptualising employee participation in organisations'. In A. Wilkinson, P. Golan, M. Marchington and D. Lewin (eds) *The Oxford Handbook of Participation in Organisations*. Oxford: Oxford University Press, 3–28.

Willman, P., Bryson, A. and Gomez, R. (2007) 'The long goodbye: new establishments and the fall in union voice in Britain'. *International Journal of Human Resource Management* 18: 1318–34.

Wills, J. (1999) 'European works councils in British firms'. *Human Resource Management Journal* 9 (4): 19–38.

Wood, S. and De Menezes, L. (2008) 'Comparing perspectives on high involvement management and organisational performance across the British economy'. *International Journal of Human Resource Management* 19 (4): 639–82.

Wright, C. (2011) *What Role for Trade Unions in Future Workplace Relations?* Acas Future of Workplace Relations Discussion Paper, September. London: Acas.

Author Index

Subject Index